Wild and Woolly Days

An anecdotal history of Luce County, Michigan 1880-1920

Caroline D. Diem

Wild and Woolly Days: An anecdotal history of Luce County, Michigan, 1880-1920

Copyright © 2020 by Caroline D. Diem. All rights reserved.

Published by: Smith Haven Books

Caroline D. Diem

Website: wildandwoollydays.com

ISBN: 978-0-578-97365-4

Library of Congress Control Number: 2021917379

Editor: Tyler Tichelaar, Superior Book Productions

Cover Design and Interior Layout: Larry Alexander, Superior Book Productions

Every attempt has been made to properly source all quotes.

Printed in the United States of America.

Dedication

This book is dedicated to my grandparents:

William Roy Diem, Jr. (1923-1978)

Martha Lou (Dowler) Diem (1924-2016)

Eileen Marie (Ryan) Steinmuller (1930-2015)

Robert Edward Steinmuller (1926-2017)

I wish you could have seen this.

Table of Contents

Introduction

FROM 2003 UNTIL 2019, I wrote the "Travelling Through Time" column for The Newberry News, a weekly periodical headquartered in Newberry, Michigan, county seat for Luce County. Founded in 1886, the Newberry News provides news coverage to a large area of Michigan's eastern Upper Peninsula, from Lake Michigan in the south, to Lake Superior in the north, from Eckerman in the east, to Seney in the west, including the Tahquamenon River Valley, the Manistique Lakes region, and all of Luce County. It covers nearly 150 square miles of territory and has been doing so for more than 130 years.

The purpose of "Travelling Through Time," a column still being written, is to review more than 130 years and 150 square miles of history for the entertainment and education of our readers. To achieve this, I spent hours squinting at yellowing microfilm and painstakingly transcribing interesting news items from days of yore. What was going on in our area twenty-five years ago, fifty years ago, or one hundred years ago? Something interesting? Something funny? Something scandalous? Something sad?

Sometimes the answer was none of the above. Sometimes the entire week's historical news would consist of little gems like "Mr. J. Smith returned from the Soo yesterday" or "Mrs. Jones hosted a card party last Tuesday." Other weeks would feature a plethora of murders, knife fights, train accidents, or tragic stories of fatal fires or devastating diseases.

The deeper I delved into the past, the further I came to realize that the old saying was true. "The more things change, the more they stay the same." For example, I read about births and marriages, new businesses, business woes, school celebrations, political infighting, and death and taxes. Merchants advertised their goods, held sales, and worried about people ordering from catalogs instead of shopping locally. Schools taught math and science, reading and writing, but were also trying to include things like drug education, current events, nature, health, and fitness. In 1907, Newberry's tenth grade English class studied Shakespeare's Julius Caesar, just as it did in 1995.

Residents griped about the state of the roads and wondered why the village council wasn't doing something about it. Parents complained about the music their children enjoyed. In 1915, the *News* quoted a Mrs. Ashbaugh, speaking on the subject. She asked, "Do you know the morality of songs? Have you thought of the vulgarity of phrase and suggestion of evil in much of the so-called popular music? Would you be willing that anyone should speak to your child in coarse or lewd language? If not, why allow it to be sung?"[1]

Eerie. Isn't it?

But I also discovered that the reverse of that old saying proved to be true, too. The more things stay the same, the more things change. There are differences, naturally, between then and now, and they are just as interesting as the similarities.

The town had a pound back then, in charge of rounding up wandering animals. But in 1889, the pound master was less concerned with loose dogs and more with the stray cows that sometimes attacked gardens and/or children. Schools closed frequently, sometimes for weeks at a time, due to outbreaks of diphtheria, measles, and other deadly diseases.* Newberry had a high school, yes, the same as today, but way back then, the "high school" consisted of four grades in one room with one teacher.

What is most different, and most delightful, was the language used in newspapers of the time. Reporters in those days of yellow journalism were quick to leap to conclusions and slow to apologize. They recited their own, personal opinions, with vast vim and vigor, as gospel truth. In doing so, they were not afraid to call a spade a spade or tell it like it was. They wore their hearts (and their prejudices) on their sleeves and kept their friends close and their enemies closer.

Reporters described events in colorful and curiously blunt terms. A suicide did not die unexpectedly; rather, he "took the neck-tie route" or "blew his brains out," all described in graphic detail. The sheriff didn't arrest suspects, he "captured evildoers." Mourners were "prostrated by the tragedy" and sometimes "crazed with grief."

These writers treated drunks and criminals contemptuously, the insane with dismissive pity, and minorities with intolerant impatience. Their friends received kid glove treatment and all the benefit of the doubt. In contrast, their enemies were objects for scornful humiliation and mocking derision.

Reporters took to the slang of the day with reckless good humor. The village council was often called, somewhat irreverently, the "city dads." Eccentrics were "cracked in the upper story." Merchants sold "nobby" goods and the "swellest" lines available. Trusting souls were "bunkoed" out of money by confidence men. In 1892, the *News*' Dollarville correspondent, after being criticized for his opinions, referred to himself as "tooting off our bazzo."[2]

Oh, those sentimental and optimistic, prejudiced and idealistic, brash and brave, foolish and passionate, clever and kind, stubborn and naïve, energetic and endearing people of days gone by. This is an attempt to share some of their stories and their language, the hopes, dreams, virtues, and vices of their long-ago days.

Caroline D. Diem

Newberry, Michigan

2020

---

* Schools closing for weeks at a time? How absurd this seemed when this was originally written, before the 2020 Covid Pandemic made the unthinkable thinkable. The more things change, the more they stay the same, indeed.

Chapter One
How It All Began

*"I had plenty of opportunity to observe the country on both sides of the straits
as we passed through. The land on both sides was covered with snow, the weather
was blustery and it was the most dismal country I ever saw."*

— William S. Locke, "Pioneer Reminiscences," *Newberry News*, June 9, 1922

THE STATE OF MICHIGAN, AS every schoolchild knows, is made up of two pieces: the Lower Peninsula ("the mitten") and the Upper Peninsula, commonly abbreviated as the U.P. Located in the center of the eastern half of the Upper Peninsula is the Village of Newberry, county seat for Luce County.

The name "Newberry," if you trace it back far enough, means "new town" from "new" and "burgh." It is an appropriate name, for, in the scope of American history, it *is* a new town. When the Declaration of Independence was signed in Philadelphia in 1776 and when Lord Cornwallis surrendered to Washington in 1781, Newberry did not exist. When the Underground Railroad ran and Sherman marched to the sea, Newberry did not exist. When Robert Fulton built his steamships, when Governor DeWitt dug the Erie Canal, and telegraph engineers ran a wire between New York and London, Newberry did not exist. Neither did Luce County.

Not that it was a pristine wilderness, bereft of people. Far from it. The Native American Ojibwa tribes had made it their home for eons, fishing, hunting, making maple syrup. French trappers, missionaries, and voyageurs had crisscrossed the area, trapping, preaching, and hauling furs about in their longboats. The explorer Etienne Brule may have been in the area as early as 1620, the same year the pilgrims landed at Plymouth. The French founded missions at Sault Ste. Marie in 1668 and in St. Ignace in 1671. Indeed, France claimed all of Michigan until 1763, when it lost those lands to the British. The British, in turn, lost the same to the United States twenty years later in 1783.

During the early nineteenth century, American engineers, explorers, and surveyors made difficult journeys through their new territory, discovering rich mineral deposits and vast forests, charting the land, and prepping it for settlement. By the 1840s, the Upper Peninsula had been thoroughly mapped, methodically measured, and laid out into thousands of 640-acre sections. But it wasn't settled country. It had no roads, no towns, no newspapers or schools or hospitals. This was a land of tangled trees and soggy swamps, black bear, black flies, mosquitoes, deer, moose, and wolves. And it was remote.

Cut off from the outside world for months or years at a time, early fur traders wandered back and forth across this land, making the eastern Upper Peninsula their home. One early settler recalled running into two trappers who, stumbling out of the woods with $1,200.00 worth of furs, immediately asked him, "Who is President of the United States?"[3]

After iron and copper deposits were discovered in the western UP. in the 1840s, a few small settlements appeared, first of all in the Keweenaw Peninsula (including Fort Wilkins in 1844). Then Marquette was founded in 1849, which was followed, over the next ten years, by Ontonagon, Houghton, Negaunee, and Hancock.

When the Civil War broke out in 1861, minerals became a huge priority. Handfuls of additional boom towns mushroomed in the western UP, around the copper and iron mines, including Escanaba, Ishpeming, Calumet, and Lake Linden.

Clinging to the eastern coastline, a fringe of tiny settlements gradually grew around harbors and the Soo locks, all of them subservient to the iron-cargo ships sailing from the west end. Congress established a series of lighthouses and lifesaving stations on the Superior Coast, beginning with the Whitefish Point Light in 1847. A few trading posts popped up here and there, serving the fur traders and attracting Native Americans and missionaries.

Yet the eastern end remained largely empty, save for the Ojibwa maple sugar camps and the occasional tiny fishing village. The land was swampy, covered in a mass of vegetation, with only a short growing season. All it had were trees.

Yes, but what trees they were: tall, thick, soaring pines and vast swaths of untouched hardwood. Many white pine trees bulged at widths of three to four feet across, and often reached up to fifty or sixty feet in height before splitting off into branches. Riches untouched, they were. Though, there was no way to access that wealth. No easy way, anyway. Not yet. Not until a railroad was built.

The lack of a railroad did not stop all lumbermen, though. A harbinger of things to come, the occasional sawmill appeared, gathering easy-to-access timber from around tiny hamlets and fishing villages like Naubinway, Manistique, or Black River (near present-day Gilchrist). If near a convenient river, they could even go in the interior a little ways. As one example, George Dawson, of Sault Ste. Marie, formed small lumber camps along the shoreline in the 1870s.

For another, Robert Dollar and George Randolph, of the American Lumber Company, arrived in the little harbor of Grand Marais in 1879 and set up a faraway lumber camp. The lumber camps, in those days, collected only the "choicest trees." The logs were hacked into rough, square beams called "waney boards" that then were floated out, loaded into ships, and sent across Lake Superior to Ontario, where they were unloaded and lashed together into rafts. The rafts were sailed down the St. Lawrence River to Quebec, where they were dismantled and again loaded into ships, bound for England this time.[4]

After founding their first Michigan camps, Dollar and Randolph snowshoed across the interior, sleeping under the stars, never washing, with Dollar wearing socks on his hands after his mittens fell in the fire. "I confess," Dollar admitted in his memoirs, "I looked more like a bum than a boss lumberman." They were "land looking," or braving the sub-zero temperatures in order to seek out promising stands of white pine.[5]

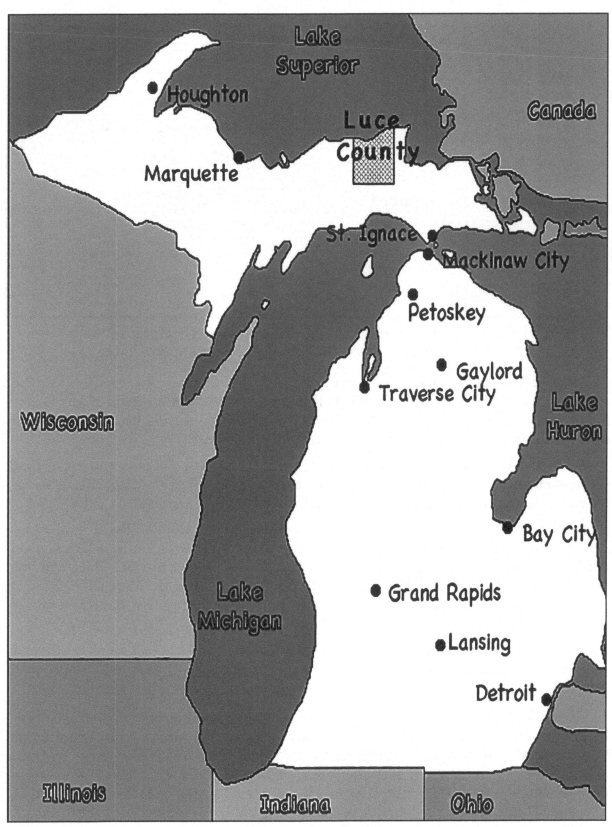

Michigan and Vicinity

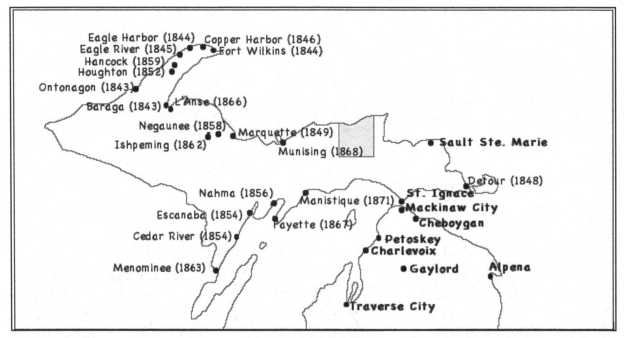

This map shows mostly the Upper Peninsula, and some of the settlements that appeared after the Civil War. All dates are approximate.

They were not alone. Other hardy men were out there, tramping the woods, looking for treasure. Once, in the early 1870s, Francis R. Hulbert discovered a prime stand of white pine—far out in the eastern UP.—just the thing he was looking for. He also discovered the snowshoe tracks of another timber cruiser who had been there a day before.

Hulbert knew he had to get to the Marquette land office first to claim the land, yet he could see his unknown predecessor's tracks winding their way northwest to Marquette, extending out 150 miles over the frozen Lake Superior. His rival had a one-day lead.[6]

Studying the tracks, Francis Hulbert bet everything on a gamble. He at once turned *southwest*, scrambling through the woods until he reached Lake Michigan. Then he hiked west until he arrived at Escanaba and the "Chicago and Northwestern Railroad," which had been built during the Civil War for iron. He took the train *back* north to the Marquette office. His roundabout gamble paid off. Francis Hulbert reached the land office first, but his frozen feet took two weeks to heal.

Getting there first to stake your claim was of utmost importance, for a railroad was surely coming to the Eastern UP. It was only a matter of time.

So the settlers began to arrive.

Irish-Canadian Robert Bryers immigrated to the United States in 1876, intending on going on to California. While in Detroit, however, he heard about the fantastic new opportunities being developed in the north and changed his mind. He sailed up Lake Huron to St. Ignace and then followed the shore to the little fishing village of Naubinway, whereupon he struck out through the woods along with Alex See, a native guide. After they traveled around the Manistique Lakes in a canoe, Robert Bryers decided that this was the land for him. In 1877, he filed for a homestead, leaving his young family in Naubinway until he could build a house on his land.[7]

Right: This tree, located in the Tahquamenon Falls State Park, is one of a very few original pines to escape the axe. According to the DNR, it is more than 185 years old, 120 feet high, and five feet in diameter. The informational plaque explains that two such trees could build an entire house. Now imagine acres and acres of such trees—and larger! Now imagine the wealth that represented. (author's photo)

Robert Dollar, in later years
(from *Men Who Are Making America*, B.C. Forbes Publishing Company, 1917).

Advertisement from *The Newberry News* of July 18, 1890, after "civilization" came to stay.

He quickly was joined by the Scottish-born Robert and Aggie Tait, their two grown sons, two grown daughters, and two hired hands (who later married the daughters). They had left Cheboygan, Michigan, in 1878, crossing Lake Michigan and arriving in the little sawmill town of Manistique, less than two decades old, and home to almost 700 people.[8]

Upon arriving, the family paddled up the Manistique River for a six-week trip featuring many delays as they portaged around vast piles of snarled driftwood. After rowing across Big Manistique Lake, they disembarked on the north end and hiked through the woods to North Manistique Lake, where they would farm.[9]

The land upon which they found themselves, described on an early surveyor's map, was mostly "swampy wet lands timbered with cedar, tamarack and some alder" surrounding a long, horizontal island of "dry land" and "high rolling sandy ridges." It was full of large birch, sugar maple, lynn (basswood or linden), elms, and hemlock trees, and featured "very little undergrowth." Furthermore, the land crossed by "deep and sluggish" streams that led to lakes of "clean and pure" water.

Here, by the lakes, Bryers and Tait would build their new homes, new fields, and their new community. It was later called Lakefield Township.[10]

By early summer 1880, when the census-taker came through, Robert Tait and Robert Bryers had been joined by six other men, all busy hacking nascent farms out of the forests. All were taking advantage of the Homestead Act, that old facet of U.S. law that promised free land to any family that, in return, would improve said land with farms and buildings.

Riley H. Fuller was one such man. He and his grown son, Ora, had disembarked at Black River in 1879, then traveled overland to the new homestead. The rest of the Fuller family arrived later, taking the railroad to Petoskey, then a steamship to Naubinway, then riding in an "ox cart over rough woods trails" through soggy lands, pursued by "clouds of mosquitoes and other stinging and biting insects" They settled on the north side of Big Manistique Lake, and within ten years, had a fine farm and a successful orchard. For a time, the area between Big Manistique Lake and North Manistique Lake (Round Lake) was even called the Fuller District.[11]

Their neighbors in 1880 included a trapper named John Stevens and his two boys; Mr. Sanford Helmer and his grown son, Gaylord; the German-born Jacob Illg (a former employee of Sanford Helmer); and the young bachelors James O. Myers and Michael Long. Dozens more would follow, not only in Lakefield, but in neighboring townships later called Germfask and Portage.[12]

In the spring of 1881, William S. Locke (a clerk at the small Black River Company store with a young family) set out to seek his destiny, snowshoeing over four-foot snowdrifts. While he stopped to gape at a broken snowshoe leaning up against a tree, Locke lost his balance, falling headfirst into the drift. Unable to get out, he was "nearly drowned" in the snow and may have died there. Fortunately, at dawn he heard a rooster cry. The bird belonged to Robert Tait. Locke called out and was rescued.[13]

The brothers George and John Smathers began to "make a home in the wilderness," as it was said, in late 1880, each one marrying and starting a family. Twenty-two-year-old Wesley Mark, and his nineteen-year-old brother, Culbert, also arrived in late 1880. Both claimed a

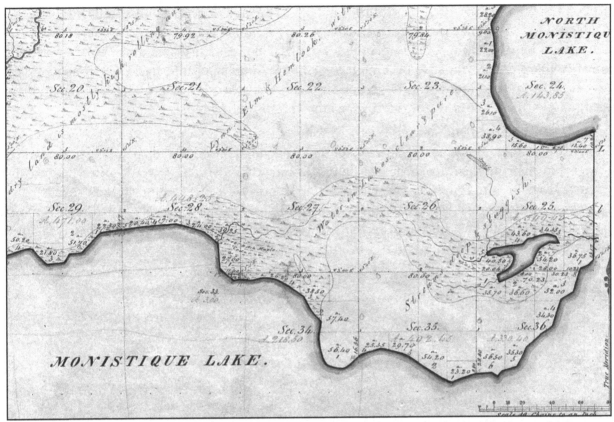

This map was prepared in 1849 by Guy H. Carleton, showing what would later become west Lakefield Township. This is the land Robert Bryers and Robert Tait settled in the late 1870s.

Left: Robert and Sarah (Ennis) Bryers (courtesy of Robert and Cheryl Teed Bryers). Right: Sarah (Gordon) Locke and William S. Locke (courtesy of Columbus Township, Luce County, Michigan).

farm on the high ground to the east of the big lake, in an area of gentle rolling hills full of sugar maple, beech, yellow birch, and fir trees. These two became prominent area farmers, and were later joined by their four younger brothers (Henry, Charles, Cornwall, and Louis) and their cousin Willard Mark, who also became farmers. Sometime later appeared their cousins Fred, George, Edward, and James Taylor, as well as their cousin Wesley Allen. The area where they lived (at one time or another) was known as the "Marks Settlement."[14]

In 1881 came the Pentland family, for whom a future Luce County township was named. Born in Ireland, Thomas and Deborah Pentland had first immigrated to Canada, and were now trying their luck with a farm in Michigan. Later, the Pentlands would offer free meals to those traveling the rough, yet ever-expanding wagon trail that wound its way south from the center of the peninsula to Naubinway and Lake Michigan. They brought with them their married daughter and her husband, and their own six sons, ranging from twenty-four-year-old Isaac to seven-year-old Moses.[15]

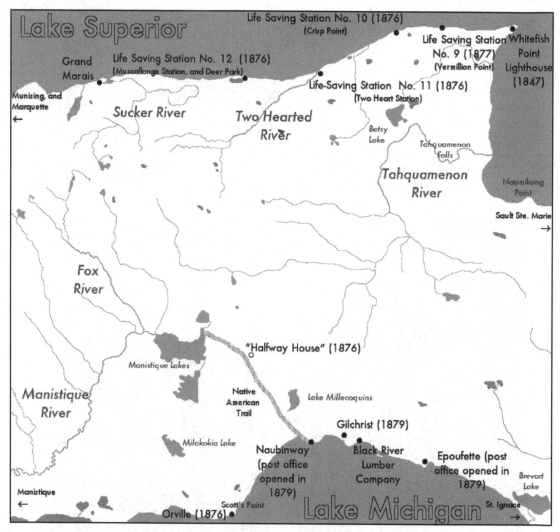

Luce County and vicinity, showing a handful of populated places, circa 1880, before Luce County even existed. All dates are approximate.

Pioneers of Lakefield Township, Luce County

Left: Gaylord Helmer, 1894 (courtesy of *The Newberry News*).
Center and Right: Jeremiah C. Holland and Harriet (Lucas) Holland
(courtesy of the Luce County Historical Society).

Right: Willard Mark, pioneer of Lakefield Township, Luce County.
Center and Right: Frederick Lewis Roat and Ada Jane (Cole) Roat, in later
years. (photos courtesy of Greg Marks).

  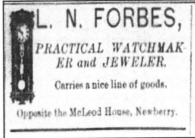

Advertisements from *The Newberry News* of
May 2, 1890 and February 1, 1890.

Frederick Roat, a Civil War veteran and Oakland County farmer, showed up in 1882 with his wife and seven small children. He then "at once selected a tract of wild land of which every acre was covered with a thick growth of hardwood and was situated five miles from any road." Immediately thereafter, Roat "cut a trail to his home, built a cabin and commenced to block out a home in the woods."[16]

Life was a hardscrabble then, full of difficulty. Besides the everyday chores of animal care, repairs, cooking, mending, and washing, the pioneers also had to fell the massive trees, remove stumps and roots, build houses, barns and fences, and dig wells.

Thousands of mature hardwood trees were chopped down and then destroyed in great, burning piles, as there was no way for the settlers to sell or otherwise use them. Jerry C. Holland (arriving in 1883) even used a pair of ponies to sow his first crop of spring wheat, the smaller animals being better able to "dodge" around the stumps left in his new fields. Once harvested, he then had to find a way to get his wheat to Sault Ste. Marie for milling into flour, a two-week journey. His neighbors faced similar problems. The nearest settlement and source of supplies, not to mention the nearest doctor, was located in Naubinway, which was only accessible by slogging an old Ojibwa trail, at least a full day's walk.[17]

These early pioneers faced winters of dangerous cold, suffocating snow, and large families crammed into small cabins. Every so often a Presbyterian minister named J. P. Mills hiked from Manistique to "Mille Coquin Lake," near Naubinway. His next stop was the Manistique Lakes. Carrying a pack weighing sixty pounds, it took him two days to get there. He often rowed across the lake. The crude roads scratched between the farms were made of "sand hill and corduroy* and mudholes." Winters were supremely isolating. "The only way out was on snowshoes," recalled Frank Kalnbach in *The Newberry News* of October 26, 1956. "The snow was so deep you would walk over fences and stumps and not even know they were there." Nine-year-old Frankie, his German-born parents, and four brothers and sisters, had moved to the area in the fall of 1886.[18]

Even if the pioneers managed to grow a successful crop, there wasn't any easy way to sell it. At the time, it took more than two weeks to transport crops from the farm to Naubinway, from which it could be shipped via boat to the wider world. With or without these crop sales, the pioneers still had taxes to pay and supplies to buy. Most of the men had to take winter jobs with the coastal lumber companies. Still, they were optimistic about the future. For the railroad, with all its associated opportunities, was coming.[19]

The end of the Civil War had sparked an explosion of frenzied industrial expansion in the United States, a growth that demanded copious amounts of lumber and steel. This new growth stirred interest in the Michigan's Upper Peninsula, which contained a virtually untouched store of raw resources. Capitalists longed to fund mines and camps to extract the necessary iron and timber from the mines and forests of the Upper Peninsula. Industrialists yearned to establish sawmills to create lumber and shingles and other finished products. Ambitious farmers' sons and new immigrants were eager to become miners and lumberjacks and factory-hands, perhaps earning enough to buy a little farm and prosper themselves. These laborers needed boarding houses and saloons, churches, and schools, doctors and lawyers, general stores, and banks and newspapers.

---

* Corduroy roads are created by laying logs together horizontally to form a bumpy, wooden surface.

And they all needed a railroad. Therefore, railroad companies were created to lay the tracks, build the engines, keep the economy moving and—most importantly of all—make everyone wealthy in the process.

Accordingly, various railroad companies formed early on, such as the Mackinaw and Lake Superior Railroad Company, and the Marquette, Sault Ste. Marie and Mackinaw Railroad Company. Unfortunately, they never made it further than planning surveys and wrangling with the federal government. One company went so far as to buy land and build a solitary hotel in what would later become Luce County. This little hotel was in the middle of nowhere, the predicted hub of a future town that fizzled before it could begin.[20]

Finally, Detroit lawyer John Stoughton Newberry, along with a group of like-minded businessmen, formed the Detroit, Mackinac and Marquette Railroad (DM&M) company in 1879.

As Newberry and his fellow investors discovered, the federal government was just as eager to bring the railroad and civilization to these woods. As an incentive, they offered the DM&M "16 sections of land for every mile of road" in the form of a land grant, which the DM&M willingly accepted. In the end, the railroad company would control more than a million acres.[21]

The grandiosely named Detroit, Marquette and Mackinac Railroad was meant to connect the now-thriving iron port of Marquette, on the shores of Lake Superior in the north central UP, to the Straits of Mackinac in the southeast UP. To accomplish this, it needed to lay 150-plus miles of track. The DM&M hired huge crews of men—the "roughest of the rough"—who walked in from St. Ignace and other ports, through the woods to the worksites. Working conditions were often execrable, plagued by rainstorms, with some worksites along the Tahquamenon River covered in swamp water three feet deep.[22] It was hard to get good workers, but those who could handle it were paid $1.50 per day. They camped in tents and shanties in the "unbroken woods" and got to work felling trees, using horse and ox teams to yank massive stumps from the ground.

The crews burned stumps, plugged holes, and leveled off hills. They filled in swamps, built bridges, and laid rails and ties. They advanced quickly. Work began on January 23, 1880, in Marquette in the central UP, and then at St. Ignace at the eastern end in May that same year.

On December 9, 1881, they met in the middle (near to present-day Dollarville). The first train, full of dignitaries and officials, pulled into St. Ignace December 9, 1881 and was greeted with flags and fireworks. The one-way trip from Marquette to St. Ignace took twelve hours.[23]

With the railroad complete, the federal government granted the DM&M its million-plus acres. In addition to the railroad, John S. Newberry and his colleagues had also formed an auxiliary business called the Peninsular Land Company into which they now transferred much of the land they had been given. It was the Peninsular Land Company that would plat the towns and sell lots to other entrepreneurs and settlers. This company had a reputation for fair and generous dealing with its customers, keeping prices down, draining swamplands, and donating plots for cemeteries, churches, and schools. The company would do everything in its power to convince settlers that Upper Peninsula lands were, indeed, perfect for farms—viable, fruitful, and fertile.[24]

The finished railroad sliced through the middle of the eastern UP and provided a funnel for all the resources that could be wrung from the land. At periodic intervals, the DM&M established "stations," like beads strung on a chain. A few were to become successful little cities with industry and streetlights and banks. Others would boast a depot and a boarding house or saloon and nothing more. A few "stations" were only promising clearings in the wilderness called "sidings" where trains could pull off and set a spell.

Having built his railroad, John S. Newberry now needed industries to use it. Therefore, in 1882—in another move of startling synergy—he helped form the Vulcan Furnace Company, which would harvest hardwood trees and roast them into charcoal.

The charcoal then would be used to turn iron ore—shipped via railroad from the iron mines out west—into pig iron, which then would be shipped—again via railroad—to wherever it was needed. These cunning capitalists would make money every step of the way.

Just where to place the *actual* Vulcan furnace was a quandary that plagued the builders. The kilns needed to be close to the railroad and close to stands of hardwood forests. On a rise of high land, the site of a former Ojibwa maple sugar camp, with rolling land and gravelly loam, timbered with maple, yellow birch, and hemlock, John S. Newberry found just the place. The little station of Grant's Corners would suit his purposes exactly. Formerly "Grant's Camp," it was only a temporary settlement, run by a sub-contractor named Grant, helping to build the railroad. It would do nicely, for it would be next door to the railroad, as well as near to stands of hardwood (besides being slightly drier than much of its swampy surroundings). So, in a modest move of self-promotion, Mr. Newberry renamed the little clearing after himself: Newberry.[25] Soon it would be the home of the new Vulcan Furnace Company.

John Newberry didn't stop with naming a town to honor himself. He also wanted to honor his family members. The first eleven streets (Harrie, Truman, John, Helen, Handy, Robinson, Parmalee, Phelps, Newberry, McMillan, and Railroad) were mostly named after the members of the Newberry family. John S. Newberry's children were Harrie, Truman, John Jr., and Helen. His mother was Rhoda Phelps, and his first and second wives were Harriet Robinson and Helen Parmalee Handy.[26]

John Newberry was hardly unique in naming his new town after himself. His fellow executives also took great pleasure in naming stations after themselves, no doubt imagining booming, modern cities growing around them, crowning their names with everlasting glory. Other DM&M executives with namesake stations included James McMillan (John Newberry's business partner), George Ingraham Seney, William Moran, George Hendrie, Francis Palms, Henry W. Sage, and Frederick Driggs. Seney, McMillan, and Moran are still villages. Hendrie, Driggs, Sage, and Palms are only names on a map.

Workmen disembarked at Grant's Corners and set to work in March 1882, clearing thirty acres of land, laying out streets, and erecting buildings in John Newberry's namesake town. An employee named W. H. Kaye set up a telegraph station in a canvas tent.

Workmen quickly erected the furnace, the purpose and primary focus of the town, on the east side of the clearing. They also built a two-story company store (the Vulcan Store, managed by R. H. Weller), and company housing on the new John Street ("twenty neat comfortable cottages"), as well as a boarding house for an additional fifty men. The township government

Executives of the Detroit, Mackinac and Marquette Railroad

Left to Right, Top to Bottom: John S. Newberry, James McMillan, George Hendrie, Francis Palms, Frederick Driggs, George Seney, Henry W. Sage, and William B. Moran.

was organized in April 1883, named after executive James McMillan, and staffed mostly by furnace employees.[27]

John Newberry and his cronies now had a railroad, stations, industry, and control over much of the surrounding land.

Newberry's new employees poured in, needing all the accoutrements that comprise a town: tools and groceries, boarding houses and saloons, churches and schools, doctors and lawyers. These and more such services were eagerly provided by the independent entrepreneurs who quickly joined them. Lots were sold, buildings were rented, and homes were built. Thus is born a town.

John Newberry himself never actually lived in his town. Instead, he lived the high life in Detroit, getting involved in politics, forming corporations all over the place, and dividing his time between a mansion in Detroit and a three-story "summer cottage" in nearby Grosse Point.[28] It is unlikely he ever even visited. Neither his wife nor any of his children ever visited either, as far as is known. In fact, the first recorded visit of a Newberry—any Newberry— was that of John's grandson, Henry B. Joy, Jr., in 1963. He had come to make a substantial donation to the town to fund the building of a new hospital, which was named in honor of his mother, the philanthropist, Helen Newberry Joy. In gratitude, Mr. Joy was allowed to lay the cornerstone of the new building in 1965.

But if the Newberry family was not keen to live in an up-and-coming clearing in the woods, others were not so skittish. Many an adventurous soul leapt at the chance to create a new community. The first family was later said to have been Thomas Miller, his wife Catherine Alice Miller, and their three-year-old daughter, Lodella. The Millers previously lived in Madoc, Ontario. Thomas was a carpenter who literally helped build his new town.[29]

The original "main street" of Grant's Corners, running parallel to the railway, was abandoned for the new Newberry Avenue, a wide expanse of stumps and brush, that ran perpendicular to the rails. The new thoroughfare was lined with plank sidewalks, hitching posts, and rowdy woodsmen celebrating their days off. Very quickly, it grew. Within a year, the street was cleared of debris and businesses lined either side. Throughout the 1880s, the new main street was extended south to the county line. Initially called "Elmwood Avenue," it was described as "large elms being on both sides of the street, their huge spreading tops almost touching the ones from the opposite side, forming a most beautiful arch and making as pleasant a drive as could very well be found." The road ran south, eventually reaching the new Pentland Township, up what was then called "Hayden's Hill," past the Peninsular Land Company's experimental farm (growing celery and oats), and past the Hayden and Zenker family farms. [30]

The village of Newberry incorporated in 1885.[31]

Unfortunately for John S. Newberry, his best laid plans didn't quite work out. Railroads were always a chancy business, being very sensitive to fluctuations in supply and demand, and requiring an enormous commitment of money and resources to maintain and run. Meanwhile, the scanty revenues, although slowly on the rise, were not enough to cover costs. A nationwide recession, peaking in 1884, did not help matters, either.[32] The DM&M went bankrupt in 1886, its assets being absorbed into a new, bigger railroad company, the Duluth, South Shore and Superior Railway, whose investors ("coincidentally") included James McMillan.

Vulcan Store Company

For Staple and Fancy Dry Goods.

It will do you good to see our White and Colored Piques, Prints and Ginghams, Hamburg Edges, Ribbons, Laces, &c.

Ready-Made Clothing.   **Suits $5.00 to $25.00.**

Orders received for Clothing to Measure.

A Splendid line of Gents' Furnishing Goods, Blue and Fancy Colored Flannel Shirts, White and Pecale Shirts, Great Variety of Styles and Prices. Trunks and Valises.

Boots and Shoes

For Everybody. Good Goods and Fair Prices. Don't fail to see them. We have almost Everything in the line of Boots & Shoes.

A large stock of Hats and Caps, including Straw Goods; also Ladies Sundowns and Children's Straw Hats.

COMMON FURNITURE

Always on hand. Orders ro'vd for fine goods. SHELF AND BUILDING HARDWARE!

Stoves, Tinware, Tools, &c. Crockery and Glassware. Drugs & Patent Medicines.

Paints, Oils, Varnishes, Brushes, Window Glass, etc. A good assortment of Wallpaper and Window Shades. Self-Act ng Curtain Fixtures.

—— IN OUR ——

Grocery and Provision

Department will be found the

:•: **Best the Markets East and West can Furnish** :•:

And at prices so Low as

Consistent with Quality.

Sugar Cured Hams, 11c per lb.

Sugar Cured Picnic Hams, 9c per lb.

All other Meats in Proportion.

Tropical Fruits and Nuts always on hand. Strawberries tow or three times times a week. **Early Vegetables via Express** in order to have them fresh.

Flour, Grain and Feed always on hand

Clover, Timothy, Millet and Garden Seeds.

Almost Everything in the Merchandise line

Our Motto is "Good Goods and Square Dealing."

Vulcan Store Co.

Detroit, Mackinac & Marquette Rail Road.

Pioneer East and West Line Through the Upper Peninsula of Michigan.

Actually the shortest line by 241 miles between Detroit, Southern Michigan and all points in the east and south-east and the great iron and copper districts of Michigan.

One express and one mail train daily each way between St. Ignace and Marquette, connecting at St. Ignace with Michigan Central Railroad, and after July 15th with Grand Rapids & Indiana Railroad, and during navigation with Detroit and Cleveland Steam Navigation Company by the unexcelled side-wheeled steamer City of Cleveland, for Port Huron, Detroit, Cleveland, etc; also with New England Transportation Company's Line for Chicago and Milwaukee, Collinwood and other places in Canada, and with other boat lines.

Coupon tickets to principal cities and towns on sale at St. Ignace and Marquette.

For information as to passenger and freight rates please apply to

F. MILLIGAN, Gen'l Fr't & Pass'r Agt., Marquette, Mich.

Detroit & Cleveland
Steam Navigation Co.

PALACE STEAMERS.
LOW RATES. QUICK TIME.

For *DETROIT, PORT HURON, SANILAC, SAND BEACH, OS-CODA and ALPENA.*

LEAVE ST. IGNACE

Wednesdays .. ..10 a. m.

Saturday...................... 9 p m.

From Detroit to Cleveland Daily, except Sunday, at 11 p. m.

Through tickets and baggage checked to destination. Our illustrated pamphlet rates furnished by your ticket agent, or address

E. B. WHITCOMB, G. P. & T. A. DETROIT, MICH.

Above: Announcement appearing in *The True Northerner*, a newspaper out of Paw Paw, Michigan, on September 1, 1882.

Left: Advertisement for the Vulcan Store, from *The Newberry News*, June 10, 1886, and an advertisement for the Detroit & Cleveland Steam Navigation Co. from December 18, 1894.

Below: A company store token good for 10 cents worth of merchandise at the Vulcan Store.

The financial woes did not appear to have affected John S. Newberry at all, however, because he had substantial investments in many, many different businesses and interests.

Despite the business misfortunes of John Newberry and the other founding fathers, the settlers of his namesake "little city" were energetic and determined. The infrastructure was already in place, after all. They were determined to make the best of it. By 1887, they had successfully petitioned the state to let them form their own county, with Newberry as its county seat. They were joined in this endeavor by their new newspaper, *The Newberry News*, and had very strong support

The Newberry Depot. This photo appeared in the October 1894 Trade Edition of *The Newberry Enterprise*.

from the farmers of neighboring Lakefield Township (those original pioneers, who were tired of hiking over 100 miles to St. Ignace or the Soo to get governmental business done).

Newberry invested in everything from seeds to electricity. When he died in 1887, he left a fortune of $4.5 million dollars.[33] His Vulcan Furnace Company was not nearly so lucrative, periodically being devastated by fire, and lurching from bankruptcy to new owner, to bankruptcy to new owner and back again.

Luce County was molded out of the western end of Chippewa County and the northwestern corner of Mackinac County (the northern half of Lakefield Township only—the southern half became Portage Township, and stayed with Mackinac). The new county's name honored Cyrus Gray Luce, Michigan's newly elected governor.[34]

Cyrus Gray Luce, Governor of Michigan, honored by the naming of Luce County in 1887. He also never visited.

Having succeeded in establishing a new county and a new county seat, the people of Luce County proceeded to elect their own officials, including a "village president," and "village trustees" for Newberry, as well as sheriffs, clerks, postmasters, township supervisors, road commissioners, school inspectors, justices of the peace, and the like. The new government set up and operated its own courts and poorhouses, drafted ordinances, and engaged in other activities designed to encourage business and improve the area.

For all the residents, the future was bright. The Duluth, South Shore & Atlantic company, after assuming operation of the railroad, built an extension up to Sault Ste. Marie, connecting the branch at the aptly named Soo Junction. (As a result of this

C. E. TIBBOTT,
PHOTOGRAPHER,
NEWBERRY AVE.
Negatives Taken in All Kinds of Weather
I WILL GUARANTEE
SATISFACTION.

· DO YOU WANT A
PIANO or ORGAN!
If so be sure and see
T. C. Winter, of Marquette,
Agent for all kinds of Pianos and Organs.

Your fare from Newberry to Marquette and return will be deducted from price of piano if you purchase of him.

Advertisement from *The Newberry News* of December 18, 1894.

Spring
House
Cleaning
is now in order.
Get
**DIAMOMD WALL
FINISH**
and **ALABASTINE**
at the
Hardware Store
of
M. R. Manhard.
The cheapest
and
Best
in the
World.
All kinds
of
Heavy and
Shelf Hardware,
Farm Implements,
Etc., Etc.

Advertisement from *The Newberry News* of May 2, 1890. Manhard's hardware was run by James C. Foster, a nephew of M. R. Manhard, who lived in Marquette, Michigan. Later named Foster's Hardware, this store continues doing business today.

A portrait of J. C. Foster that appeared in *The Newberry News* of November 4, 1892.

Newberry Avenue, 1890s, looking south from the railroad tracks (photo courtesy of Sterling McGinn).

extension, in 1888 a town called "Corea" was planned, but it never materialized). Spurs and narrow-gauge tracks now branched off the main line in a myriad of places, penetrating the interior, the better to bring out that precious, prized lumber.[35]

By 1890, Newberry had more than 1,600 residents, a ten-month graded school, three churches (Catholic, Methodist, Presbyterian), water works, a fire department, municipal water main nine blocks long (that had replaced the old village pump), four hotels, several boarding houses, and a business district replete with general, grocery, drug, shoe, and hardware stores. Here you could find doctors, lawyers, barbers, a photographer shop, Chinese laundry, newspaper, cigar shops, pool rooms, more than a dozen saloons, and a post office. A fine brick bank was going up at the southern edge of town, which was to include an "opera house" on the second floor. Past the village limits to the west was a village dump for rubbish and beyond that a solemn cemetery for the dead.[36]

Economic expansion exploded out around Newberry into the surrounding areas. North of Newberry was thirty miles of cedar swamps, white pine forests, beech, birch, maple, elm, and hemlock.

This section housed dozens of lumber camps, temporary communities of a busy, boisterous, and noisy nature. At any one time, hundreds of men could be in residence, living and working in the woods.

Where the timber ended, Lake Superior began, its shoreline studded with lumber mills at Deer Park, Shelldrake, and Emerson, as well as lighthouses and "life saving stations" at Crisp Point, Whitefish Point, Deer Park, and Vermillion. These were lonely, faraway places, yet many were also thriving. For example, at the mill run by A. M. Chesbrough on the mouth of the Tahquamenon River, the town of Emerson was filled with thirty houses, a store, school, post office, and 109 people in 1890.[37]

In the 1890s, Deer Park had more than 300 people and enough families to support its own two-room schoolhouse. Its mill—illuminated by electric lights—ran "day and night," and a thrice-weekly stagecoach made the fifty-mile roundtrip down to Newberry, carrying mail and passengers. West of Deer Park was Grand Marais, no longer a tiny, lonely harbor, but a lumber boom town of its own, which peaked in 1899 with a population of about 3,000.[38]

During these boom years, dozens of satellite communities sprang up around Newberry. Robert Dollar, now owner of the Robert Dollar Lumber Company, founded his own company town, not a mile west. Like John Newberry, he believed in self-promotion and named it: Dollarville. Here he built a lumber mill in 1882. According to historian Charles Sprague Taylor, Robert Dollar's very first load of lumber was traded to farmer Robert Bryers for 100 bushels of potatoes. Later, Dollarville also hosted many additional mills, a railroad station, stores, saloons, a school, and hundreds of workers in rented houses owned by the mills.[39]

DM&M executive James McMillan had his own little namesake village—founded in 1885 fifteen miles west of Newberry and originally named Hornick's Camp—which was quickly surrounded by homesteading farmers. Beyond that was Seney, a notoriously wild lumber town, and Germfask, another farm community. East of Newberry, the railroad continued on until Soo Junction, where one could go north to Sault Ste. Marie, or south to St. Ignace.[40]

This postcard, dated 1909, shows the bank building on the corner of Truman and Newberry, which was built in 1890. Besides the bank, this building also had retail space (in the bottom right corner) and an "opera house" on the second floor (author's collection).

Just beyond Soo Junction, the Hulbert family centralized its own timber operations around a particularly lovely lake Francis Hulbert had discovered during his frozen race to Marquette a dozen or so years earlier. Although it was, as his son later said, little more than a "a small black hole in a hemlock forest, on the edge of a swamp," the village of "Hulbert" did have a few log cabins, cottages, and a sawmill.[41]

Then there was Sage Station, one of the largest of the experimental farms run by the Peninsular Land Company. The farm's purpose was dedicated to discovering ways of turning the cutover lands into prime farming territory. The Peninsular Land Company had already discovered that celery was particularly well suited to the climate, and was experimenting with other crops. By demonstrating the fertility of the land and the viability of cash crops, the Land Company hoped to better lure farmers to the area. The farmers then would (hopefully) purchase a farm from the Land Company. Later, naturally, the same farmers would use the railroad for all their shipping and traveling needs.

To the southwest of Newberry was Lakefield Township, now a well-established farming community made up of those initial, optimistic pioneers, growing oats, potatoes, and hay. Lakefield Township had, at various times, post offices named Seabrook, Ennis, and Helmer (the last two named for Sarah Ennis Bryers and Sanford Helmer). Lakefield also boasted the Fuller District and the Marks Settlement. They soon had their own churches and schoolhouses. The farmers were determined to better themselves, and in 1889 began work on the "Tait" Road to Pentland Township. No more would it take two days by oxen (or one day by horse) to reach Newberry.[42]

South of Lakefield, over the county line, even more communities sprang into being, such as Rapinville (founded by the Rapin family), Donald, Kennedy Siding (later Engadine), and Portage (later Curtis). Stagecoaches ran five times a week, bumping their way down to Naubinway, carrying mail and passengers.[43]

Pentland Township, just to the south of Newberry and east of Lakefield, was home to more farmers and more wood camps. One particularly grand camp was established in 1889 by the Vulcan Furnace company to cut cordwood. Dubbed "Woodville," it was accessed by a narrow gauge railroad line that ran seven miles southeast of Newberry.

By 1895, Newberry was thirteen years old, as exuberant, excitable, and infatuated with technology as any teenager. The village was just about to get the newfangled and ultra-modern electric lights for its businesses and streets (described as lovely "bouquets of light").* The "city fathers" had recently installed a sewer system. And the village had just won a seven-town competition to become the site of a potentially lucrative state facility: the Upper Peninsula Hospital for the Insane, a massive facility intended to house hundreds of inmates as well as their attendants and doctors.

Newberry was a new town, a young town, full of energetic, progressive, optimistic citizens, and it had established economical cornerstones in timber, industry, government, the "insane asylum," and a prospering farming community.

The future had unlimited potential.

Log train in Dollarville (photo courtesy of Dr. James Surrell).

---

* By Marjorie Morrill, waxing nostalgic in 1936, even as she was celebrating "Fifty Years of Progress" in the *Newberry News.*

Dollarville Sawmill, 1888 (photo courtesy of Sterling McGinn).

Horses.

A full car load of heavy draft and farm horses will be for sale at the stable of the Dollarville Hardwood Lumber Co., Dollarville, Mich. for two days only, Dec. 18 and 19. Time given if so desired; satisfaction guaranteed.

HAMMEL, KANN & HAMMEL.

A Car Load of

BUGGIES

JUST ARRIVED

All Kinds, Styles and Prices

We have some extra good bargains and can discount values offered by any mail order house..............

Phone 18   **J. C. FOSTER**

Advertisements from *The Newberry News* of June 23, 1905 and December 15, 1905.

This photo, discovered in a drawer at the office of *The Newberry News*, is labeled simply "Horse and Buggy, circa 1907."

Chapter Two
Peopling the Place

"Newberry is peopled with intelligent, accommodating, refined, progressive and whole-souled citizens, and the stranger who visits Newberry for the first time is favorably impressed with the intelligence and friendliness of its inhabitants."

— Ed Jones, Editor, "An Embryo City's Future,"
Newberry Enterprise, February 15, 1894

"We have built an ordered civilization out of those days that are gone, and we are proud of it and its splendid institutions—built it with hardship and with struggle, and sustained it with as fine and progressive a people as may, I think, be found anywhere."

— Dr. Frank P. Bohn, "This Was the Forest Primeval,"
Michigan History Magazine (Winter 1937)

BEFORE LUCE COUNTY WAS ESTABLISHED and populated with energetic pioneers, its original inhabitants, the Ojibwa, made the land their home. They were a nomadic people who moved regularly, with favorite trails and camping places, but no real fixed settlements. They hunted, fished for sturgeon and whitefish, gathered blueberries and cranberries, and sometimes raised corn and potatoes. In the spring, they camped on the high ground near what it is now Newberry, the better to tap maple trees and make maple syrup.[1]

In his book *Tahquamenon Country: A Look at Its Past*, author Charles Sprague Taylor relates several traditional stories from the Ojibwa of the area. One legend relates the story of a rival group of Menominee warriors. Intent on bringing battle to their enemies, they canoed seventy miles up the Manistique River, then portaged over to the Tahquamenon River, toward their prey. With them was a woman, born Ojibwa, who had been captured as a young child and raised among the Menominee.

The war party never arrived. As they paddled down the Tahquamenon, their young captive led the troops in rousing song—all the better to drown out the rushing and roar of the approaching waterfall (the famed Upper Tahquamenon Falls, about twenty miles northeast of Newberry). The entire group plunged to their deaths.

Another legend, related by Taylor, tells of a race of giant sturgeon with human heads that lived in the cascading Lower Tahquamenon Falls, four miles beyond the larger Upper Falls.

Whenever a solitary fisherman disappeared, it was said that he had accidently been caught by one of these creatures, and been claimed by them and turned into a human-headed sturgeon himself.[2]

The most famous tale of the area, one that brought the nation's attention to the eastern UP, is, of course, *The Song of Hiawatha*. The epic poem, written by Henry Wadsworth Longfellow, was extremely popular when it was published in 1855. For a long time, nearly every schoolchild in the country was familiar with Hiawatha and his adventures around the "Tahquamenaw River," his childhood exploits, his wooing of Minnehaha, and other escapades.

Left: Upper Tahquamenon Falls (as it looks today), where marauding Menominees once met their doom (author's photo).

Right: Lake Sturgeon could grow up to seven feet long, up to 250 pounds, and could live over 100 years. They no longer can be found frolicking in the falls because their habitat was destroyed by nineteenth-century logging operations (U.S. Fish & Wildlife Service).

Longfellow based his poem partially on the Ojibwa stories of Manabozho or Nanabozho, a trickster and demi-god. Many of these stories had been collected and published by Henry Rowe Schoolcraft several years earlier. Schoolcraft was the "Indian agent" at Sault Ste. Marie, who learned the native languages from his Ojibwa wife, Jane Johnston, and later authored the exhaustive six-volume, *Indian Tribes of the United States*. His collection of translated legends provided the inspiration for Longfellow's magnum opus.

While Longfellow's poem is Native American in inspiration, and set around the Upper Peninsula, it is not particularly authentic in execution. The name Hiawatha itself comes from a *completely different tribe*, the Iroquois, and belonged to a completely different personage (Schoolcraft and Longfellow had simply *assumed* it to be the same person). Nevertheless, *The Song of Hiawatha* was so very much beloved that the name Hiawatha and Longfellow's poem have continued to be linked to the Upper Peninsula to this day.[*]

With the coming of European-Americans, with their permanent villages and condescending attitudes, many Ojibwa left the area, some to Canada.

---

* Another major inspiration for Longfellow's poem was the Finnish language epic *Kalevala*. Very interesting, considering the future influx of Finnish settlers to the UP.

Left: Four miles downriver from the Upper Falls is the Lower Tahquamenon Falls, home of the human-headed sturgeon (author's photo).

Right: Chief Shingabowossin (ca. 1763—ca. 1830) was an important Ojibwa chief living in and around the eastern Upper Peninsula (picture courtesy of the Luce County Historical Society).

Others chose to stay and formed the basis for the Bay Mills Indian Community of today, located a few miles west of Sault Ste. Marie on the shores of Lake Superior.[3]

Ah, but which of the European invaders came to the New World first? The traditional approach, the one believed by most nineteenth-century Michiganders, was to assert that it was Christopher Columbus, an Italian working for the queen and king of Spain. He discovered the New World (or at least the Caribbean Sea) while looking for a sea route to India. He found it for himself, certainly, even if he never did realize where exactly he was. In any case, his voyages revealed the "New World" for most other fifteenth-century Europeans, most of whom had no idea that the Americas existed. However, he wasn't the first European to bump into the Western Hemisphere.

It is almost certain that the Vikings tried to settle along the northeastern coast of North America (later called Newfoundland) in the 1000s. They quickly failed, and promptly and mostly forgot that they had ever been there. Nineteenth-century historians had heard these Viking tall tales before and dismissed them. Archaeological proof was not unearthed until 1968 in L'Anse aux Meadows, Canada.

Besides the Vikings, Europeans had told each other even more shadowy stories of Brendan the sixth-century Irish monk, and Madoc the twelfth-century Welsh prince, each who are said to have sailed across the Atlantic. Then there are even wilder theories about Ancient Egyptians who were said to have built boats of papyrus (paper made of reeds), and in 1970, ethnographer-adventurer-author Thor Heyerdahl proved it was indeed possible to cross the Atlantic this way.

Occasionally, across the United States, stones are unearthed with markings that resemble Egyptian hieroglyphics or the Ogham runes of early Ireland. So either ancient peoples were quite the world travelers or we have a rash of hoaxes on our hands. Maybe both.

Luce County's own little contribution to the speculation about who first "discovered" the "New World" came in November 1896. According to a report in *The Newberry News,* Jake Gordon and George Howe, while "digging for a mink under the upturned root of a cedar tree" unearthed what they initially thought of as the "petrified remains of three persons." Further investigation showed they were not human remains, but three small statues, between two and three feet high. Subsequent digging unearthed a "tablet of stone covered with hieroglyphics."[4]

This incredible discovery was a sensation and a half. The statues and tablet were hauled into Newberry, where they were displayed in a store window. The townspeople came to gawk and speculate. Clergymen gave their opinions, claiming the tablet to be a "very valuable… historical relic" which "may reveal something of great importance." "The work on the tablet is too artistic to be ascribed to any of the Indian tribes," said the editor of *The Newberry News,* in a stupid and blatantly racist remark. "It must have been done by some people of a higher order of intelligence." Photos were taken and sent to the Smithsonian to be studied by "long haired scientists" and other "experts for translation" while locals waited anxiously for their opinion.[5]

The opinion, when it came, was anticlimactic. The Smithsonian basically shrugged its shoulders, leaving the impression that they thought it was a hoax. Many of the townspeople now agreed, having a "strong suspicion that it was the work of a bunch of jokers with time on their hands and an inclination to raise hell." Not everyone was so skeptical, though. A "Chicago Lecturer" named J. Frank Pickering stopped in Newberry in 1916 and theorized that the items were the work of a lost tribe of Palestine who "grew to be a mighty race" of white people before being destroyed in an epic "war of extermination" in Michigan's vicinity. Later researchers claimed the language to be Hittite, Etruscan, or Phoenician. Others just as passionately insist that it was a prank.[6]

There is curiously little interest in these stones, and they are usually not taken seriously. Yet, there has never been any suggestion that Jake Gordon, George Howe, or their employer John McGruer, had the talents, knowledge, or inclination to fake such a thing. McGruer had so little regard for the stones that he allowed them to crumble in his barn for forty years before they were moved to a tourist trap in St. Ignace. Today, the remains are on display in the Fort du Buade Museum and Gift Shop in St. Ignace, Michigan.

Whoever carved the tablet and stones, whether a misplaced Egyptian wanderer or a mischievous nineteenth-century scholar, remains a mystery.

Following Columbus's voyages (and those of the Vikings, monks, and Egyptians) other explorers came, many founding colonies up and down the Atlantic coast. Slowly, surely, they penetrated into the interior. The French were especially fond of the Great Lakes.

Duluth, South Shore & Atlantic Ry.

"ZENITH CITY SHORT LINE."

Direct Route between the East and South
east and the great Northwest and
all points on the South Shore
of Lake Superior.

LEAVE NEWBERRY AS FOLLOWS:

GOING WEST.

10:55 a m. EXPRESS MAIL, daily, for Ne-
gaunee, Ishpeming, Republic,
Champion, Michigamme, L'Anse,
Baraga, Houghton and inter-
mediate points, connecting at
Houghton with Mineral Range
railroad for Hancock, Calumet,
Red Jacket and Lake L

2:17 p m. FAST EXPRESS, daily, for Negaunee, Ishpeming, *Republic,
Champion, Michigamme, Nestora
Superior, West Superior, Duluth
and intermediate points, connecting at Duluth for all points west
and southwest. Wagner Palace
cars through to Duluth without
change.

GOING EAST.

3:15 p. m. MIXED, except Sunday for Au-
Train, Munising, Seney, Newberry, St. Ignace and intermediate points.

11:35 a. m. FAST EXPRESS, daily for Sault
Ste. Marie and intermediate point
connecting with the Canadian Pacific express for Montreal, Boston
New York and all New England
points. Wagner Palace sleeping
cars to Sault Ste. Marie without
change.

5:03 p. m. EXPRESS MAIL, daily for Sault
Ste. Marie, St. Ignace and intermediate points, connecting at
Mackinaw City with the Michigan
Central and Grand Rapids and
Indiana railroads, for all points
in lower Michigan and the east
and southeast. Wagner Palace
sleeping cars through to Detroit.

TRAINS ARRIVE IN NEWBERRY AS FOLLOWS:

FROM THE EAST.

10:54 a. m. EXPRESS MAIL, daily from
Detroit, St. Ignace, Sault Ste.
Marie and intermediate points.

2:17 p. m. EXPRESS daily, from Boston,
Sault Ste. Marie and intermediate
points.

12:30 a. m. ACCOMODATION, except Sunday, from St. Ignace and intermediate points.

FROM THE WEST.

11:35 a.m. EXPRESS, daily, from Duluth
and intermediate points.

5:03 a. m. EXPRESS MAIL daily, from
Houghton and intermediate point.

—*Except Sunday.

For rates, Time Tables and other infor
mation apply to Ticket Agents.

W. F. FITCH,   C. B. HIBBARD,
Gen'l Manager.   G. P. & T. A.

DSS&A Timetable from *The Newberry News* of December 19, 1890.

Vulcan Store Company !

For short time we will make

LOW :-: PRICES !

To close our stock of medium and low priced

Overcoats, Pea Jackets,

And Ladies, Misses' and Children's

Wool Lined Over Shoes

Our stock is complete in the following lines:

Groceries, choice canned goods, green apples, dried fruits, flour, family drugs
and patent medicines, hardware,
tinware, cuttlery, clothing,
boots, shoes and rubbers, hats, caps, &c.. &c.

Our motto is: Good Goods and Fair Prices.

Vulcan Store Company.

TO THE PUBLIC.

We are now prepared to take con-
tracts for all kinds of
PLASTERING & KALSOMINING
Centres, Circles, and Cornishing a
specialty. Give us a call.
Alex. McLean & Co.

Advertisement from *The Newberry News* of September 1, 1887 and June 24, 1886.

Advertisements from *The Newberry News* of December 19, 1890 (left) and October 29, 1915 (center and right).

Advertisements from *The Newberry News* of May 12, 1887.

Left: Sanford N. Dutcher (circa 1894), for decades the Luce County Prosecutor, put away many an evildoer.

Center: Alexander Main (circa 1894), a Scottish carpenter and contractor who built many of Newberry's early buildings. He also became a probate judge and was active in church, community, and school matters.

Right: "His Corpulence" himself, Donald N. "Dan" McLeod (circa 1894), hotelier, lumberman, businessman, and local bigwig.

Left: Dr. George Trueman, ca 1900. He lived in Newberry in the late 1880s (from *Men of Progress: Embracing Biographical Sketches of Representative Michigan Men*, Evening News Association, 1900).

Center and Right: Joseph Liberty and Mrs. Hannah (McConnell) Liberty (courtesy of the Luce County Historical Society).

So by the 1700s, France claimed much of Michigan. French voyageurs, fur traders, and missionaries all visited the area, but few stayed. Still, as late as the 1880s, many families of French-Canadian and Chippewa origin lived along the shores of Lake Michigan, fishing and hunting as they had for generations.

These families had arrived in the Great Lakes area in the 1700s and early 1800s. Now their descendants lived at Naubinway, Scott's Point, St. Ignace, or Mackinac Island, sporting first names like Jean Baptiste, Victoire, Josephine, or Theophile and last names like Aslin, Beaudin, Rapin, Vallier, Paquin, Goodreau, or Derusha. Some worked as coopers, building barrels for fish. Many were illiterate and most worked as fishermen.

A brief period of British rule in the late 1700s brought a handful of soldiers to the Great Lakes area, but they had little influence. After the 1793 Treaty of Paris, of course, "Michigan" was officially ceded to the United States, as part of the "Northwest Territory." During the first half of the nineteenth century, American surveyors and governmental officials (like Douglass Houghton and Henry Schoolcraft) made visits to the Lake Superior coastline, exploring the geography and mineralogy of the new American land. They did not stay permanently, either. Later on, Protestant missionaries tried to set up new Christian Ojibwa communities in the days before the Civil War. A Baptist minister of Sault Ste. Marie named Abel Bingham and his assistant, James Douglas Cameron, endeavored to establish a settlement near the mouth of the Tahquamenon River, but it was destroyed in a cholera epidemic in 1849. The Methodist Rev. John Pitezel set up a similar community on Lake Superior's coast at Naomikong Point (about twenty-five miles east of what would one day become Newberry). In 1849, his little parish featured a schoolhouse, mission house, and several homes. At its peak, it was the center of a sixty-person community, but it, too, soon declined.[7]

Then, of course, came the 1880s and the railroad, and a heady influx of energetic, permanent residents, eager to build and stay. It was not unusual for a new resident to move into the area first, and then invite family members to join him. Many of the children of these families, those who stayed in the area, married into other pioneer families. Thus, early Luce County and the village of Newberry became the home of a vast web of interconnected brothers and sisters, parents and children, in-laws and cousins.

Luce County's earliest settlers included: two Smathers brothers, six Mark brothers, and six Pentland brothers. Early correspondence often referred to Dollarville's "Beaudin Colony" from Gaspe, Quebec, which included at one time or another Louis, Fred, Emma, Albert, and Frank Beaudin, plus their second cousin, Josephat Beaudin, as well as Oliver and Edmund Beaudin, who may or may not also be relations.

Later, Newberry had the Jenney brothers, Labombard brothers, Liberty brothers, Barber brothers, Henderson brothers, and Surrell brothers. Most of the Canadian Costley siblings (specifically, Frank, James, William, Edward, Mary, Lizzie, Isabella, and Hugh Costley) made Newberry their home at one time or another in the late 1880s, as did many of the Trueman siblings (William, James, Mary, Joseph, and George). Sanford N. Dutcher, an early prominent lawyer, enjoyed the company of his brother, Furman Dutcher, as well as Mrs. Dutcher's brother and sister, Milton and Eva Beurmann.

Angus McLeod was joined by his grown children: Mrs. Christina McKay, Mrs. Sarah McLean, Angus Jr., and John, along with their spouses and children.[8] Dan McLeod (no relation)

Advertisements from *The Newberry News*, May 12, 1887, May 2, 1890 and June 24, 1886.

Advertisements from *The Newberry News*, July 18, 1890 and December 19, 1890.

Advertisements from *The Newberry News*, November 18, 1892 and December 19, 1890.

and his sisters—Theresa "Tracy" McLeod and Mrs. John McCuaig (and family)—all came to Newberry. So did Mrs. McLeod's sister and brother-in-law, Mary and Robert Langstaff.[9]

Webb and Harry Latham were followed by their brothers-in-law, Hibbard Ingalls and Herman Chamberlain. William Crocker and his brother-in-law, David Davern, and sister-in-law, Miss Sarah Amy, came to stay as well. Yet another family arriving to try their luck in the new town was William T. Murphy, his sister Mary Ann Gormely, her husband Francis, and Francis's sister Elizabeth.[10]

Mrs. Lucy Hubbert and her sister, Mrs. Evelyn Bettes, both moved to Newberry, as did their husbands, children, father William Darcy, and brother Will. Siblings, children, parents, cousins, in-laws, nephews and nieces, aunts and uncles all banded together to move to and build up this new country.[11]

Friends and neighbors came, too. In the 1870s, Robert Dollar (future lumber baron) and Robert Bryers (future farmer) were both living in the same small town, Bracebridge, Ontario, which had been founded very recently and served as home to only a few hundred people. Hugh Robert McInnes, another early resident, also appears to have been from Bracebridge.[12]

The carpenter Thomas Miller (possibly Newberry's very first permanent resident) hailed from Madoc Township in Ontario, Canada (named after the legendary Welsh prince). So, too, did Mr. and Mrs. Joseph Liberty (and his brother, Louis), who arrived with the railroad and helped clear the new townsite, felling logs. Another Madoc resident, Miss Ida Fretz, arrived a few years later to open a millinery (ladies' hats) shop. Her mother, Mary, and brother, Will, joined her there.[13]

Luce County soon hosted an ever-changing kaleidoscope of people, ebbing and flowing, moving in and moving out: Americans, British-Canadians*, Irish-Canadians, French-Canadians, and "Sweedes." Finns began arriving in great numbers in the 1890s. A significant "colony" of Kentuckians (most from Greenup and Carter Counties) came in the 1910s, specifically recruited by the Lake Superior Iron & Chemical Company (successor to the Vulcan Furnace Company). Indeed, many Kentuckians moved not just to Luce County, but all over the eastern Upper Peninsula. At various times, Newberry also hosted Poles, Armenians, Russians, Belgians, Norwegians, Italians, Chinese, Swiss, Germans, Danes, Austrians, French, British, and Irish.[14]

In 1900, two-thirds of county residents were immigrants or the children of immigrants, mostly from Canada (roughly divided evenly between those of British and French origin), as well as a growing number of Swedes and Finns. But they all eventually became Americans together, their descendants becoming known as "Yoopers."**

---

* Those Canadians of British origin included first and second-generations from Ireland and England, but especially from Scotland. This accounts for the preponderance in early Newberry of surnames like McClellan, McDonald, McKay, McKinnon, McLeod, McLean, McPhee, Campbell, Cameron, and favorite Scottish first names like Alexander, Angus, Archie, David, Donald, Duncan, Malcolm, Neil, Robert, Agnes, Minnie, Margaret, Jessie, Jean, Janet, and Catherine.

** The term "Yooper," refers to a resident of the Upper Peninsula of Michigan, "the UP." Although the term is fairly recent (it did not become common until the late 1970s), it is now ubiquitous throughout the region and acts as a term of self-identification as well as a source of good-humored pride.

The six Pentland Brothers came with their parents to the future Luce County around the year 1880. All six grew up to be prominent local farmers. Back Row: William John, Moses, and George. Front Row: Isaac, Alexander, and Thomas (photo courtesy of Roxanna Pentland Transit).

New Tailor Shop!

FREDERICK B. STADE,

THE TAILOR.

I wish to inform the People of Newberry and Vicinity that I have opened up a new Merchant Tailor shop in T. V. Case's old stand and hope to get your patronage.

In have the finest and newest samples ever put before the public. Call and examine. Prices moderate. All work guaranteed, and done in the latest style.

Advertisements from *The Newberry News* of
November 11, 1892 and December 7, 1906.

The Canadians (both French and British) came because they had had much experience lumbering in Quebec and Ontario and could put their talents to good use here in this up-and-coming area. The French-Canadian loggers ("Frenchmen"), with their red sashes, were especially skilled in hacking pine logs into the square beams known as "waney boards." The early lumber barons (many of them Canadian-born themselves) imported large crews from Quebec. Many of these men would move on, but many also stayed, marrying, having children, and putting down roots.[15]

Their French-Canadian accent is one of the sources of the modern "Yooper" accent of today. The French-Canadian exclamation "hein" becoming the "eh" of today and their "tuque" becoming "chook" (knitted winter hat). In the 1890s, Robert H. Wright, who lived in Newberry at the time, wrote a series of comical articles in the "French Canadian dialect" under the pen name of Pete Pareau. They were very well received in their time, but are nearly unreadable today, due to the extreme phonetic renderings of the words and the unrelenting dullness of nineteenth-century tariff politics (Wright's favorite topic). The following sample, from an 1890 edition of Wright's upstart paper, *The Newberry Independent*, may give an idea of the nineteenth-century French Canadian accent (as rendered by an English speaker). In it, Pete Pareau had traveled to Washington, DC to talk to President Harrison.

> "Hallo, Ben," ah say, "bah goah am glad to see you. Ah suppose eet surprase you to see me. You have de honair to meet Pete Pareau from Luce kountay. Shook han's hagain, Ben. How ees you waff an odder relashun?"
>
> "Mah waff ees well, Mistaire Pareau," de president reply.
>
> "Am glad to hear dat. Ah suppose eet ees veray pleasant for you to be een position where you can spend your day surround bah all you relashun?"
>
> "Mistaire Pareau ah will considair you happlication for office latair on."
>
> "Tank you, Ben. Ah wrote you several lettair on de subjec' of mah happointment to offeece but ah suppose dey was los' as ah did not geet reply from you. Ah hear dat you will be candidate for de nomination hagain een aighteen-hondred an 92. Eef de report ees true an you geet de nomination eet will be to you hinterest een Luce Kountay to happoint me to fat offeece. Ah got great deal hinflence wid de Frenchman."[16]

Another major source for the Yooper accent was the Finnish, Swedish, Norwegian, and (to a lesser extent) Danish immigrants. They provided the "ja" or "yah" for "yes" and reinforced the "dis and dese" for this and these. Scandinavians immigrated to the US throughout the nineteenth century, mostly for economic opportunity. Sweden and Norway, for example, suffered a surplus of young adults and a lack of farmland. This made emigration more attractive. Swedes were considered good immigrants, praised by the locals for their honesty and cleanliness. "Their houses are models of cleanliness," *The Newberry News* gushed in 1890, "in fact some of our native working men could take lessons from them in that respect." The editor went on to explain that "these people make good citizens, are perfectly honest and upright, their word being as good as gold."[17]

V. C. KEITHEN

—DEALER IN—

Watches, Clocks Jewelery, Etc., Etc.

Keep on hand a nice line of goods and invites the public to look over stock.

Repairing of all kinds.

Done in a workmanlike manner. Give me a call when in want of jewelry. Located in Jones & Holt's store

First National Bank,

o—OF—o

ST. IGNACE, MICH.

—o—

CAPITAL.................$50,000.00
SURPLUS and PROFITS.   6,000.00

—o—

Offers most Favorable Terms for Opening Accounts.

Pays Interest on Certificates of Deposit.

Buys and sells Foreign Drafts.

Has Facilities for Collecting Times Equal to any Bank on the Peninsula.

O. W. JOHNSON Pres.
WM. SAULSON, V. Pres.
EDW. L. DURGIN, Cashier

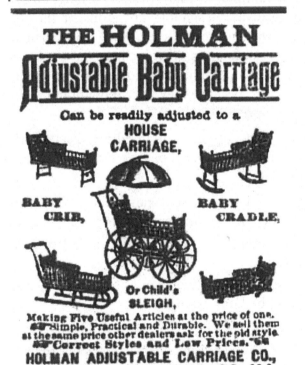

THE HOLMAN
Adjustable Baby Carriage

Can be readily adjusted to a
HOUSE CARRIAGE,
BABY CRIB,
BABY CRADLE,
Or Child's **SLEIGH,**

Making Five Useful Articles at the price of one. Simple, Practical and Durable. We sell them at the same price other dealers ask for the old style. Correct Styles and Low Prices.
HOLMAN ADJUSTABLE CARRIAGE CO.,
275 Wabash Ave., CHICAGO, ILL
Illustrated Catalogue sent free.

GRANT BROS.,
PHOTOGRAPHERS

PHOTOS   FOR XMAS

GET your photos taken now and have them ready for the Holidays. Bring Children to the Studio at 10 a m., but not later than 2 p m., owing to the short days this season of the year photos cannot be promised short of ten days after plate is made.

Studio Fitted to Make Photos from a Post Card to 14x17 Direct

Advertisements from *The Newberry News* from (top left, clockwise):
May 12, 1887; September 1, 1887;
December 19, 1890; and December 7, 1906.

Finland, too, was plagued by the same conditions as Norway and Sweden: a burgeoning peasant class and limited farmland with which to support them. In addition, Finland was under the political control of Russia, which was becoming increasingly heavy-handed toward the Finns. The Russians policy was one of "Russification." "In his own country he is kept under subjection with a stern hand," remarked *The Newberry News* of the Finns in 1907. "His liberty is curtailed, his possessions are few, and the hand of authority sees to it that these conditions remain so." Later on, the Russian lords forced many young Finnish men into their army, which was busy desperately losing World War I.[18]

And so many emigrated, rather than submit to Russian rule. In 1917, a party of four (unnamed) Finns landed in Newberry and reported to the newspaper a thrilling story about how they had fled their country, rather than be drafted by the Russian Tsar. Waiting until dark, they launched themselves and a small motorboat into the Gulf of Bothnia, off the Baltic Sea, where the motorboat broke down in the ensuing storm. The Finns then rigged a sail, but that blew away and they drifted along until the boat sank. Swimming, they made it to a deserted island off the coast of Sweden, where they were rescued by "kindhearted peasants." Thereupon, they made their way to the US and eventually found themselves in Michigan.[19]

Of all the immigrant groups in northern Michigan, Finns suffered the most prejudice. Finns had relatively more difficulty communicating with their neighbors. Swedes and Norwegians spoke a Germanic-based language, a distant cousin of English. French-Canadians and Germans spoke a language that was at least familiar to their American neighbors, as French and German were commonly taught at more advanced schools. The Finns, on the other hand, spoke Finnish, a language nobody knew that was most closely related to Hungarian and Estonian. They also had strange customs that no one else had ever heard of like a propensity for saunas. The Finns had more trouble assimilating and, thus, were more homesick and thought to be more quarrelsome, liquor-crazed, and stab-happy. Because they were thought to be more quarrelsome and stab-happy, they experienced more prejudice.

In 1891, for example, *The Luce County Democrat* reportedly ran an editorial stating that "the average Finlander in the upper peninsula is little better than a beast... they are a curse to the country and a disgrace to any civilized community."*

The French-Canadians seemed to harbor a special intolerance against the Finns. Fights between the two groups were not uncommon. Bosses in the lumber camps and the factories tended to arrange ethnic groups together in the same shifts, to alleviate the tensions and increase cooperation.[20]

Many of the immigrants to the UP tended to Americanize their names to a certain extent. The Finnish Matti Kumpulainen became Matt Campbell, for example.**

---

* No copies of this particular newspaper are known to exist. The quote comes from a letter to the editor written to and published in the *Newberry News*, the *Luce County Democrat*'s bitter rival. In the letter, the anonymous writer condemns the editorial and urges everyone to "exercise a little more charity towards his erring fellow men." Of course, *The Newberry News* probably ran the rebuttal more out of a desire to bash the *Democrat* than from any inclination to promote friendly feelings (please see Chapter 9).

** Newberry actually had two such men. Both were born Matti Kumpulainen in Finland (one in 1878, the other in 1880), both were married to women called Mary, and both died in Luce County, having changed their names to Matt Campbell (one in 1915, one in 1958).

What You "AUTO" Have is a good ROCKER

and right here is the place to get them.

From $1.00 to $20.00

We have the choicest variety and the highest standard of quality and design. We guarantee to save money on any article. Just come in.

G. Rosenthal & Son.

A Foot Stool Sale.

A Foot Stool adds considerably to the appearance of any room in the house. You know that.

I have a few very pretty stools left over from the holidays that are selling now at reduced prices. They are really chic. Call in and see them.

W. C. Jenkins

Undertaking. Embalming

BANK BLDG.

You Need Wood.

I Sell Wood.

16, 18, 24 and 48 inch good sound body hardwood in lots of from 10 to 500 cords at lowest market prices. Special prices made on orders of 50 cords or over. Orders filled promptly.

Wholesale and Retail.

Full Measure.

T. H. Ferguson.

W. R. STEWART,
LAND LOOKER
Residence on JOHN St. - Newberry

Advertisements from *The Newberry News* of February 12, 1904.

Narcisse Lambert Pelletier sometimes listed his first name as Nelson. His son Theophrede Pelletier became Fred or Alfred. Euclide Larivee sometimes went by Joe Rivers. Frank L. Harris, prosperous businessman, was born Louis Strohauer to German parents. And finally, Pierre Sicard was known locally as Peter, Anders Hedberg as Andrew, and Kjerstan Hedberg as Christina.[21]

Others clung proudly to their heritage. Swedish John Stark gave five of his American children the decidedly foreign names of Bror, Ingrid, Olafva, Svea, and Gota (the sixth was Edward). Norwegian-born Hjalmar Johnson, valedictorian of the Newberry High Class of 1898 and resident of Michigan since he was a small child, never Anglicized his first name.

Finnish language services continued in Newberry's Finnish Lutheran church until well into the twentieth century. In 1891, it was reported that many former Canadians were flying the Stars and Stripes and the Union Jack together, and no one thought the worse of them for it. In 1900, the Swedish community held its own Fourth of July celebration with ice cream, coffee, food, and a "patriotic program" full of songs and recitations.[22]

First-generation immigrants tended to work together, worship together, live together, play together, and marry each other. Although Newberry was too small to have any true ethnic enclaves, it did have its "Swede town" on West John and West Helen streets, beyond the John Street school, where many Swedish speakers built houses. Newberry also had its "Finn Town" concentrated on East Truman, around the Finnish Lutheran church and Herman Anderson's grocery store.[23]

So the Swedes had their sewing circles, youth groups, and Fourth of July picnics, and the Finns had their temperance society, Monday night dances, and even their own small lending library with books in English and Finnish.

"The Finns stayed down at their end (of Truman Avenue) with their sauna baths and not much else," reminisced Louis Foster about his childhood in the 1910s, "and never was there a social event attended by both groups." Prejudice was slow to die. Even in the late 1920s, Louis Foster believed, teachers still gave "preferential treatment" to sons of the "Scottish Presbyterian establishment" over those with Swedish and Finnish last names.[24]

It was not until the third and sometimes fourth-generations that their American descendants, schooled together, began to mix. The Finns, however, may have had the last laugh, as today there is a decidedly Finnish bent to the Upper Peninsula.

Chapter Three
Lumberjack Life

"Once was a time when the river hogs
Rode with ease the bobbing logs.
About the Big Falls throbbing roar
A boom was tied from shore to shore.
Down the dark Tahquamenon
In tall calked boots and mackinaw
The French and the Irish shanty-men
Shouted their songs again and again."

— Marjorie Huntoon Morrill, from her poem "Dan McLeod" (1931)

REGARDLESS OF WHERE AND WHEN they came, all immigrants to the new Luce County were hoping to build a successful life, to grab a piece of the growing wealth that accompanies new industries. And of all the industrial cornerstones that supported the new county, timber was the most important, and the most ubiquitous.

Trees and their byproducts supported not only the logging camps, but also the sawmills, charcoal kilns, saloons, hotels, railroad stations, all of their employees, the shops, doctors, lawyers, schools, and just about everything else. Logging reigned over all things.

Large concerns associated with the railroad like the Vulcan Furnace Company and Peninsular Land Company operated lumber camps. So, too, did independent companies like the Robert Dollar Lumber Company, Chicago Lumber Company, Danaher & Melendy Company, Chesbrough Brothers, Mason Brothers, Con Culhane, Morse & Son, Reed & Green, Cook & Willson, and many others.

There was plenty of room for small businessmen as well. The smallest lumbering camps employed as few as eight to ten men. Thus, they attracted many men who were already established in other professions. For example, Adam G. Louks was a "sheriff and lumberman." Joseph Stafford was a "druggist and lumberman."[44]

Jeremiah Holland was a Civil War veteran and member of a surveying party that had explored and mapped the UP in the 1860s. In the 1880s, he returned, purchasing both extensive timberlands and farmland on Manistique Lake. He was a "farmer and lumberman." Dan McLeod was a hotelier and lumberman. He owned and operated the Clayton House (later the McLeod House) from 1885 until 1896. He also bought tracts of timberland, organized lumber camps, and cut "millions of feet of pine." Sometimes, these men would contract with the bigger companies, hiring themselves out as "walking bosses" for the corporations. At other times, they would be independent operators.[45]

Lumberman ran two types of logging camps: the pine camps and the hardwood camps.

In the early days, white pine was the most valuable of all the trees and much sought after by the logging companies. As a softer wood, it cut more easily, and because it floated well, it was easier to move around, using the streams and rivers of the forest. Hardwood was cut, too, but not as much, and mostly for the charcoal industry, which didn't care about quality (since the wood would be burned up anyway). Because hardwood did not float as well, hardwood camps tended to locate closer to Newberry, the railroad lines, and the kilns.

Camps ranged from tiny groups of less than a dozen men to massive outfits with several hundred employees each. The camps were under the charge of a woods boss, who used clerks to handle the paychecks and order supplies, blacksmiths, and saw filers to look after the tools, and most importantly, a cook. The rest of the men were an assortment of log cutters, log haulers, road builders, etc. and their pay ranged from $15 to $30 a month.[46]

Accommodations for the woodsmen ranged from shacks in the woods to veritable villages. Especially in the early days when trees were still plentiful and waste common, many men would often live in log cabin bunkhouses. Others made do with tar-paper shacks. Larger camps also built a cook shack for cooking and eating, complete with oilcloth-covered tables, as well as barns and granaries for the animals, a blacksmith shop, a camp store, and an office for the boss.

The earliest camp workers subsisted on a diet of pickled pork, corned beef, flour, tea, and coffee. Beans were a favorite staple, and butter and sugar were luxuries. Later on, the meals grew much more elaborate, featuring steak and eggs, bacon, roast pork, pancakes, and lots of pie. A good cook became essential for any lumber camp's success.[47] Woodsmen's lives were lit by kerosene lamps and heated by red-hot woodstoves. The smell of coffee, pine sap, tar, wood-shavings, and wet wool socks permeated the camps. The woodsmen's workdays began before dawn with a hearty breakfast and continued until past sundown, the men being in bunks (often straw ticks and blankets) by 9:00 p.m. Their only time off was Sundays, Christmas, and New Year's Day.[48]

One of the most substantial camps was a hardwood camp first established by the Newberry Furnace Company (formerly the Vulcan Furnace Company). The camp's workers hauled the hardwood by narrow gauge railroad to Newberry and the kilns. Their camp was dubbed "Woodville." To work these camps, the Newberry Furnace Company employed almost 400 people. The single men lived in a boarding house, while the families were housed in twenty "modest little cottages." About twenty children went to the Woodville School, which was set up especially for that purpose. Miss Alice Skinner of Traverse City was imported to be its teacher. The children loved her, and at night, she turned her attention to twenty-six "full-grown men and women taking advantage of this means to secure an education that perhaps was denied them in their youth."[49]

By 1891, when the Newberry Furnace Company sold the camp to the Mason Brothers, the "village" consisted of forty wooden buildings in three "streets," including a general store and blacksmith and carpenter shops. This little community, and others like it, were not meant to be permanent. Even as the community was being built, *The Newberry News* lamented that

Logging Camp (courtesy of the Tahquamenon Logging Museum).

A Con Culhane lumber camp
(courtesy of the Tahquamenon Logging Museum).

"everything is so comfortably and pleasantly situated that it is to be regretted that they cannot be utilized for a much longer period." Woodville would disappear when the lumber ran out.[50]

"Landlocked" Woodville was somewhat unique. Other lumber operators, especially the pine cutters, made sure to set up their camps near to rivers, especially the big three of the area: the Tahquamenon, the Fox, and the Betsy.

In the older, white pine camps, most woodsmen began work in the fall, the "sawing season," when the coming winter and preponderance of ice made hauling logs easier. The lumberjacks sawed all winter long, through the frost and snow. Using sleighs and animal power, they hauled the logs down "ice roads" to the nearest convenient river for "banking."

Work continued until winter ended and ice roads turned into mud roads. Many lumberjacks were let go for a time, until the ice melted in the rivers and the "spring drive" began. During the spring drive, woodsmen required real skill since they faced the dangerous, frustrating task of riding and poling the buoyant pine logs downriver. This was a tense, risky job, and accidents were common.

Local historian George Rintamaki, writing in 1984, described it best as "an activity which was akin to riding on top of a restless horse standing up." He further explained, "In order to keep the logs moving along with the current, the men actually stood on the logs as they bobbed along, sometimes jumping from log to log to get to a spot where a tangle or jam threatened. Experienced river hogs, as the men were commonly called, became so adept and skilled at this that they hardly ever 'went for a swim.'"[51]

In 1915, when the era of the river drive was ending, a nostalgic *Newberry News* described it thus:

> "Clad in hobnailed brogans and wielding 'pike poles' and 'peavies,' the lumberjacks piloted millions of feet of lumber down the river on the crest of the spring freshets. Log jams were daily occurrences, and many of the woods men lost their lives when the drives were shooting through rapids or traveling in narrow channels where the swollen streams were swift and treacherous."[52]

There were three categories of workers in the spring, who were paid up to $2.00 per day. The Sacking crew came up behind, trying to find straggling logs and send them on their way. The River Drivers kept the logs moving in the middle, and the Jam crew tried to head off log jams up at the front of the pack. They wore "red shirts, overalls cut or torn off nearly up to the knees," and "nail-studded driving boots," explained *The Newberry News* in a short, reminiscent article called "The Passing of the Lumberjack" in 1917. They were "open and aboveboard sort of fellows who could and would work, swear, drink or fight on the square," and "rugged, big-hearted fellows who despised a shirk or a sneak."[53]

Spectators would watch in awe as logs as thick as two-feet across would come barreling down the Tahquamenon River, shoot over the Tahquamenon Falls, and sometimes crumple like matchsticks. Once the logs reached Lake Superior, they would either be sawed into lumber then and there at one of the various remote, river-mouth sawmills, or be bundled up and shipped out as they were. [54]

The couple is identified by the Luce County Historical Society as Jeremiah and Harriet Holland. However, the Germfask Township Sesquicentennial book lists them as their daughter, Cecil Ray Holland, and her husband, Neil McEachern (photo courtesy Luce County Historical Society).

Logging Camp (photo courtesy of the Luce County Historical Society).

Another particularly grand camp was set up by Donald N. "Dan" McLeod. A popular fellow, he moved to Newberry in 1885 to start a hotel with, as he said, "One wife, one child and $1.50 in cash." A host with boundless energy, his hotel was one of the most successful businesses in town. Even so, in the 1890s, he gave up the hotel business altogether to become a lumbering boss. He logged everywhere from the shores of Lake Superior to Rexton in the south.[55] In the fall of 1900, he was hired by the logging company Hall & Munson to cut timber for them on the Sucker River, near Grand Marais, for two years.[56]

McLeod eventually employed almost 200 men in three different camps. Unlike his predecessors, he practiced a modern and up-to-date approach to logging. Instead of building ice roads in winter to get the logs to the river, his workers laid ten miles of narrow-gauge railway (his engines were dubbed "Big Alice" and "Little Alice"). With a railroad, his employees could cut and haul year-round, not just in winter. Instead of waiting for the snowmelt to flood the rivers, the workers built a dam to better control the river's level and the flow of water. By 1901, his workers were moving more than 100,000 feet of logs a day. McLeod's neighbors were both skeptical and impressed over the "considerable outlay of money" that he poured into his camps. He even employed a "chef" named Ben Ward, who could "give many a good housewife pointers," in the opinion of a 1901 news article in *Newberry News*.[57]

McLeod was a genial man, fond of practical jokes, who loved to laugh. He was a generous man, known to donate wagonloads of supplies to poor widows. He was also a rotund man, sometimes referred to (with great affection) as "His Corpulence." Everyone loved Dan McLeod. His obituary noted that "Even though the skies were overcast, for him the sun was always shining, and his infectious laugh was a dispeller of gloom."[58]

The bosses of the timber camps were hearty, larger-than-life figures, at home both in the woods and in town. Another memorable camp boss, David Ranson, had first established himself in Grand Marais with Robert Dollar and stayed there until 1885, whereupon he moved to near the Tahquamenon River. As a child, he was the ill-educated son of a Canadian stevedore, unable to write his own name. As a man, David Ranson had wealth, power, and influence, and he knew more about timber than anyone else in the peninsula. At his busiest, he ran five different camps, each with seventy-five to eighty men and fifty horses. According to historian Ida M. Spring, writing in 1947, his claim to fame was that he had once killed a bear with an axe.[59]

Camp Boss John "Norwegian Jack" Ryland became notorious for his slick operations, deceiving his workers, superiors, and local merchants alike. He is said to have cheated bartenders by treating the entire room and then refusing to pay. He abused employees until they quit to save on their salaries, and he deliberately inflated the number of logs he had cut to his bosses.[60]

Perhaps the most beloved camp boss was Cornelius "Con" Culhane. He had arrived in the United States in 1847, a poor, Irish immigrant child, his penniless family fleeing the famine. By the time he was twenty-five, he had a small farm in Michigan, but it was in the woods where he found his calling. He spent nearly two decades logging in lower Michigan before moving up north, where he was considered a near-legend.

Culhane was a hands-on boss and spent a great deal of time in the woods, supervising his crews. He built a handsome home in the woods near to his logging operations for his wife, Ellen, to whom he was devoted. Ellen was popular with the men, who called her "Ma."

Logs plunging over a waterfall during the spring river drive
(photo courtesy of the Tahquamenon Logging Museum).

A more modern way to transport logs
(photo courtesy of the Tahquamenon Logging Museum).

Con Culhane worked his men hard and forbade them both cigarettes and liquor. He spoke in a thick Irish accent and was fond of wrestling and roughhousing.

Nothing could stop Culhane. One winter, he moved his entire operation to its new location by placing tracks across the frozen swamp, running his train across, and then stopping, picking up the pieces at the back, and reattaching them in front. Just like a cartoon. He loved his little train engines, naming them the Ellen K and the Con C. He was so celebrated and admired that he almost had a township named for him. The name "Culhane Township" was proposed as early as 1893 and would have been located in the far north of Luce County. Unfortunately, it did not have enough permanent settlers, so the plan never came to pass.

By 1903, Con Culhane was sixty-one and widely considered to be a millionaire. He owned hundreds of acres of forestlands, sawmills, and his own logging railroads. Although planning his retirement, he had not yet decided to stop work. One fateful day, he was riding on his beloved trains, when—and no one knew quite how it happened—the train jolted. Culhane lost his balance, fell under the wheels, and was instantly killed.[61]

While the pine lasted, pine camps dominated the scene. After the turn of the century, the great pine stands were vanishing—by 1903 "only a few scattering bunches remain(ed)" and lumbermen turned more and more to harvesting hardwood, or cedar, and producing pulpwood. New types of saws and new railroad lines made hardwood easier to harvest, and more and more of these camps rose to fill the gap left by pine loggers. Still, the industry was on a smaller scale than before.[62]

Rivers and river drives were still used to get the logs to the sawmills, but it was a cumbersome process involving lashing heavy hardwood logs to more buoyant pine logs so that both would float. Narrow-gauge railways were much less trouble; thus, more and more of these little rail lines were built until even the area's great stands of hardwood had vanished.[63]

As the lumber industry was beginning to wind down, it became more challenging to find men to work in the woods. The brawny French-Canadian and Scottish lumberjacks who had dominated the field in the 1880s had grown older, or moved on, following the remaining pine trees westward. Other immigrants, especially Finns, came in to fill the gap. These were often recruited by agents working in big cities, who were not above exaggerating and/or outright lying to the newcomers about both salary and working conditions.[64]

"Camp jumping" became more of a problem. The lumber companies would send train tickets to immigrants recruited in the cities. When the men arrived, however, they often found that working conditions and salaries had not lived up to their promises. Many refused to honor their contracts, and just as understandably, many companies were not about to let the cost of the train tickets go to waste. Often, the immigrants were threatened with jail unless they came back to work—at least until their fares had been paid for. The misunderstandings and lies did nothing but increase unease and stiffen prejudice about those difficult Finns.[65]

Left: Cornelius "Con" Culhane, one of the most famous of the area's lumber bosses. Right: Lumbering Tools
(photos taken at the Tahquamenon Logging Museum).

Above: A "big wheel" used to move logs. This one is on display at Pictured Rocks National Lakeshore (author's photo).

Luce County and Vicinity in 1890. Two major new railroads and dozens of new communities.

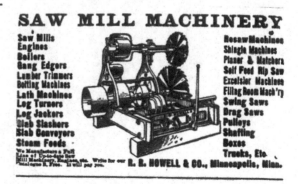
Advertisements from *The Newberry News* of July 15, 1892 and August 28, 1908.

Chapter Four
Wild and Woolly Days

*"Those were pioneer days. Days when men partook of both work and
pleasure in a whole-hearted, strenuous manner, and in which the tenderfoot had
no place."*

— William G. Fretz, Editor, *Newberry News*, July 16, 1915

I N THE EARLY YEARS, WHEN lumberjacks were thicker than mosquitoes, they traditionally would be at loose ends when the logging drive ended in the spring. Some, of course, went home to their families and farms to put in a summer of work. But others would hang around town, letting off steam.

After each period of work, Newberry would be inundated with "five or six hundred strapping, big men." Most such men would pile into town, where each one's "first act was to sandwich a shave and a bath between two drinks," before he "sallied forth to paint the community a deep, dark crimson. And he usually succeeded admirably." Cleaned up, they hit the stores, replacing clothing and equipment, canthooks, peavies, hobnailed boots, stag pants, Mackinaw coats, and "bright red or rough gray Mackinaw socks."*

The woodsmen proceeded to spend the "balance of their stakes in one roistering, rollicking, roaring time" at Newberry's hotels and saloons (claimed by old-timers as numbering twenty-one), where drinking, dice games, and card games abounded.[66]

Twenty-one saloons may have been a bit of an exaggeration, but there were indeed quite a few. Eleven licenses were granted in 1890, and sixteen in 1893, although it should be noted that these numbers also included four or five hotels, and did not take into account anything located outside the village's limits (smaller communities sometimes had saloons of their own).[67]

Still, most of the blocks nearest the depot were devoted to saloons and hotels, clustered around East Helen Street, while still more could be found on the northern edge of Newberry Avenue. These included such establishments as the Board of Trade Saloon, the Arcade Saloon, the Railroad Saloon, the Palace Saloon, the Newberry Liquor Store, the South Shore Saloon, the Oriental Saloon, the Bank Sample Room, the Blue Front Sample Room, and others.

Saloons never seemed to be managed by any one person for very long. They passed from manager to manager, like a weird game of musical chairs. The Board of Trade Saloon, for

---

* A canthook is a logging tool made of a long wooden handle and an adjustable metal hook used for turning logs. A peavey is very similar to a canthook, but has a spiked end alongside its hook.

example, was run in succession by Fred Reed, Webb Latham, Matt Surrell, Peter Beaulieu, Charles Henderson, Charles Little, and Frank Quinn, all between 1889 and 1899.[68]

One of these former owners, Fred Reed, went on to run the Oriental Saloon and the Marquette City Saloon. Charles Little had previously owned the Railroad Saloon.

Matt Surrell later owned the Palace, which also had been owned by Harry Abbott, Nicholas Mertes, and F. L. Harris. And F. L. Harris had also owned (at one time or another) the Bank Sample Room and the Blue Front Sample Room.[69]

Ed Ryan was perhaps one of the most newsworthy of the saloonkeepers. Notorious for having a bad temper, he operated at various times the Arcade Saloon, the Oriental Saloon, and the Newberry Liquor Store. In February 1899, he got into a "row" with his bartender, John McDonald, and punched him in the face with a beer bottle. McDonald promptly sued Ryan, asking for $2,000 for (reportedly) "spoiling his beauty." *The Newberry News*, much amused, concluded wryly that Ryan was "in trouble again."[70]

Ryan took exception to this quip and the threatened to sue if an apology was not issued. In the April 7, 1899 edition, William G. Fretz, who had been editor of the paper for only a few months, gamely complied, writing:

> Edward Ryan takes exception to the statement in THE NEWS that he was in trouble, and we hasten to retract the statement. It's no trouble whatever for Mr. Ryan to smash a fellow being's face with a beer bottle, club or anything else that comes handy, but is rather more of a pastime. In fact, Mr. Ryan never had any trouble in his life, except to shoot straight, and he is a very poor marksman. The idea of Edward being in trouble over such a small matter as being sued for $2,000 for spoiling his bartender's beauty is simply ridiculous, such an infinitesimal affair as this could not possibly cause him moments of worry or trouble. There is only one thing that we can think of that troubles Edward, and that is how to get rid of his coin, so we presume it will be no trouble for him to "dig down" should a verdict be rendered against him. Mr. Ryan rather intimated that unless we retracted we might have a libel suit on our hands, so we have hastened to comply with his wish and hope this will appease his wrath and that he will allow us to do business a little longer. It's all a mistake. Edward is a real nice fellow, and runs the quietest saloon this side of hades.[71]

The case came to trial in May, but all charges were dropped because John McDonald failed to appear.[72]

Many unfortunate altercations involving bartenders and saloon owners were reported on over the years. For example, the September 6, 1907 edition related how at the Riberg saloon, the "mixologist" named Andrew Lake saw the pound master hauling off John Riberg's cow. Lake snuck up behind the pound master and "biffed" him on the neck, knocking him down and taking the cow. What exactly he hoped to accomplish is not clear and he was probably not sober. Anyway, within an hour the sheriff hauled Mr. Lake in and he was fined $50.[73] (Keep in mind that the average woodsman made less than $30 a month).

Almost all the saloons offered the "choicest selection" of "fine domestic and foreign Wines, Liquors, and Cigars," but a few were fancier. The Palace offered "champagne on ice," bourbon,

CASE'S DRAY LINE.

Draying done at reasonable rates.

Pianos and household goods handled with care.

ORDERS

Left at residence on Helen street will rreceive prompt attention.

DAVID CASE.

NEWBERRY - - MICH.

LITTLE HORSE

HARNESS SHOP!

GEO. J. RYAN, Prop'r.

MANUFACTURER OF

Truck, Lumber and Farm Harness,

A Specialty made of Light, Single and Double Harness in all the Latest Styles of the day.

Dealer in Robes, Blankets, Surcingles, Whips, Lashes, Etc.

Newberry Avenue, - Newberry, Mich.

GROCERY DEPARTMENT

WHEN YOU THINK OF COFFEE, THINK OF

Monarch

THAT'S ALL

Advertisements from *The Newberry News* of July 18, 1890 and September 13, 1907.

F. ROSENTHAL

Has just received a large stock of Spring and Summer

Clothing, Dress Goods, Furnishing Goods, Carpets, Etc.

Which I am selling at Lower Prices than ever before.

Elegant Furniture a Specialty.

THE PEOPLE'S ONE PRICE STORE

Judge of Artists!

If you want a good shave,
Call on the Judge,
He harbors no malice,
He bears no grudge.
He shaves with care the tender face,
And as an artist he leads his race.
His shop is as nice as any in town,
On Newberry avenue he may be
i n found;
His razors are sharp,
So give him a call,
For his dandy hair cuts are pleas-
-ing all.

JAMES VANMERE, Prop.

David Somerville,

Cor. Trueman ave. & Handy st.,

DOES A GENERAL

Blacksmith Business.

A specialty made of

Horseshoeing and Repairing

☞ All work guaranteed satisfactory and prices reasonable. A share of your work solicited.

Somerville.

Advertisements from *The Newberry News* of November 25, 1890 (top and center) and July 18, 1890 (bottom).

sour mash rye," and "imported brandies." The Arcade carried "bottled beer for family use." The Bank Sample Room boasted of "mixed drinks of every description to order."

Some had lunch counters, pool rooms, and slot machines. The Blue Front Saloon boasted "a fine picture gallery in the rear" for the enjoyment of its patrons, while the Palace had "some fine specimens of Italian and Egyptian statuary." Nearly every "drinking establishment" proclaimed itself to be a "quiet and orderly place," but that can't have been the case all the time.[74]

The legal saloons—those properly licensed and owned by more or less respectable citizens—brought enough problems to the village. Illegal houses were even worse. Although it was not mentioned overmuch, Newberry did have its very own "bawdy house" or "house of ill fame." (Other popular euphemistic terms included "house of ill repute" or the slangier "ranch.")

About a mile northwest of town was the "Swamp Forty." During the summer, when work was light at the lumber camps, a kind of shanty town sprung up, full of out-of-work lumbermen camping, eating beans out of cans, fighting, gambling, and enjoying other unsavory activities.

The centerpiece of this ad hoc shantytown was the "Swamp Hotel," located on a small body of water called Angel Lake. It was, reported *The Newberry News* in 1900, "one of the lowest dives we believe that exists in this peninsula, rivaling the far-famed Seney brothels for all-round toughness." Here the woodsmen could find cheap booze, gambling, and "soiled doves." (Five "doves" were arrested in 1893 and eight in 1894). Fights and skull-crackings were common. Woodsmen on their days off could rent a horse at the livery stable and then ride out over rough roads to the "ranch." There, they would release the horse (which would find its own way home) and enjoy their evening. The respectable citizens of Newberry were disgusted by the existence of the "hotel de swamp," but tolerated the place since it was out of sight. This "house of ill repute" existed until at least the 1920s.[75]

Such shenanigans would *not* be endured in town, though that did not stop some from trying. Any boomtown attracts its share of less respectable entrepreneurs, and Newberry was no different. One of the most infamous was a woman known as "Pinky."

Pinky was born Clara Wilkinson in 1854, the oldest daughter of James and Sarah Wilkinson, semi-literate farm laborers in Lapeer County in the lower peninsula of Michigan. At sixteen, Clara began her marital career, getting hitched to William S. Griswald. The marriage did not last, and Clara went on to marry Milan Canfield in 1873, Franklin Salisbury (1877), Charles Harrington (1880), and then William Rust (1882). She had three children, two of whom died young.[76]

Clara's connections to the Tahquamenon area began in the mid-1880s when, according to *The Newberry News*, "things were wild and woolly." At this time James Alvin "Al" Demarest came up from downstate, intending to open a saloon. With him came Clara, or Pinky, now known as "Mrs. Al Demarest," whom the newspaper termed "a notorious character" and "a bad lot." She was only in Newberry a few years, but her memory cast a long shadow. Together, Al and Pinky opened their saloon on Helen Street in January 1887 and lived together in a house just south of the Village.[77]

Their saloon was of the wilder sort. Within a month, Al was arrested for "keeping a house of ill fame," but the charge was dropped when the complaining witness failed to show up for court.

Left: Advertisements from *The Newberry News* of January 11, 1907 (top two) and February 11, 1904.

Below: Advertisements from *The Newberry News* of June 23, 1905, September 1, 1887, and November 18, 1892.

By that summer, a second charge had been filed, and warrants were issued for his arrest. The charge once again cited him for keeping a "house of ill fame." Not surprisingly, Al and Pinky fled the area. They left behind their horses, which were seized by their attorney for payment of fees.

Al was seen in the area a year later, skulking about his former house, and "and officers made an attempt to retake the law-breaker," storming the place at 3:00 a.m. They were not successful. As the May 24, 1888 *Newberry News* reported, "The slippery, oily, fat but nimble Demarest saw them when some distance from the house and started on a run." Al Demarest was known for being a fast runner. In 1886, he had come in second place in the "fat man's race" held on the Fourth of July. His skills came in handy now. Over fences and stumps, through the woods and brush, he was followed by the officers for about three miles, when he entered a swamp and the trail was lost." Al was never seen in Newberry again.[78]

Pinky's reputation was such that, whenever a tidbit came his way, Newberry's newspaper editor wrote it up to keep his readers informed of her wrongdoings. Reportedly, after leaving Newberry, Pinky and Al returned to Al's hometown of Gaylord, Michigan, where they ran another saloon and livery stable. In 1889, their relationship deteriorated. One hot July night, Pinky barricaded the door against Al, who tried to break in. Pinky grabbed a shotgun and shot into the air, trying to "frighten" him. As it happened, she had just shot an innocent passerby—a "respectable man with a family"—through the bowels.[79]

Pinky always claimed she was trying to reform, but she never did manage it. In 1891, she married Peter Augustus Spooner, and in 1894, Joseph Lanway. She was famous for operating "houses of ill fame all over the state."[80]

In the late 1890s, Pinky returned to the UP with her latest paramour, who called himself Thomas Collins, accompanied by her son, Walter, about twenty, and a four-year-old child named Roy.

The family moved to Deer Park, where they began to sell illegal liquor until the sheriff broke up the "gang." They were "heavily fined and told to clear out," but Sheriff Crocker was suspicious that little Roy, "a strikingly handsome child," was no child of Pinky's. He began to investigate and learned that "Thomas Collins" was really named Thurman Strowbridge. Roy was *his* son—not Pinky's—and together they had kidnapped the child from his estranged wife while she lay sick in bed.

Sheriff Crocker confronted the couple, who now were living in Grand Marias, Michigan (then a town of about 3,000 people), where Pinky operated another "house of ill-fame," employing two women. "Thomas Collins" got work as a berry picker and fisherman. The couple did not resist and the sheriff was immensely pleased to return little Roy to his overjoyed mother.[81]

In 1901, Pinky Collins got into an argument with another berry picker named Williams (or Mitchell) and "blazed away at him with a rifle." She was arrested, found guilty, and sentenced to two years in prison, "the first time they have been able to convict her." At this point, she disappears from the historical record.[82]

In 1903 *The Newberry News* reported that Pinky's paramour, still going by "Thomas Collins," was caught stealing wood camp supplies. He was sent to prison for two years. He eventually

Reed & Beaulieu

——DEALERS IN——

Wines, Liquors and Cigars.

The best in the village

Newberry avenue.

-:- CALL -:- AND -:- SEE -:- US -:-

Dressmaking:

I have rented rooms at the Newberry Hotel and will engage in the Dress-making business here, and having had considerable experience can

Guarantee a Good Fit

And First-Class Workmanship.

Call at my rooms and get prices, when in need of a dressmaker.

MISS BELL McKAY.

Above: Advertisements from *The Newberry News* of September 1, 1887 and November 18, 1892

Below: Advertisements from *The Newberry News* of September 1, 1887 and May 12, 1887.

B. ZENKER.   GEO. ZENKER

Zenker Bros.

Painters and Paper Hangers.

~~All Kinds of~~

Painting, Upholstering

Cabinet Making and Paper Hanging

~~Done in a workmanlike manner~~

☞ If you have anything to do in our line it will pay you to get our prices.

ZENKER BRS., Newberry. Mich.

James Somerville,

GENERAL

BLACKSMITH!

Cor. Trueman ave. & Handy st.

All work in my line promptly and and satisfactorily done.

Well Driving

-:- A SPECIALTY -:-

For Sale.

A store building and lot; desirable location; situated on the principal street in the village of Newberry near the depot. An excellent stand for a saloon, restaurant or general store. Address or enquire of

W. E. MURNEY, Newberry, Mich.

reconciled with his wife and child and lived with them at Whitefish Point and the Soo until his death.[83]

Not all of the "wildness" was quite so vulgar, though, and much was of an innocuous and relatively harmless sort.

William Fretz, then a young newspaper employee, related how he was once awakened by a man "stealthily creeping along the roof of the wood house." Will called out a warning (along the lines of "What the devil are you doing there?") and the drunken man whined back, "O, it's only me, Will. Some son-of-a-gun has tied the hall door shut and I had to climb out of the window." The man climbed down the side of the house and faded into the night. The inebriated stranger was never identified.[84]

Tomfoolery often made the news. According to a *Newberry News* report from December 23, 1910, a party of "Finlanders," angry at being fired, broke into the Dollarville Depot and proceeded to slash opens bags of flour and spread it all around. They were arrested when some stalwart citizen noticed "four men, covered with flour," fleeing the area.[85]

Then there was the April 9, 1915 tale of the Engadine lumberjack who became "gloriously full" after a winter's work, broke into an undertaking parlor, and fell asleep in a coffin. "He was arrested the following day and paid a small fine."[86]

"Wild and woolly" men (and women) created a burden on Newberry's new infrastructure. A considerable problem was "tramps" and other out-of-work woodsmen who deliberately caused a disturbance of the peace just so they could be locked up and have a place to sleep and a meal. The Luce County Board tried to deter them by installing a "stone pile" in 1905 and ordering "petty offenders to earn their board by breaking stone." When this failed, Judge H. L. Harris informed would-be offenders that if it happened once or twice, the "tramps" would be discharged and ordered to leave town. If it happened a third time, he had no compunctions about sending the loafers to prison in Detroit. This must not have worked very well because about a decade or so later, *The Newberry News* happily announced a "cruel surprise" upon all the "tramps, bums and loafers." Now they had to labor on the public roads![87]

Oftentimes, wild behavior and copious drinks led to more serious crime, but most of it was of a simplistic and petty nature. More often than not, the crimes were the result of crowding together large groups of uneducated, underpaid men. Their employment was of a precarious and temporary nature, and many of them were homesick immigrants working dangerous jobs in extreme conditions. "They were in the main a big-hearted, good-natured class" and carousing was "their means of diversion after a hard winter's labor," *The Newberry News* remarked indulgently in 1911.[88]

But not just the seasonal workers got into the act. The factory hands who worked in the charcoal kilns and sawmills could be just as troublesome. They also had tough lives and rough pleasures. Quarrels, stabbings, and beatings were common and all made worse with alcohol. Fights broke out over the most trivial matters.

Drunk and disorderly, the violent and the crude cavorted in the streets. According to *The Newberry News* of September 22, 1905, a group of "four Frenchmen" took umbrage with Marshal Charles Carlson for trying to break up their fistfight. After the marshal was accidently punched in the face, several stalwart citizens jumped in to assist, and all four "landed in the cooler."[89]

Interesting Spring Specials

Ladies' Suits and Skirts in a bewildering profusion to choose from............

Summer Wash Goods in every weave imaginable from the heavy material to the lightest, flimsiest fabric made, ranging at 35c 25c 20c 15c and 9c

Spring Dress Goods A variety that none can surpass, in every fashionable weave, such as Mohairs, Poplins, Panamas, Voiles, Serges, Etc., at 19c 39c 50c 69c and up to $2.00 per yard.

Spring Linens at Rock-bottom Prices. Get in touch with our Linen department and you will be money ahead.

G. ROSENTHAL & SON

"Where your dollar does its duty."

S T A N D A R D

BINDER TWINE

We sell it in any quantity.

We sell it at reasonable prices.

Phone 18   J. C. FOSTER

WE EXPECT TO HANDLE A CHOICE LOT OF

Field and Garden Seeds

this spring and will order anything special that we do not happen to have on hand in field seeds so kindly place all orders early so that we will be able to get them here in time.

PHONE 3   **H. E. SMITH**

Galvanized Barb Wire

$2.75 per hundred in 500 lbs
Lots or over.   *x*   *x*

AGENCY FOR THE

Sharpel's Cream Separator

Best Separator on the market.

Phone 18   J. C. FOSTER

For Your Easter Dinner

Strawberries, Pineapples, Oranges, Bananas, Celery, Lettuce, Raddish, Asparagus, Green Onions Vegetable Oysters, Parsley and Pieplant

Saturday we will have a fresh lot of XX

Easter Lilies, Plants, Violets, Sweet Peas, Roses, Carnations, Hydrangeas.

MEAT DEPARTMENT

Peacock Ham and Bacon
Beef, Pork, Mutton and Veal
Chickens

KREMPEL & TAYLOR

PHONE 15.

Above: Advertisements from *The Newberry News* of August 4, 1905 and April 21, 1904.

Left: Advertisements from *The Newberry News* of April 21, 1904.

In another incident, reported on August 15, 1890, the citizens of Dollarville were awakened by a woman's shrieks coming from W. J. Pentland's saloon, where she was being confined against her will by several men. A neighbor came to the rescue of the woman (who was "of doubtful reputation") and "sheltered her until daylight."[90]

Only the next week, the "most disgraceful affair that ever took place in this village" happened at "Pentland's dive" in Dollarville. The August 22, 1890 *Newberry News* described it as follows:

> The inmates of the resort in the swamp took possession, with the consent of the proprietor, of that notorious back room connected with the bar-room, about three o'clock in the afternoon, and with male companions they settled themselves for a debauchery spree. Their actions from then until near eleven o'clock was nothing short of a regular brothel, the women being drunk and staggering upon the street after men and using the vilest of language. The worst of the slum holes in any large city could not have shown more depravity than was exhibited there, and William John smiling and enjoying it all. When Deputy Sheriff Barbour, who had been attending the caucus at Newberry, arrived, he was notified. He proceeded to the saloon and ordered Pentland to get rid of his customers, who apparently intended to make a night of it, as they were located both upstairs and down. Pentland done as requested, but our citizens consider that if the deputy sheriff had done his duty, as he should have done, he would have had a case for the prosecuting attorney.[91]

Scores of similar episodes occurred over the years, as *The Newberry News* most assiduously informed its readers. In 1906, a lumberjack by the name of Pat O'Malley went on a "jag" on Christmas Eve and decided it would be a good idea to snatch a Mackinaw coat from the front of Leighton's store in Newberry. The sheriff tracked him to the back alley. While trying on his new coat, O'Malley spotted his would-be captor and apparently decided it would be a good idea to attack the sheriff with a razor. Theorized the reporter, "a terrific punch in the jaw caused O'Malley to suddenly (change) his mind and he was locked up without further trouble." Perhaps in the Christmas spirit, Mr. Leighton refused to press charges and O'Malley was only locked up for ten days—for being drunk.[92]

All kinds of petty crimes were reported on throughout the 1880s and 1890s. Charles Doughtery "helped himself to a suit of underclothing belonging to Tom Allen" and was jailed for thirty days. James Carter and John Cook beat each other up over ownership of a dog, a "measly cur." A notorious fellow called Jim Robinson "filled up with bug juice" and punched out "three unoffending Frenchmen." Among Robinson's other reported crimes were assault, stealing snowshoes from children, robbery, "forcibly injecting large doses of ... moonshine" into a man named Green, and jail breaking.[93]

Even professionals could sometimes act a bit wild and woolly. In 1894, for example, a lawyer and a doctor were each accused of assault in two separate incidents.

Frank H. Peters was one of Newberry's earliest attorneys. One day in March, he set out from town in a hired rig, trying to track down "a Frenchman" who owed him money. He drove all over the outskirts, never finding his client—who happened to be in town, conscientiously paying said bill. Finally confronting his missing man, Attorney Peters demanded that he reimburse him for the money to hire the rig, as well as the time spent in chasing him, but the client

Above: Advertisements from *The Newberry Enterprise* of November 15, 1894 and *The Newberry* News of August 28, 1908.

Left: Advertisements from *The Newberry News* of September 13, 1907 and December 25, 1908.

refused. According to the March 2, 1894 *Newberry News*, Peters lost his temper, threatened to "knock the stuffin' out of him," and then attempted to do just that. The respected lawyer was nearly arrested for assault, although he wasn't because the "irate Frenchman" clearly had the upper hand.[94*]

Then later that fall, Dr. Leighton of Grand Marais accused Dr. Bohn of poaching one of his patients. Dr. Bohn "stoutly denied" any such action, so Dr. Leighton "struck at Dr. Bohn with a brass weight, knocking him down and cutting a deep gash over his right eye."[95]

Many otherwise stalwart citizens winked at the laws regarding liquor, especially selling it; violations happened left and right. Saloonkeepers kept on dispensing drinks on Sundays, election days, and holidays, which was prohibited. Farmers sold illegal moonshine to the lumberjacks.

Although in later years the old-timers were wont to wax nostalgic about these days, at the time, they were not so forgiving. Newberry, unlike Seney, had very quickly become its own county seat, and with that came the responsibility for law and order. It had its own village marshal, sheriff, deputies, justices of the peace, night watchmen, judges, jails, and courts. Justice, though, was initially something of a casual affair. During Dollarville's first year of existence, for instance, the village celebrated its first Independence Day in 1883 with "bad whiskey" and a "free-for-all fight."

The Justice of the Peace arrested two of the men, but he had no place to keep them. Robert Dollar suggested locking the men in a vacant boxcar overnight. The next morning, however, officials discovered the boxcar was gone. It had been hauled away by the railroad company to Marquette, along with its inadvertent passengers. Writing in his memoirs, Robert Dollar commented, "When told they were in Marquette, they took to their heels and disappeared in the town, so we had a Good Riddance."[96]

Joseph Lucas had a warrant issued for his arrest in 1893 because of his "wife-beating proclivities." Whenever officers came to his shack to arrest him, however, he jumped down into a tunnel he had dug especially for that purpose and fled into the woods. When the officers left, he returned home, threatening his long-suffering wife into silence. Eventually, the officers wised up and met the fugitive at the end of the tunnel, announcing their presence with a "Come along Joe, you're caught this time."[97]

In 1887, as *The Newberry News* reported, Marshal William T. Crocker and Deputy Holmes were escorting the previously mentioned James A. Demarest—arrested for keeping a house of ill fame on Helen Street—to jail, when he was called over by Justice Miner L. McKinley, who wished a few private words with the accused. When the marshal checked on them a few minutes later, both men were gone.[98]

---

* It must be noted that Charles Brebner, the editor of the paper, and Atty. Peters belonged to opposite political parties and did not care for each other. Indeed, in return for Brebner having dared to criticize something he had written, Peters once threatened the editor with the "worst licking we ever got in the course of our lifetime…emphasizing his remarks with language unfit for publication; in fact, a blue stream run clear through his exhortation." Peters was furious about the Frenchman story, retorting that it was "entirely untrue," that he had "exercised my God-given right of self-defense when I was assaulted" and his financial arrangements were "nobody's business," and insulted Brebner's manhood. (see *Newberry News*, May 20, 1892 and "Letter to the Editor by Frank H. Peters," *Newberry Enterprise*, March 8, 1894)

Above: A most forgiving shopkeeper, Perry Leighton in 1894 (courtesy of *The Newberry News*).

Left: Advertisements from *The Newberry News* of November 18, 1892.

Below: Advertisement from *The Newberry News* of June 23, 1905.

Justice McKinley had arrived in Newberry in 1886 from Gaylord, under contract to paint the new schoolhouse. He stayed, working as a housepainter and establishing a successful laundry business. As Justice of the Peace, he had presided over the weddings of several local couples. Additionally, he and his wife were founding members of a local chapter of the Good Templars, an organization dedicated to temperance. What the connection was between the two men was never made clear, but Justice McKinley apparently skipped town soon after the aforementioned "discussion" with Demarest, leaving behind Mrs. McKinley and four little daughters. He reportedly turned up again in Illinois ten years later, accused of running his own house of ill fame. Then, in 1896, he was arrested for bigamy because he had taken a second wife while the first Mrs. McKinley was still alive and well and furious in Chicago. So it seems probable that he also had been involved in the Demarests' nefarious doings.[99] Both families were from Gaylord, it should be noted.

Had Marshal Crocker managed to bring his man to jail, he may not have succeeded in keeping him there. The jail was disparagingly referred to by the *News* as an "old dry goods box" and about as secure.[100]

This was illustrated rather embarrassingly in the spring of 1888 when the jailer left on an errand, leaving his unnamed prisoner quietly whittling in his cell. The jailer failed to realize that what the prisoner was whittling was a wooden key, fine enough to turn the lock and open the door.

Having gained his freedom, the prisoner sauntered back into town where he bought himself some tobacco. Satisfied, he then returned to his cell, relocked the door, and destroyed his handiwork.[101]

Not all prisoners were so considerate. Once, in the spring of 1890, the jailer was "amazed" to find the jail's entire population (four inmates, including the notorious Jim Robinson) had all escaped into the woods. No one knew quite how they had managed it. Although the County offered a $200 reward for all four men, only one prisoner was recaptured a month later near Escanaba, where had been working on the river drive.[102]

During an August 1891 infamous incident, Arthur Salmon was the jailer, and he had three inmates under his protection. Peter Lindholm was a "Sweede" who had been arrested for "a stabbing affray" and Mr. and Mrs. John Calvin were awaiting trial for keeping a house of ill fame. Jailer Salmon was collecting their dirty dishes after dinner one night, and while the door was open, Lindholm grabbed a pile of ashes and flung them into the guard's eyes. The two men rushed out, but the half-blinded Salmon grabbed Calvin and refused to let him go. Lindholm then somehow got ahold of a knife and stabbed Salmon four times. In spite of this (and while still holding Calvin), the jailer sprang at Lindholm, kicking him, and knocking him down three times. The last kick went wild and Lindholm was hurtled out through the screen door (which "smashed into smithereens") and into freedom. Calvin also broke away, because now Salmon was occupied in preventing Nellie Calvin from joining in the jailbreak. Although a posse quickly formed, they were unable to track either man. No reward was offered, because as *The Newberry News* phrased it, "Luce county is well rid of the two toughs anyway, whether they are captured or not."[103]

Another exasperating jailbreak occurred in 1894 after Thomas Pool (arrested for attempted rape) tried to commit suicide by eating broken glass. When that failed, he and a fellow inmate

Frank H. Peters in 1895
(from The Memorial Record
of the Northern Peninsula of
Michigan, Lewis Publishing
Company)

Left: A Newberry jail cell, now maintained by the Luce County Historical
Society (author's photo).

Newberry Avenue, sometime after 1900. The man in the foreground is Dr.
Perry, carrying his doctor's bag (photo courtesy of Sterling McGinn).

pried the floorboards up and escaped into the night. Thomas Pool (described as a "wife beater and a low-lived worthless brute" and "one of the lowest thugs that ever disgraced God's Footstool"*) was not recaptured for another six months. This would not have happened, opined the *News* on November 9, 1894, if the jail had been made of stone walls and cement.[104]

Fortunately, once Newberry became the seat of its very own county, it was possible to build itself a fancy new courthouse, along with a fancy new jail and sheriff's residence in 1891 and 1894 respectively. The two buildings were constructed in red sandstone in the "Queen Anne" style, typical of the high Victorian era, with turrets, porticoes, and gables aplenty. Justice now was represented by two elegant and solidly sturdy stone buildings.[105]

A fancy new jail did not solve the jailbreak problem entirely, however.

Seven years later, the *News* reported that Sheriff Cyr had ordered one inmate (Alex McLeod) to stack a pile of wood. Instead, when the sheriff's back was turned, he "took leg bail," vanishing from sight. Or, in the picturesque words of the *Soo News Record*, he "took to the tall timber and was seen no more."

That is, he was seen no more until the next spring. Sheriff Cyr just happened to be waiting at the train station in Sault Ste. Marie when Alex McLeod just happened to come sauntering by.

So Sheriff Cyr just happened to arrest him, whereupon the unfortunate McLeod spent the next three years in prison.[106]

Ridiculously, a few months later, almost the exact thing happened. In December 1902, another inmate (Andrew Peterson, a Finn arrested for assault) was ordered to clean out his cell by the turnkey (jailer's assistant). Seizing the opportunity, Peterson "dashed a handful of pepper and salt in the turnkey's eyes and took to his heels." He made it almost as far as the Danaher Plains (more than thirty miles to the west) before being recaptured.[107]

In 1913, the *News* reported how Sheriff William DeLill let out his prisoners for an "airing" in the jail yard, under the watchful eye of a "trusty." Then he went back inside to take a bath. While enjoying his bath, one of the prisoners (Roy Edwards, arrested for burglary) made a mad dash for the woods. No trace of him was ever found.[108]

The types of crimes committed were, for the most part, rather mundane: disturbing the peace, public drunkenness, vagrancy, fighting, stealing chickens, using improper language in front of a lady, insulting a lady, striking a lady with a piece of cinder, selling liquor without a license, and the occasional bastardy case.[109]

Frequent newspaper articles during these wild and woolly days indicate that robberies were not uncommon: a fur coat snatched from a store window, $50 picked from a train passenger's pocket, silverware disappearing from a boarding house. Once a thief broke into a candy kitchen and made off with $30. John Little took a watch belonging to C. B. Noble and refused to give it back.

Three teenage boys living in a shack in McMillan were detained for counterfeiting poor-quality nickels. In 1917, a housekeeper named Mary Tebo was arrested for stealing a roll of

---

* Thomas Pool may not have been guilty, as Governor Pingree was considering him for a pardon in 1900. According to an article in the *Detroit Free Press*, the governor believed he was only convicted due to the machinations of a vindictive wife. Many Newberry people, however, appalled by the governor's actions, had no doubt at all that Pool was indeed a "worthless brute" and guilty as charged.

TWO HUNDRED DOLLARS REWARD!

NEWBERRY, LUCE CO., MICH., APRIL 25, 1890.

Two Hundred Dollars Reward is offered for the arrest and detention or information that will lead to the arrest of the following described parties:

THOMAS FISHER, aged 56 years, 5 feet 6 inches high, full beard, sandy complexion, small squint eyes, weight 140 lbs. In for attempt to murder. Reward: One Hundred Dollars.

CHARLES PHENDELL, aged 27 years, 5 feet 8 inches high, dark moustache, dark suit of clothes, sharp nose. In for Larceny. Reward: Fifty Dollars.

THOMAS COPELAND, age 21 years, dark complexion, thin beard, 5 feet 8 inches high, eyes black and peculiar, weight about 145 lbs. In for Larceny. Reward: Twenty-five Dollars.

JAMES ROBINSON, aged 30 years, 5 feet 10 inches high, small sharp eyes and nose, eyes bluish grey, weight 170 lbs., flat face and broad chin. In for Robbery. Reward: Twenty-five Dollars.

The above described prisoners all broke jail this (Friday) morning.

A. G LOUKS, *Sheriff.*

Advertisement that appeared in *The Newberry News*, May 2, 1890.

James Vanmere, The Barber.

East Side of Newberry Avenue.

Advertisement in *The Newberry News*, January 15, 1892.

bills from her employer while he slept—she also, for good measure, shaved off his moustache before fleeing.[110]

Childhood crime did not appear to be rampant, but when noteworthy, it made the news. In 1899, a gang of children snuck into the furnace company, stealing the "brasses from the friction boxes of flat cars," worth "upwards of $1.50 each," and sold them to unsuspecting local merchants. Several prominent citizens were humiliated, as they were forced to plead guilty for receiving stolen goods. A ten-year-old named Bert Schram stole "nuts, fruits and candies" and was sent to the Lansing Reform School. According to the *News*, this action was intended to free him "from the evil influences with which he was surrounded, more than as a punishment for his crime."[111]

In the more settled areas, crime tended to leave the more respectable citizens alone. Miscreants mostly confined themselves to hurting other miscreants, but not always. Quite alarming were reports in 1893 of a "gang of toughs," "gamblers," and "sharpers" led by a man named "Dutchy, alias Hook," that made the town of Trout Lake their headquarters. Trout Lake sat at the intersection of two major railroads, far from any law enforcement. Their modus operandi was to ride the rails and engage fellow passengers in rigged games of Three-card Monte. Should a passenger refuse to play, the gang would (in the words of *the Detroit Free Press*) simply "knock him down and turn his pockets inside out."[112]

In another example, the *News* reported in the late 1890s that a "gang of toughs" had begun to hang about Dollarville, bumming rides and intimidating the farmers going about their errands. The threats sometimes turned into criminal acts. In August 1898, John and Otto Sanderlin were returning from church when they were "brutally assaulted…by three young toughs." Those bullies were arrested and sent to jail, but the rest of their gang remained at large. One warm spring night the next May, two inebriated farmers were robbed. According to the *News*, "a couple of questionable characters" were suspected by the authorities, but the farmers were "too drunk to be able to give a clear account of the affair" and nothing came of it.[113]

Nothing, that is, until July 1899, when the "questionable characters" approached and begged a lift from Mr. Amasa Grover (who had been to town to see the circus and was now on his way home). The toughs requested a ride, and Mr. Grover amiably assented.

While on board, the delinquents began rummaging through Mr. Grover's belongings. Naturally, Mr. Grover asked them to stop and, just as naturally, they asked him to fight. Being a "strong and well-built man," Mr. Grover agreed and proceeded to thrash three of the men into submission while the other two fled. The farmers had no more trouble after that.[114]

Truly serious crime was actually not all that common in Newberry and the surrounding area, but it did happen. And when it did, *The Newberry News* was quick to inform its readers.

For example, in 1904, when James Fitzpatrick attempted to crash a Christmas Eve party being thrown in the woods by a "gang of Finlanders," they unceremoniously ejected him. He "retaliated by firing a load of buckshot through the shanty." The sheriff came out to investigate the attempted murder, but found Fitzpatrick long gone.[115]

In 1911, John Pahfanen entered John Hill's boarding house and demanded a free meal. When he was refused, he "drew a wicked-looking knife and made a murderous attack on Hill,

A 7558 Court House and Jail, Newberry, Mich.

ROSS LEIGHTON, PUB.   SHERIFF'S RESIDENCE AND COURT HOUSE. NEWBERRY. MICH.

Two postcards that show the original, very grand Luce County Courthouse and Sheriff's Residence/Jail. The sheriff's residence survives today as the Luce County Historical Society's museum. Regrettably, the courthouse was demolished in the 1970s (author's collection).

the owner of the place, inflicting an ugly gash in the forearm." Then he "calmly sat down at the table and proceeded to eat a hearty meal." He was arrested and sent to prison. Fortunately, no one was killed. Murder may have been intended, but murder was not accomplished that day.[116]

Another murder attempt occurred when Jack Connors, a blacksmith from Naubinway, became obsessed with Mrs. Agnes Roddick, a widow who ran a restaurant in Newberry. He had taken to hanging around the place, insulting and threatening men he believed to be her admirers (whether they were or not) and "drinking heavily." On June 4, 1912, as the *News* reported, Mrs. Roddick came home from a visit to the Soo and walked down the street to her restaurant. She found Connors waiting for her, demanding to know where she had been. They argued. He then put a gun to her head, exclaiming, "Then you'll die right now," and fired twice. Fortunately, he was "a mighty poor marksman" and Mrs. Roddick ran out into the street and into Marshal DeLill, who overpowered Connors and arrested him. Mrs. Roddick insisted there was never "anything between her and Connors, and that the talk of jealousy is pure bunkum." Connors was sent to prison.[117]

However, not all murders were thwarted.

The earliest tale of murder in Luce County has all the trimmings of legend. All of the stories agree on the most basic of facts: a French trapper had built himself a little cabin on a stretch of high ground next to the Tahquamenon River, about ten miles downriver from what would later become Newberry. The trapper was slain and his bloody body chucked into the Tahquamenon.

Writing in 1984, local historian George Rintamaki provided a detailed account of this murder, one that he had heard from eighty-six-year-old George Olsen, who had heard it from his father, Bernard Olsen (1860–1947). This version of the tale takes place around the turn of the century. In it, the Frenchman was named Joe LaPoint and his bloated body had been discovered by two lumberjacks. The murderer was theorized to be LaPoint's friend, Dick Pomeroy, an unsocial fellow whose dog packs terrorized both deer herds and woodsmen alike. Pomeroy seemed to be the most likely suspect at the time because he definitely did murder another friend, Alphonse Rodette, and was sent to prison in Marquette. He apparently never spoke a word about either murder. It's a colorful tale, but unfortunately, there is no trace in census records or otherwise of any of these three men.[118]

An earlier account of the slain trapper, written in 1931 by *Newberry News* reporter Oakley Rivers, claims the murder took place in the early 1880s, while the railroad was being built. The solitary, unnamed French trapper was known to have a "rapidly increasing cache of pelts and sum of money." Feeling lonely, the Frenchman had taken a "pardner" and soon after had vanished. Visitors found plates laid out on the table, and blankets laid out on the beds, but no men, no furs, no supplies. They also found that:

> from the door of the cabin down the pathway to the river and then out onto the ice was a deep groove, as if a heavy body had been dragged. In the groove a trail of crimson was frozen into the ice. Out on the surface of the river the trail ended, and here was plainly visible, now frozen over, a red-rimmed hole!
> ("Mystery of the Tahquamenon" by Oakley Rivers, *The Newberry News*, August 7, 1931)

A Selection of Luce County Sheriffs

(Many of these men also served as undersheriffs, deputies, and marshals.)

Left: Adam Louks, sheriff from 1886–1890, 1893–1896, 1905–1908.

Middle Left: William T. Crocker, sheriff from 1896–1901.

Middle Right: Arthur A. Henderson, sheriff from 1890–1893.

Right: Ed Cyr, sheriff from 1901–1905.

Left: William DeLill, sheriff from 1912–1917.

Center: John Turnbull, sheriff from 1908–1912, 1918–1921.

Right: William Krempel, sheriff from 1917–1918 (photo courtesy of Jeff Chown).

WILLIAM H. KREMPEL

CANDIDATE FOR

Sheriff of Luce County

AT THE GENERAL ELECTION, TUESDAY,

NOVEMBER 7, 1916

Your Support Will Be Appreciated.

Left: Campaign card, 1916 (courtesy of Jeff Chown).

Right: Advertisement from *The Newberry News*, February 1, 1890.

COURT HOUSE AT NEWBERRY, MICH.

Above: This postcard, incorrectly labeled "court house," is another view of Luce County's sumptuous sheriff's residence. The jail, with its barred windows, is attached to the back (author's collection).

Below: An advertisement from *The Newberry News* of June 25, 1909.

CHOOSE WISELY...

when you buy a SEWING MACHINE. You'll find all sorts and kinds at corresponding prices. But if you want a reputable serviceable Machine, then take

the · WHITE ·

27 years experience has enabled us to bring out a HANDSOME, SYMMETRICAL and WELL-BUILT PRODUCT, combining in its make-up all the good points found on high grade machines and others that are exclusively WHITE—for instance, our TENSION INDICATOR, a device that shows the tension at a glance, and we have others that appeal to careful buyers. All Drop Heads have Automatic Lift and beautiful Swell Front, Golden Oak Woolwork. Vibrator and Rotary Shuttle Styles.

OUR ELEGANT H. T. CATALOGUES GIVE FULL PARTICULARS, FREE.

WHITE SEWING MACHINE CO.   CLEVELAND, O.

For Sale by J. C. FOSTER, Newberry, Mich.

Newberry Avenue, sometime after 1900 (photo courtesy of Sterling McGinn).

John Barber

Drayman

HEAVY and LIGHT DRAYING DONE ON SHORT NOTICE

AGENT FOR

Norse's Soft Drinks

CALL 'PHONE 59

THE RIGHT HOUSE.

Is celebrating the New Year by offering its entire stock of

Men's Boys Children's and Oacks'

Clothing, Etc

At and Below Actual Cost.

————ALSO OUR————

BOOT AND SHOE STOCK

AND AN ELEGANT LINE OF DRESS GOODS

Will be disposed of at greatly reduced prices. This sale is made necessary on account of the unfavorable weather leaving us greatly overstocked in all lines. No such bargain will again be offered. Take advantage of the at once.

HENDERSON BROTHERS.

Advertisements from *The Newberry News* of August 28, 1908
and May 2, 1890.

The earliest printed account comes from a short article called "A Trip on the Taquamenaw," printed in the June 21, 1894 *Newberry Enterprise*. After describing the beauty and geography of the river, the uncredited author relates the following story:

> Among others who has made this a hunting ground was one who was well known some year ago by the name of 'Snakes.' He made his home some five miles above the Sage Branch on the east side of the river on a high and dry knole (sic). He built his cabin and made himself comfortable and even cleared off the timber from eight or 10 acres of land. He lived here all alone for five or six years, occasionally going out to dispose of some furs and bring back some necessary supplies. He was considered to be a harmless, half-demented man, making no friends or asking no friendship of anyone. After a while parties going up and down the river missed him from his usual haunts and could see no signs of him having been at his cabin for some time. Someone venturing to make a close inspection found that he had not apparently been there for months. Two land lookers going north of the river, a mile or so west of 'Snake's' place some two months before, remember hearing two shots fired in quick succession in the direction of his cabin. Sometime after it is said that two strangers sold a package of furs at St. Ignace, which is believed to have been stolen from him at the time of the murder, if murder it was. At any rate he has never been seen since, alive or dead. The two shots fired were very likely his death [sic], his body was probably weighted and sank to the bottom of the muddy stream.[119]

There was no newspaper in the early 1880s, and no one seemed to have recorded the tale until much later. A brief account written in *The Newberry News* in 1940 stated that "all the early settlers who claimed to know anything about the circumstances are dead."[120] As Rivers concluded in his article, "No one will ever know the answers to these questions. Only the peaceful waters of the Tahquamenon saw the tragedy." But the Frenchman's little clearing in the woods is still known as "Deadman's Farm."[121]*

Other murders followed, of course, but most happened in the woods and in tiny, out-of-the-way communities. A brief news item in 1888, from up north in Deer Park, tells how August Oleson (a "Sweede") drew a knife during a drunken brawl and his companions beat him to death with clubs. A 1906 *News* article details a dancing party thrown by Finnish woodsmen, which was crashed by a man named Thomas Duke and his loutish friends, all "pretty well filled up with fighting whiskey."

Duke arrived at the party and began to insult the girls until he was whacked over the head with a "piece of a 2x4 scantling" by Toivo Avelangi. In a daze, Duke wandered into the woods, where he died.[122]

---

* An alternative, less grisly version of the story, offered by Oakley Rivers in 1931, claimed that the Frenchman had merely loaded up his canoe with his furs "and rounding a bend in the river, disappeared forever from the sight of man," whereupon he was either murdered or drowned. The old-timers that Oakley Rivers was consulting may have mixed up the story of Deadman's Farm with that of John Cook, "an old man who has been employed by J.H. Hunter watching a set of camps." In 1904 he met a party of hunters as he was "paddling down the Tahquamenon in a boat" and was never seen again. (see "Fears for His Safety," *Newberry News*, November 18, 1904).

This postcard, dating from around 1906, shows a DSS&A engine and snowplow, as well as the drifts that resulted. The anonymous collector made the rueful notation "Glad I visited the place in summer" (author's collection).

This photograph from 1914 shows a large crew of men and machinery attempting to drain a piece of swampland near the Tahquamenon River (courtesy of *The Newberry News*).

Still other murders and equally heinous acts were reported on in *News*. According to a November 6, 1891 article, Jacob Hungisto and two companions were, after an evening of drinking, following the railroad tracks back to the wood camps. While doing so, they ran into a party of five woodsmen on their way into town. As the three men passed by, each one was asked if he had any whiskey. Each one replied in the negative. After the third "no," the men evidently grew angry, and somehow (no one quite understood how), Jacob Hungisto was stabbed to death. The paper noted that all of Jacob's worldly possessions amounted to some scrap paper, three bottles of alcohol, and two cents. It was difficult to get to the bottom of the affair since none of the men spoke English, no one admitted to seeing anything, and all were drunk. In the end, only a Jacob Reini was convicted of manslaughter.[123]

A horrific report came out of Emerson, the little sawmill community on the shores of Lake Superior, in the winter of 1892. The workers there were celebrating Washington's Birthday— with whiskey, naturally—and had become quite drunk. As the reports went, they partied their way to a house of ill fame, grabbed Lucy Webb (its owner), and locked her in a smoldering kiln for five hours. She died a few minutes after being rescued. Word of the outrage spilled out and was published in newspapers throughout the Midwest. The authorities were said to have been investigating, but no follow-up was ever reported. One hopes that this was just a tall tale taken too seriously.[124]

Newberry village itself did not experience a murder until 1894. As reported in the December 28, 1894 edition of *The Newberry News*, on Christmas Eve a group of woodsmen came into town, cashed their paychecks, and set up shop in the Board of Trade Saloon. Isaac Stetcher and Timothy Kane had a long history of not getting along, and this night was no exception. They insulted and threatened each other until a fight was about to break out. But the bartender objected and friends intervened, convincing Kane to let it go. He finally agreed and left the bar, but Stetcher could not resist and called out one final insult. Kane ("a bad tempered man") rushed at Stetcher ("a coward"), who backed away, begging "Don't you strike me, Kane, I'm not a match for you, don't strike me." Stetcher followed this plea by pulling a knife and stabbing Kane twice. Kane died almost instantly, and Stetcher began to sob, crying, "What have I done, boys, what have I done? I didn't want to kill anyone."[125]

It could be argued, though, that this was not murder, but manslaughter, happening in the heat of the moment. A far more cold-blooded and definite murder occurred in June, 1897, as the result of a quarrel involving Alexander Boulton, a seventy-three-year-old businessman, and Richard Palmer, a "shiftless, quarrelsome" man. Mr. Boulton had hired Palmer's friend, William Duval, to cut shingle bolts for him. Palmer wanted in on the deal, too.

Duval and Palmer invited Mr. Boulton to Riberg's saloon to talk over the arrangements. Boulton, however, was not enthusiastic, as Palmer had recently been released from jail after beating his wife. Palmer remonstrated, but Boulton held firm. He absolutely refused to hire Palmer, so Palmer stabbed him four times. Crying out to his son, "Tom, I'm done for," Alexander Boulton fell to the floor in a puddle of blood.

"The murderer made no effort to escape," marveled the *News*, "but sat coolly down on the chair he had occupied before the stabbing and sullenly watched the life blood flow from the dying man and spread over the floor in a large pool around him." Sheriff Cyr arrived almost at once and arrested Palmer, who pled not guilty, in spite of fourteen witnesses who

Advertisements from *The Newberry News* circa 1918 and circa 1894.

The saloon at the Murphy House in May, 1902. The child in the left corner is Harvey Gormely, while the man in profile (standing next to the bartender), is his father, Francis P. Gormely, owner of the business.
Please note that the bearded man sitting in the doorway sports a wooden leg. Legend has it that this leg was removed and burned during a drunken brawl.
(photo and identification courtesy of Sterling McGinn).

said otherwise. He was convicted of murder in the second degree and, although sentenced to twenty-four years in the Marquette prison, very soon was transferred to the Michigan Asylum for Insane Criminals at Ionia. There he died in 1922 from a combination of heart disease and syphilis.[126]

Another murder occurred on July 27, 1907, at the Johnson House near the railroad tracks. According to the News, two teamsters began to quarrel. Henry Colburn had accused Frank Montgomery of stealing his harness rings. Colburn had recently come up from downstate to work and had a wife and child in Bay City. Montgomery, "a man of powerful physique," had recently been released from prison for burglary and had a history of violence and arrests. The argument escalated to "blows being exchanged" and the bartender kicked both men out into the street.

Colburn, however, stopped to pick up a knife, and upon stepping outside, stabbed Montgomery twice, once in the ear and once in the lung. Montgomery roared, "I ought to kill you for that!" He then launched himself at Colburn until he "had his opponent down and was pummeling him." A bystander eventually pulled the two men apart, and only then did Montgomery notice he was seriously wounded, exclaiming, "Bert, he has cut me."

Montgomery was taken across the street to the Hotel Murphy, where he died at 10:30 that night. Colburn was arrested and "nearly collapsed" when he was told Montgomery had died. He pled guilty to manslaughter and was sent to prison at Jackson.[127]

With all the murders and stabbings, shouting and mayhem, the wild and woolly days were exciting while they lasted, but they weren't comfortable, or desirable, and they certainly weren't respectable. The reputable and upright citizens of the region were determined to stamp them out.

Chapter Five
To Drink or Not to Drink

"There has been considerable loud talk and threats of terrible doings by the saloonists and their usual complement of whiskey suckers towards us for the stand we are taking in exposing the disregard with which they have shown for the laws regulating the sale of liquors.... Our action in this matter is backed up by our best residents who have all decided that their feelings have been outraged too long already by the wantonness of the present saloonists and have resolved to call a halt."

— Dollarville Correspondent, Newberry News, August 22, 1890

AS AN OBSERVANT READER MAY have noticed, most of the local crime and wild behavior had one thing in common: liquor, alcohol, "boose," "bug juice," "moonshine," "the ardent," "fighting whiskey," "the flowing bowl," and "king barleycorn." Most every one of the murders, manslaughters, and knife fights was intensified one way or another by alcohol, a fact well known by most of the early residents.

One of the great moral and political questions of the age was prohibition. A favorite debate topic among the local folk was whether or not to outlaw alcohol. Proponents of prohibition were called "Drys." They saw liquor as a literal demon, something that seduced weak men away from the wholesome pleasures of hearth and home. They opined that alcohol not only led to a burgeoning population of thugs and miscreants, but also spawned houses of ill-repute, gambling and bar fights, battered wives, and ragged children.

Liquor was the root of all poverty and misery. At the very least, it caused drunkenness and hangovers, which due to the delicate, dangerous working conditions of the time, were to be discouraged. As proof, Newberry Drys may well have pointed to not just the crimes, but the scores of unfortunate incidents sprinkled across the early days, assiduously reported on by the paper.

A distressing number of drunken mishaps involved trains, proving that large, heavy machinery and intoxication are a disastrous mix. An early *News* report described a misadventure involving a man named James Clockesy, who had "for two or three days past been imbibing too freely of bug juice." During this bender, on a cold October afternoon in 1886, Clockesy, wandered away from his companions and took a nap on the railroad tracks. The ore train came rattling by, and although the engineer braked and Clockesy woke up, neither could avoid an accident. The train struck the man, "tearing one ear completely out by the roots and tearing a gash the whole width of his forehead." Almost miraculously, Clockesy recovered. Very few others were quite that lucky.[128]

Patrick McBride, "in a state of intoxication," tried to steal a ride by jumping onto a moving train in February 1889. He missed, "mangling both legs in a horrible manner," and died in agony. The citizens raffled off his gold watch to pay for the burial.[129]

Another man, whose name was never discovered, fell off the freight train in October 1900 and was run over. "His body was literally ground to pieces, his head being severed and the body mutilated in a horrible manner…the remains were strewn along the track for some distance," reported the newspaper. The "partially intoxicated" Julius Trombley, while walking back to work at the wood camps, was hit by a train. The poor man's head was "crushed and (his) body ground to a pulp." Calie Richards was "cut to pieces" in October 1911. The sheriff discovered his body literally *in pieces*—first a foot, next a head and shoulders, then an arm.[130]

In 1913 a lumberman called Gust Carlson died after falling asleep on the tracks near Sage. Two months later, the same thing happened to James Toby. In October, the "stupidly drunk" George Asland also lay down on the tracks. He was roused by workmen and shaken awake, but "staggered back on the track after they had passed and again went to sleep." He was "instantly killed by the 6:30 passenger train going east"—a terrible experience for both George and the train's passengers.

In 1917, the *News* reported the sad case of Finnish immigrant Jalo Hainari, who had been having a grand time at the Swamp Hotel, but later fell asleep on the railroad tracks. Two young men, who also had been drinking, happened along. They woke up the inebriated Finn, robbed him of $114 in Canadian bills, and let him go. The newly impoverished and still-drunk Jalo finished off his night by laying back down on the railroad track and later was run over by the freight train at three o'clock in the morning. Railroad workers discovered his "horribly mangled" corpse a few hours later.[131]

Between 1886 and 1920, at least twenty men were killed by falling off or falling under the train, and more than half of them were known to have been drinking. But trains were not the only things that did not mix well with alcohol. Not by a long shot. Saloons, hotels, boarding houses—really, any public gathering place—could be dangerous to a drinker's health.

In 1902, a Finn lumberjack named Antti Juvonen wandered into the Luce County poorhouse in a dazed condition after being "roughly handled" by his companions, all of whom had been "filling up on bad whisky." He died the next day. Another lumberjack named John Kelly was enjoying his evening at the saloon at Soo Junction before passing out. When he awoke, he found his $200 savings was missing. He claimed he had been given "knockout drops," but the $200 was long gone in any case. While on a "glorious drunk," a Trout Lake saloonkeeper "took a hatchet and proceeded to chop up the residence of John Cline" and, less amusingly, assaulted a thirteen-year-old girl and skipped town. Two brothers, discovering a jug lying by the side of the road near Deer Park, began "imbibing pretty freely" and then proceeded to beat each other up in a "savage fight." In 1916, a group of laborers working at a road construction camp drank from Saturday night until Sunday afternoon. A fight broke out and Dave McCarty drew a knife, cutting Tim Sullivan "quite severely about the arms and chest." Sullivan retaliated by biting off McCarty's nose.[132]

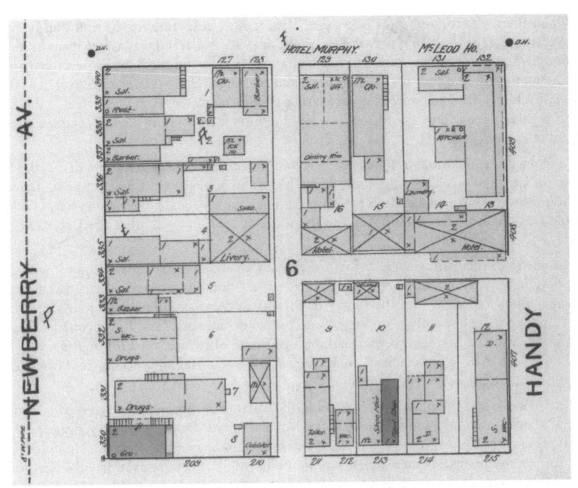

In 1893, the Sanborn Fire Insurance Company drew up a map of Newberry, showing its streets and buildings and the businesses they contained. This portion shows two of the hotels, and five of the saloons, all in close proximity to each other (original digitized by the Library of Congress).

Advertisement from *The Newberry News* of October 29, 1915.

Then there was the report of Abe Sager, who was so desperate for a drink that he broke into Nels Anderson's saloon one dark June night in 1900. Anderson was asleep upstairs, but he woke up when he heard the drunken stumblebum. "On opening the door he perceived a form advancing toward him through the darkness, and rushing at the intruder he delivered a couple of terrific blows with telling effect, stretching the intruder senseless at his feet." Abe Sager never regained consciousness and, as the *News* piously stated, "king alcohol...added another victim to his long list."[133]

As long as degradations and outrages were confined to those who chose to drink, the Drys could turn a blind eye. They might not like it, but they could accept it. And, after all, the taxes on liquor brought in a tremendous amount of money for the local government, but, of course, sometimes the degradations did fall on the innocent, and that was what the Drys could not abide.

In one such incident, George Cook of Pentland Township took his horse for a wild drive one day in 1907. Drinking and driving, even with a horse and wagon, turned out to be a mistake. Cook ran right into the buggy of Mrs. Isaac Pentland, who was going for a drive with a young neighbor child. Her buggy was "totally demolished" and the occupants received "numerous bruises, besides a severe shaking-up," while Mr. Cook sped off on his merry way. Cook was said to be "a perfect gentleman when sober, but a wild and reckless fool when under the influence of liquor."[134]

In 1889, Mrs. C. A. Dean, wife of Dollarville's schoolteacher, was menaced by a drunken lout who broke into her house. In 1907, Matt Hakala, full of "fighting whiskey," wandered into a gathering at the Finnish Temperance Hall and broke up the meeting. He then stumbled home and threatened his wife with a butcher knife before the officers arrived to take him to jail. Thankfully, none of the Finnish Temperance supporters, nor Mrs. Hakala, Mrs. Dean, Mrs. Pentland, or the child, were seriously hurt, but other victims of the demon drink did not fare quite so well, with often fatal results.[135]

One such tragedy occurred in November 1900. Thomas Pentland was seventy-one-years old, the patriarch of a large family of pioneers. The readers may recall that Pentland Township was even named for this prominent citizen. Now in his twilight years, he was "crazed with liquor." Grabbing his rifle, he let off a few shots at his sixty-one-year-old wife and grown son, Moses. He missed Moses, but Deborah was fatally injured and died a few days later, mourned by her heartbroken family.[136]

Then there was the sad story of Mr. and Mrs. Matt Anderson. Mrs. Anderson had had a mostly miserable life. She was born Sanna Liisi Riberg in 1874 in Finland to David and Liisi Riberg. The Ribergs, with their five children, immigrated to Newberry in the 1880s, where her father operated one of Newberry's wilder saloons. The children did not attend school much, and they all grew up to lives of liquor, bad marriages, and neglected children.[137]

Sanna (also called Susie, or Lizzie) was married at sixteen. Her first husband committed suicide in 1897, hanging himself in an old shack, where his body was discovered by their six-year-old daughter. The impoverished widow then married Matt Anderson, a day laborer and drunkard. Between her two husbands, Sanna had seven children, but by September 1910, five had died, the last baby of "marasmus," or severe malnutrition.[138]

The bar at the McLeod House (photo courtesy of Dr. James Surrell).

ORIENTAL SALOON!

FRED REED, Prop.

The finest furnished saloon in the city of Newberry.

Nothing but the very purest

Wines and Liquors,

Goes over the bar.

CHOICE CIGAR,

Is what you will get if you call for one.

Come in and see me in our new quarters.

Next Door to the Bank.

FRED REED, Prop.

PALACE SALOON,

H. F. ABBOTT, Prop.

—NEWBERRY AVENUE.—

The Finest Bar in the Village stocked with the choicest brands of

Wines, Liquors, Cigars

A Specialty made of Greenway's

Detroit Ale and Porter, and Schlitz Ex. Beer,

Unequalled for Family Use.

When in the city for a little time,
Come to the Palace and leave a dime;
If you drink our goods and go to bed,
You'll not wake up with a big head.

Nothing but pure, unadulterated goods goes over the bar.

H. F. ABBOTT.

Advertisements from *The Newberry* News of March 16, 1889 and July 18, 1890.

Deborah and Thomas Pentland, sometime prior to 1900
(photo courtesy of Roxanna Pentland Transit).

Below: Part of the Annual Liquor Report for Luce County for the year 1908.
Saloon licensing brought in $8,250 per year for county operating expenses.
Today that would be the equivelent of more than $200,000.

Name of Person, Corporation Association Company, or Copartnership paying a tax	RESIDENCE	KIND OF BUSINESS	PLACE OF DOING BUSINESS	Amount of Tax Paid
Chala Esterholm	Newberry, Mich	Selling or offering for sale spirituous or intoxicating liquors or mixed liquors by retail, or any mixture or compound excepting proprietary patent medicines, which in whole or in part consist of spirituous or intoxicating liquors, and any brewed, malt or fermented liquors.	Lot 3, Block 2, Newberry	$500 00
Bert Koontz	McMillan, "		2, 3, " 6, McMillan	500 00
J. E. Quinlan	Newberry, "		" 16, " 6, Newberry	500 00
Nels P. Anderson	" "		" 1, " 6, "	500 00
Wilfred Nantell	" "		" 4, " 6, "	500 00
M. S. Nackerman	" "		" 3, " 6, "	500 00
John Hunt	" "		" 1, " 5, "	500 00
William Green	" "		13, 14, " 6, "	500 00
Albert Randa	" "		" 6, " 1, "	500 00
Henry Hartwick	" "		" 2, " 6, "	500 00
V. Maki and T. Hakala	" "		" 7, " 1, "	500 00
Alexander Pentland	Dollarville, "		" 6, " 2, Doll'rville	500 00
John K. Mackey	Newberry, "		" 9, " 7, Newberry	500 00
John H. Johnson	Soo Junction "		ne ¼ of se¼, s 35, t 46 n, r 8 w	500 00
Frank L. Harris	Newberry, "		Lot 1, Block 1, Newberry	500 00
Philip Grondin	McMillan, "		" 10, " 7, McMillan	500 00
Harvey Nelson	Newberry, "		" 1, " 5, Newberry	250 00

Now it was Christmas Eve, 1910, and Matt and Sanna had spent the entirety of the day drinking "bad whiskey" along with her brother, John Riberg, and a few friends. After a night of debauchery, Matt decided that he did *not* care for the way Sanna was flirting with his friends. He picked up a kerosene lamp and hurled it at her. Mrs. Anderson promptly burst into flames. After "some time," someone finally went for Dr. Perry, who found the woman laid on "a filthy mattress flung in one corner of the room" in agony, surrounded by "a scene of utmost squalor and filth." The friends had vanished and her husband and brother were so "stupidly drunk" that they could do nothing to help. Sanna died the next day. Matt Anderson was charged with manslaughter, sent to prison, developed pneumonia, and died after only four months.[139]

A Soo Junction Saloon (photo courtesy of Sterling McGinn).

A pool room in McMillan
(photo courtesy of the Luce County Historical Society).

John Riberg, the brother, apparently did not learn his lesson about the oft-deadly consequences of binging. Two years later, he spent all evening drinking with his own wife, Lena, and a friend in a shack near the woods camps. Around midnight, with the three of them passed out, a defective chimney caught fire. Johnny, their ten-year-old son, woke up with his hair burning. The boy managed to awake the adults and the men dashed out of the shack and fled into the night. Johnny's mother also stumbled out, but then changed her mind and went back inside for the baby. Unfortunately, seven-year-old Victor followed her. Lena, Victor, and nine-month-old Dyyna did not come back out. So "completely consumed by the fire" was the family that their remains could be "gathered up in a basket."[140]

These unfortunate occurrences, and others like them, reinforced the Drys' arguments for abstention, temperance, and prohibition. They reasoned that without alcohol, none of these calamities would have happened. Probably. Therefore, the Drys concluded, a great deal of poverty and misery could be eliminated by outlawing liquor. It was a simple solution to a tragic problem.

As can be imagined, there was massive opposition to such an idea. Prohibition opponents were called "Wets." Some Wets' opposition was based purely on economics. For example, many local government officials argued that their revenues counted a great deal on liquor taxes.

Another Wet faction was based on the struggling farmer, whose solvency often hinged on the profit he made from selling grain to the brewers. The brewers, meanwhile, made profits from selling their alcohol to the saloonkeepers. And naturally, the most vociferous of Wets included those same saloonkeepers, whose wealth and very livelihood depended on their ability to serve that whiskey.

Other Wets included scores of immigrants who came from countries where pub life was an integral part of their culture and a welcome respite from the unending drudgery of their days. If an honest workingman wished to relax with a glass of beer after long hours of backbreaking, dangerous labor, then who was to say otherwise? Some fancy, patronizing stuffed shirt? Some boss man who lived a life of ease and comfort? Not likely, they figured.

The Drys, on the other hand, were often earnest, educated men of authority (and their wives) who wanted a brighter, better world. They truly believed that without access to alcohol, the drunk who drank up his wages, beat his wife, and ignored his children would transform into the sober man who saved his money, kissed his wife, and played with the children. If the honest workingman had to give up his liquor for lemonade, then wasn't that a fair price to pay?

The Drys were fighting to protect women and children and prevent tragedies, as well as to enhance productivity (which would help them make money). The Wets were fighting to be treated as adults and equals, as beings able to make their own decisions and run their own lives. Many were fighting for the right to sell whiskey (which would help them make money).

Emotions between the Wets and Drys ran high, and conflicts were often ugly and fierce. For example, in 1898 the *News* spent a large amount of ink ridiculing Marshal R. J. McDonald for his "absolute worthlessness," as he had been "appointed to protect the saloon keepers, and not the public" and often looked the other way while "drunken men…reel around on the streets and swear and obstruct the sidewalks." Marshal McDonald, sniffed Editor Brebner, "is well termed the 'wooden man,' for he is about as useful as a wooden man would be in his place, and does about as much to earn his salary of $50 a month." The editor continued to refer to the poor marshal as "the stick" for months afterward. Brebner further railed against the village trustees who had appointed him, griping that "these men have no regard for the rights of the public, and it would be like casting pearls before swine to try and reason with them."[141]

Advertisements from The Newberry News of November 18, 1892.

Advertisement from *The Newberry News* of October 24, 1889, January 4, 1890, and May 5, 1887.

Yet the ugliest incident of all happened in the tiny village of McMillan, a few miles down the road from Newberry, in what became known as the "McMillan Firebug" scandal.

When the railroad was being laid, and the Vulcan Furnace Company ruled supreme, McMillan had been planned to be another charcoal town, like Newberry. Several kilns were built early on, but quickly were abandoned. By 1900, McMillan was a small stopping point on the D.S.S.&A Railroad, home to about twenty families, mostly farmers, a handful of railroad employees, and folks living in some assorted lumber camps in the woods. Its character was quite rural in nature. During a particularly bitter political feud in 1887, H. D. Moore of Lakefield referred to his rival, William S. Locke of McMillan, as a "Chore Boy in the service of the King of Potatoville," describing McMillan as a place that was only "disturbed by the contented grunts of the festive porker roaming through its grass-grown streets."[142*]

In any case, it was a fairly quiet little community. Things began to change in 1903, however, when the Northern Cooperage Company built a factory in McMillan. This was a major investment in the village's future, as plant officials hoped to employ between forty and sixty men. Additionally, the Danaher Lumber Company had established a sizeable camp to the west of McMillan, where it planned to employ up to 100 more men. McMillan began to prepare itself for the influx.[143]

The farmers primed themselves to take advantage of the situation, many forming small businesses meant to capitalize on the newcomers and grab a bit of the coming riches for themselves. William S. Locke built a rooming house, as did David H. Galligher. Henry Mark (one of the Lakefield Marks) opened a saloon and a boarding house. His brother, Culbert Mark, founded a meat market. William Michaels, a popular blacksmith, opened his own shop. Six-foot wooden sidewalks were planned, as well as a new township hall. The hamlet was "putting on metropolitan airs."[144]

Merchants from Newberry also flocked to the area. Mr. Ostrander set up a drug store and Wesley Robinson a barbershop. James C. Foster opened up an auxiliary branch of his famous Newberry hardware store, while Dr. Bohn and Dr. Perry opened a branch of their drug store. A livery stable opened. County Clerk John Tait (who, besides being the county clerk, also owned a farm nearby) purchased up cheap plots of land, which he later sold at a profit. Many new homes sprang into existence. But relations between the old-timers and the newcomers, between the farmers and the factories, soon began to sour.[145]

Political control of McMillan and the surrounding Columbus Township remained in the hands of the old farmers, where it had always been, at least since 1893, when, after five years of fighting and pleading (and the failed attempt to combine with Lakefield), they had broken off from McMillan Township to form their own government. Now, they were said to "run things to suit themselves," including letting the saloons run in a "free and easy fashion."

---

* Locke retaliated by calling Moore the "Great I am" and concluding in a letter to the editor: "I will say that as far as brains is covered, we do not claim more than an ordinary amount, but we can spare a few for the empty scull of his lordship." Locke and D. L. West (the "Potatoville king") wanted the village of McMillan to detach from McMillan Township and join Lakefield Township. Moore wanted nothing of the sort. Each accused the other of falsifying petitions and lying to their neighbors. Eventually, Locke and his allies won out. The village of McMillan detached itself from McMillan Township and formed its own government: Columbus Township.

This postcard, dated 1914, shows McMillan with its metropolitan airs
(photo courtesy of the Luce County Historical Society).

A McMillan factory, dated 1913
(photo courtesy of the Luce County Historical Society).

The Dry side included John Tait (county clerk) and Donald McDonald (who worked for the Danaher Lumber Company), along with the factory, lumbering, and railroad bosses. "County Clerk Tait, the Cooperage Co. and lumber companies operating in the township," reported the News, "have made several attempts to wrest the political control from the gang without success, which has still further embittered the feelings between the two factions."

Henry Mark was the leader of the farmers, the old timers, who decidedly represented the Wet faction. One of McMillan's bigwigs, Mark farmed and dabbled in lumbering while his wife (a former schoolteacher) ran their boarding house. At one time, he set up a lumber camp near North Manistique Lake, and another time, he owned a small sawmill at Locke Lake.[146]

At the time, *News* Editor Fretz was firmly on the side of the Drys. He wrote (in a shockingly hyperbolic fashion) that Columbus Township's "political machinery…is said to be about as rotten as could be imagined…. If half the stories in circulation are true, there is no crime the gang would scruple at in order to maintain their sway."

Having failed to take over township government and banish liquor from Columbus Township, the Drys began filing court complaints against the saloons. Henry Mark was fined for "violating the liquor laws" and his saloon was closed by Luce County authorities. The mistrust and anger between the two factions deepened.[147]

Matters reached a boiling point in early 1906 when Fred Smith, a millwright working for the Northern Cooperage Company, filed a complaint with county officials claiming that Henry Mark was running "a house of ill fame" and continuing to violate the liquor laws. The authorities agreed and arrested Mark. He pled guilty, was fined $60, and again was forced to close his "free and easy house." Mark is said to have vowed vengeance and made threats against all his enemies. His friend, William Michaels, "while crazy-drunk," threatened to shoot County Clerk Tait the next time he stepped off the train. Ill feeling abounded.[148]

On a warm June night in 1906, the D.S.S.&A. depot burned to the ground and a bundle of kerosene rags was found nearby. The next night, fires started in two barns belonging to County Clerk John Tait and another at Northern Cooperage Company, but by this time a "strict watch" was in place and not much damage was done. Still, on yet another night someone set fire to the schoolhouse, as well as a house belonging to the Northern Cooperage Company. These fires, too, were discovered and extinguished. In each aborted fire, remnants of kerosene-soaked rags were found.

County residents almost panicked, believing that some kind of madman was at large, "some partially demented being possessed of a mania for setting fires." A vigilance committee was formed and kept, but the fires seemed to have abruptly stopped.[149] Soon, some people began to believe that the "reign of terror" was not due to a lunatic, but was, in fact, "spite work." Someone—it wasn't revealed who—hired the Smith Detective Agency out of Grand Rapids to investigate, and the agency sent two agents up, William Warner and H. A. Fishleigh, to hang about and collect gossip.[150] The detectives ingratiated themselves with Henry Mark, buying illegal moonshine from him and listening to him plan to reopen his "ranch." Henry reportedly said:

> If McDonald makes any holler we'll spike some of his logs; they'll go down to
> Dollarville and zip will go a band-saw and maybe two or three heads. If that
> don't settle him I have got a good gun and I'll lay in the bush some night and

P. Beaulieu,

Dealer In

Wines, Liquors & Cigars.

The finest equipped refreshment room in town.   A first-class pool room in connection.

Drop in and see me in my new place.

P. BEAULIEU.

Corner Newberry Ave. and Helen Street.

The Railroad Saloon!

JOHN LITTLE, Prop.

HELEN STREET.

My Bar is Stocked With the Finest Brands Of

Wines, Liquors and Cigars.

—A Specialty Made of—

The Celebrated Milwaukee Beer.

n4tf   *JOHN LITTLE.*

M. SURRELL,

Proprietor of

BOARD OF TRADE

SALOON.

The most elegantly fitted up place n the village. Our bar is stocked with a full line of

Choice Wines Liquors & Cigar

Foreign and Domestic.   Lunch counter in connection.   M. SURRELL.

Advertisements from *The Newberry News* of October 24, 1889, and (bottom two) December 19, 1890.

Locke and Galligher,

GENERAL - STORE !

McMillan,   -   -   Michigan.

All Kinds of

Produce taken in Exchange for Merchandise, and Highest Price paid for same.

New potatoes on hand, at market price.   Also all kinds of vegetables, such as Turnips, Carrots, Rutta-beggas, Beets, Etc.   Cordwood cheap-er than can be bought elsewhere.

Marquette City Saloon

FRED REED, Prop.

The finest furnished saloon in the city of Newberry.

Nothing but the very purest

Wines and Liquors,

Goes over the bar.

A CHOICE CIGAR,

Is what you will get if you call for one.

Come in and see me in our new quarters.

Next Door to the Bank.

FRED REED, Prop.

For Sale by all leading dealers.

Right: Advertisements from *The Newberry News* May 5, 1890, December 12, 1890, and December 27, 1912.

shoot his damn head off. He'll lay still then. And if that blankety-blank Tait butts in, we'll dynamite him.[151]

That seemed to be enough. Lawmen swooped in and arrested nine men: Henry Mark, Culbert Mark, William Michaels, William S. Locke, Wesley Allen, James Taylor, John Rutledge, George Fletcher, and George W. Dunlap.[152] The nine men were examined by Judge Harris, who quickly dropped the charges against Locke and Fletcher, who had not been involved at all. The justice also dismissed the case against William Michaels, who admitted overhearing many of the plots and schemes, but not participating in them.

Michaels testified to the court that the Mark Brothers and Wesley Allen had told him they were "going to give certain parties a touch of 'high life'" and also that "there will be a blaze tonight!"[153]

At the end of the justice's examination Henry Mark, Culbert Mark, John Rutledge, Wesley Allen, and James Taylor* were bound over for trial. Henry Mark somehow came up with his $7,000 bail money, but most of the others did not. Henry was free to go home. Coincidentally, or not, the very next week Henry Mark's own $2,000 barn was completely destroyed by a fire. A bloodhound was brought from St. Ignace to track the arsonist, but the trail ended at the roadway. Whether revenge or a transparent attempt to divert suspicion, no one would say.[154]

The trial, the most sensational ever held since the county's formation, began when the next term of circuit court opened in October. Joseph H. Steere served as the presiding judge. Louis Fead (of Newberry) and F. P. Sullivan (of the Soo) appeared for the prosecution, while the defendants hired P. H. O'Brien (of Laurium), F. T. McDonald (of the Soo) and J. J. McNeil (of Newberry). It proved very difficult to get an unbiased jury, and more than fifty men were rejected. Eventually, "twelve good men and true" were chosen: James Holt, John Teed, Thomas Miller, Peter Johnson, Charles Walker, Thomas B. Smith, Justin Robinson, Bernard Olsen, James Welsh, A. J. Townsend, A. B. Pratt, and Charles Carlson.[155]

Testimony lasted a full week, with forty-plus witnesses being called, but the prosecution's star witness was William Michaels, who previously had admitted to overhearing all kinds of juicy details. When called to the stand, however, he categorically denied everything to which he had previously sworn. Moreover, it was clear that he was completely sloshed. The exasperated Judge Steere ordered him to jail to sober up, but the next day he was still denying his previous testimony, especially anything that incriminated Henry Mark. The rest of the prosecution's testimony was "circumstantial in nature and contradictory in its detail."[156]

The jury was out for more than twenty-eight hours and, in the end, reported a deadlock. Eleven were for conviction; John Teed of Lakefield was for acquittal, and he would not be budged. With a mistrial declared, the prosecution brought charges again.

The venue changed to the Soo, and a new trial was scheduled, which was held in March 1907. By this time, however, the excitement had pretty much died out. The accused had prepared a stronger defense, while the prosecution could find nothing new to add to its case. Henry Mark was acquitted, along with his cronies.[157]

While the second trial was going on, John Rutledge confessed to the sheriff that he had started two of the fires and that William Michaels started two of the other fires (Michaels

---

* Wesley Allen and James Taylor were Henry Marks' cousins on his mother's side.

Louis Fead of Newberry,
later a judge (photo courtesy of
Sterling McGinn).

A most tenacious juror: John R.
Teed of Lakefield
(photo courtesy of Robert and
Cheryl Teed Bryers).

Judge Joseph Steere
(from the
Michigan Manual of 1915).

Advertisement from *The Newberry News* of
December 7, 1906.

denied this). Rutledge was sentenced to one to three years at the Michigan State Prison at Jackson. With that, the scandal was over.[158]

But the feuding did not end with the closure of the case.

Henry Mark demanded (and received) a retraction from *The Newberry News* to the effect that he had never run "a house of ill repute."

The *News*, in its June 26, 1908 edition, admitted that it "acknowledges itself to have been misled" by "what it considered a reliable source" and further acknowledged that Mark had received a "complete vindication" in court. Henry Mark was not satisfied. He went on to sue *The Newberry News* for defamation of character. The court agreed, awarding him damages of six red cents.[159]

The prosecutors, annoyed perhaps at being cheated out of their victory, slapped William Michaels with perjury charges and he went to prison for two years. The once energetic and hardworking blacksmith never seemed to recover, although he did return to Newberry after his term was served. Formerly a respected citizen, "the inventor of Michaels road sprinkler, and one of the best blacksmiths that ever pounded iron," one whose "smiling phiz" was always welcome in town, Billy Michaels was now considered "unsavory" and he was arrested for theft in 1916. Thereafter he left Newberry, moving to Marquette, where he became known for his fine "artistic wrought iron work." He died in 1930.[160]

Henry Mark was thrown in jail for contempt of court when he refused to testify against William Michaels. He was not let out until he answered the questions the court put to him. Shortly thereafter, Henry Mark once again was accused of violating the liquor laws.[161]

Then, in 1915, Henry and Culbert Mark were themselves accused of perjury. Columbus Township had been forced, via a citizen's petition, to require a "personal bond" from every applicant for a saloon license. The gleeful *News* explained:

> The dry forces in Columbus figure that an applicant for a saloon license will have a very hard time securing a gilt-edge personal bond, as most of the people who are qualified are either holding some public office or would refuse to become a bondsman from principle. In this way they feel confident of being able to put the one and only saloon in the village out of business.[162]

Undeterred, Henry and Culbert had clubbed together to fund the surety bond for McMillan's lone saloonkeeper, Thomas Whalen. The Drys now claimed that the brothers had lied, and that they did not, in fact, have the money to be a surety. Yet once again, the brothers were acquitted. Henry Mark dropped dead of a stroke two years later.[163]

The Drys continued their assault. They formed temperance societies and built temperance halls, restaurants, and hotels. They organized rallies, pressured politicians, wrote editorials, and gave sermons. In 1910, a countywide election was held on whether or not to make Luce County dry. It lost, but only by thirty-one votes. They were gaining ground.[164]

Eight years later the entire state of Michigan voted in prohibition, and all the remaining saloons were forced to close. Some tried to switch over to serving "cereal beverages…that look and taste exactly like beer, only the kick has been extracted." Others converted their bars into restaurants. Still others closed up shop all together, and a few saloonkeepers would even "express themselves as being rather pleased to get out of the business."[165]

Tuesday, April 30, 1918, marked the last day for drink in Michigan. Noisy and intoxicated, but relatively well-behaved and good-natured, large groups of men crowded into the saloons "four and five deep before the mahogany." At eleven o'clock, the "saloon men put on bargain sales and auctioned off the odd lot of liquors they had left to the highest bidder." The last of the liquor was "carried away (in) good-sized loads, some inwardly and others in bottles, jugs, etc."[166]

The next week, the sheriff and prosecuting attorney followed up by conducting thorough inspections, scrutinizing cellars and backrooms, and searching for anything that had been overlooked or hidden after the law went into effect. They found only "one lonely case of wine" at the Newberry Hotel that belonged to an out-of-town guest, and a "dray load of booze" at the Murphy Hotel, which Landlord Quinlan insisted belonged to his wholesaler and not him, explaining that he was only awaiting instructions for its disposal.[167]

Michigan's prohibition was followed by a national law in 1919, an actual amendment to the Constitution of the United States, ushering in nationwide prohibition. Thus did the era of the saloon end.

The Drys appeared to have won—but not really. For the era of the saloon made way for the era of prohibition, of speakeasies, blind pigs, moonshine, rum-runners, organized crime, and whole new levels "of violating the liquor laws." Effective December 5, 1933, the 21st Amendment to the Constitution repealed national prohibition, which was considered to have wildly failed. The debate over whether to drink or not to drink, to indulge or not to indulge, whether alcohol, cigarettes, drugs, gambling, or any other potentially hazardous activity, continues to this day.

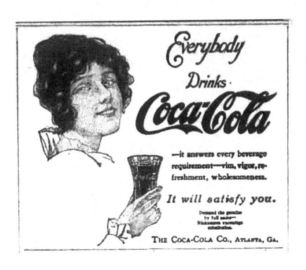

Chapter Six
That Old Time Religion

"My trips have to be made largely on snow shoes. My field is too large for one man, but I know you cannot afford the support for another, and I am going to cover it if it doesn't stretch me so thin as to crack in spots. This is yet a wild country between settlements... One cold day, with the mercury thirty-six below at noon, I walked fifteen miles, visiting settlers, and at night, with mercury near forty below, had a good meeting with a dozen. You would not do better in some large towns."

— Rev. J. Payson Mills, "Wolves and Snow Shoes,"
The Church at Home and Abroad, Volume 3, 1888

IN LATER YEARS, THE PIONEER citizens of Newberry were wont to look back with affection on all those crazy, drunken fools and their shenanigans. At the time, they were not so indulgent. They wanted respectability, decency, orderliness, and dignity. They wanted civilization. So they committed to the two great forces for civilization they had: church and school. While the next chapter will focus on Luce County's educational endeavors, this chapter is devoted to...well, the devoted.

In the early days, Newberry was still very much a company town. It had a company store and company housing. Most of its early governmental officials were company employees. The first "president of the village" was John H. Sherman, who also worked for the railroad's "land department." The second president, James Gandsey, ran a hotel owned by the "land department." The Village Trustees of 1886 included the druggist Hibbard Ingalls and merchant Amos Jones, as well as Royal A. Jenney, Sidney Wight, and David Donaldson, all three of whom worked for the Vulcan Furnace Company.[168]

In any case, in the beginning the Village of Newberry's founders (who remained in far-off Detroit) took a supportive and paternalistic interest in their little namesake. Newberry's first church was Presbyterian, and was paid for by Mrs. John Newberry herself.[169]

The twenty-four-member congregation had gathered itself together April 1, 1883, meeting in the schoolhouse for its first religious service. Within a year, with the help of the Newberry family, members had their church built and were planning a parsonage. They also organized a Sunday school and Ladies' Aid Society.[170]

Mrs. Newberry continued to send support, donating a bell inscribed with the words, "O come Let us Worship." She also paid off the mortgage and later donated money to build a chapel. Even so, for the next ten years, the congregation struggled. It accumulated debts and was unable to hold a pastor, all while the membership waxed and waned. The entire organization was only kept afloat by the zeal and determination of the Ladies' Aid. Not until 1894, under the direction of Rev. Vahan K. Beshgetoor, was the Presbyterian Church considered financially stable.[171]

Newberry's second house of worship was the Methodist Episcopalian church. In 1883, the Methodist Annual Conference of Detroit sent north the Rev. Guy M. Bigelow with $100 to start a church society, which he did in November 1883. Rev. Bigelow and the original twelve members raised $1,000 and moved into a small store on Newberry Avenue, which would serve as the first Methodist church. Membership grew quickly, and by 1886, the church offered a Sunday school with fifty-five children, as well as a "young people's group" with another twenty-four members. By 1890, the congregation had grown so large that it built itself a bigger, better church on Phelps Street, along with a parsonage for the minister. Like the Presbyterians, Methodist ministers never stayed very long. By 1889, the Newberry Methodist church been led by five different men. Ministers continued to change over every two to three years.[172]

The many Methodist and Presbyterian church pastors were, on the whole, a decent and dedicated group. The Methodist Rev. Ernest Scott, in 1914, memorized the marriage ceremony in Finnish for the benefit of the delighted Finnish-speaking couples. The Newberry Methodist church often hosted a guest speaker, a Mrs. E. Norine Law, who toured the nation during the 1890s giving sermons promoting temperance. Rev. Beshgetoor, of the Presbyterian church, had an interesting life. He had been born in Armenia, the son of a Christian minister. At age twenty-two, he had been arrested and imprisoned by the Turkish government for publishing a newspaper, the contents of which it did not approve. He escaped to the United States in 1886, learned English, and graduated from college as a minister. Newberry was his first parish, and he worked very hard. Within two years the once-beleaguered and near-bankrupt church was solvent and successful.[173]

Other ministers were a bit eccentric, like the Methodist Reverend Joseph A. Cottam, who lived and preached in Newberry from 1910 to 1912. In June of 1912, a fire broke out in the parsonage, ruining furniture, destroying furnishings, and gutting several of the rooms. Also, during the excitement, a "sneak thief" made off with $40 from the minister's desk drawer. The church, as owner of the parsonage, eventually received $700 from its insurance company for repairs, and Rev. Cottam personally received an additional $300 for damaged furniture, as well as many financial gifts from his neighbors and parishioners.[174]

Afterwards, Rev. and Mrs. Cottam left for England for several months for his health. He returned in August and declared himself much improved and eager to return to his duties. A week later, he announced his intention of leaving Newberry, saying his doctors recommended a change in climate. He suggested that he might go to "Porto Rico." Instead, he took a post in the Dearborn Methodist Church. Two years later, his parsonage burned to the ground while he was preaching a sermon next door entitled, "Why I Am a Protestant."[175]

Newberry's first Presbyterian church
(picture courtesy of Dr. James A. Surrell).

Presbyterian Church

Subject for Sunday morning services, September
the Eighth. Hour 10:30

"Bible Words Not Always a Safe
Guide."

You are cordially invited to attend both morning
and evening services.

Evening Scrvice 7:30.

OYSTER SUPPER.

The Ladies Aid Society of the Presbyterian church will give an oyster supper on the evening of Friday Nov. 11th, in the chapel of the church. Supper will be served from 6:30 to 10 o'clock p. m. Lovers of the molluscuous bivalve may expect a treat. Admission only 25 cents.

Above: Advertisements from *The Newberry News* of
September 13, 1912 and August 28, 1908.

It was definitely a deliberate act. Firefighters had noted the "pungent fumes of gasoline" at the time. Moreover, an attempt to ring the church bells failed because the bell pull had been cut, as had the electric wires. Rev. Cottam blamed a fanatic—someone who hated Protestants and/or ministers who advertised their sermons through posters. The police, however, blamed the reverend and charged him with arson, noting that his valuable library had been moved into the barn the day before. Thereafter, Rev. Cottam became "critically ill with brain fever."[176]

Newberry citizens followed the trial from far away through the Detroit papers. "Mr. Cottam is a bombastic egoist," reported *The Newberry News* doubtfully, "but people are loath to believe he was also criminally inclined." The people seemed to have the right idea. A few months later, Rev. Cottam (who had recovered from his "brain fever") was acquitted after a jury deliberation of only twenty minutes. After a lengthy battle with his insurance company, Rev. Cottam eventually received $3,000 and later wrote a book about his ordeal (*Why We Are Protestants; and, An Account of the Burning of the M.E. Church Parsonage at Dearborn, Mich.*).[177]

In general, the Methodists and the Presbyterians got along well together. They quarreled, occasionally, but at other times would loan each other money or collaborate on Sunday School Conventions or other projects.

Initially, Newberry Catholics had to make do with an occasional priest from St. Ignace, more than seventy-eight miles away, but the increasing numbers of French and Irish Canadians (estimated at sixty-five families by 1887) began to press for a church of their own. They got one in September of 1886 when an energetic young priest named Father John Manning arrived in town. Father Manning was the son of Irish immigrants who had fled famine and rebellion to Canada. He had always been rather frail, so he was sent to Michigan in the hopes that the climate would improve his health. He certainly did not take it easy. By "arduous effort and unceasing exertions, tramping around lumber camps, organizing amateur opera troupes," Father Manning raised $1,500 for a new church to be built.[178]

Francis Palms, an executive of the Peninsular Land Company, donated two building lots on West Harrie for this purpose, plus $500 of his own money, more than the average annual salary of a workingman. The church, St. Gregory's, and "glebe house" (priest's home) were built and completed in time for the 1886 Christmas services.[179]

Newberry's Catholics enjoyed their new church for all of one month before a defective chimney reduced the entire building to ashes. Father Manning at once announced his intention to rebuild, creating a bigger, better church. Unfortunately, the building was only insured for $700, as a larger policy for the completed building had not yet been approved.

The community rallied behind him, contributing $300 in the first two hours to the "Burnt Church Fund." He then went into a frenzy of fundraising, trolling the lumber camps for donations and organizing fairs and plays, including "the domestic drama, *The Toodles*." Poor and rich alike responded generously, and even the bigwigs of the DM&M, including Francis Palms, James McMillan, William B. Moran, and Mrs. John S. Newberry, each gave "magnificently." The second St. Gregory's was built on the same site within six months.[180]

Father Manning remained in Newberry until 1889, conducting Catholic services in Newberry, Seney, and Naubinway. He was one of Newberry's most beloved figures, serving on the school board and helping to organize the volunteer fire department. A "fluent and witty speaker," his Fourth of July speeches were remembered fondly years later. His mother and

Left: The initial plan for Newberry's second Methodist church
(drawing courtesy of *The Newberry News*). Right: Rev. Kishpaugh, who
served in Newberry from about 1892-1894 (photo courtesy of Tom Whalen).

Left: Rev. Cottam, who served in Newberry from about 1910–1912
(*Detroit Free Press*, December 8, 1916). Right: Newberry's Methodist church, in a
postcard dated 1910 (author's collection).

Methodist Manse, postcard dated 1910 (author's collection).

sister, Helena and Minnie, lived with him, and were also very well liked. The popular priest was later sent all over the peninsula, serving in Republic, Houghton, Calumet, Gladstone, Gould City, Iron River, Naubinway, and Rapid River before his health failed and he died at the early age of fifty-nine.[181]

Catholics, Presbyterians and Methodists all had their houses of worship now, but members of a fourth religion were arriving in increasing numbers: the Lutherans.

As early as 1887, Newberry's first Finnish immigrants sent for Rev. Jacob J. Hoikka of Republic to come down and hold services every so often (borrowing the Presbyterian church for a night), but they yearned for a home of their own.[182]

So, the most prominent and well-established Finns in the community, including the grocer Herman Anderson, saloonkeeper David Riberg (called "the Finn king," since he appeared to boss the others around), and ten others organized a church society. By 1889, they had raised enough money to begin construction. John Pakka, another Finnish immigrant, served as the contractor, and the church was completed and dedicated January 6, 1890. It was known as the Finnish Lutheran church, or Bethlehem Lutheran church, and was located on East Truman Street on the edge of town.[183]

Services in this church were held in Finnish, which was agreeable to the Finns, but less so to the increasing number of Swedish-speaking Lutherans. They wanted a Swedish language church. As a result, "The Scandinavian Lutheran Church Society" formed in the early 1890s and sponsored a Swedish pastor to come to town (Rev. A. Wihlborg). Six years later, the "Swedish Lutheran Church" was dedicated officially, with sermons in English and Swedish. The church, located on West John Street, was described as "a handsome edifice, one of the best in the town, and is a credit to the congregation."[184]

A small group of Episcopalians also held services from time to time. The members borrowed a church from one of the other denominations, sometimes the village hall, and once a "Chapel car" by the railroad tracks. In 1892, they purchased a plot of land in the hopes of building a church for themselves, which they were finally able to do in 1901, erecting "a beautiful little place of worship" on West Truman.[185]

Newberry also had a small but significant community of Jewish residents, the most prominent of which were Gustave and Fanny Rosenthal, who ran the People's One Price Store (and owned other buildings about town). They had moved to Newberry in 1887, attracted by the new town's incipient prosperity.

Fanny's brothers, Isaac, Morris, and Samuel Newmark, later joined them, along with her sister and brother-in-law, Mollie and Charles Sheer. Another prominent Jewish villager was Charles Rosenthal, presumably a relative of Gustave's, and Charles's brother-in-law, Max Coplan. Charles and Max ran the Boston Store.[186]

In the 1890s, Gus Rosenthal hired Max Bloom to live in Newberry and be a "teacher of Hebrew to the young Rosenthals and Newmarks" and also act as "stable boy, and general roustabout." In 1892, however, "Rabbi Bloom" had a violent quarrel with Gus, which spilled out into the streets in a "stream of Hebrew, Russian, Polish, Dutch, low Dutch, broken English and unbroken hatred," as the amused newspaper reported. Max Bloom sued the Rosenthals over assault and back wages, and the Rosenthals accused Bloom of violating village ordinances,

Left: The first St. Gregory and Rectory, 1887
(photo courtesy of Dr. James A. Surrell).
Right: Father Manning, an Irish dynamo (photo courtesy of Dr. James A. Surrell).

Line Drawings of St. Gregory's and Rectory (*Newberry News*, September 1, 1887).

Left: The second St. Gregory's (photo courtesy of Dr. James Surrell).

Right: Inside St. Gregory's in 1899, celebrating First Communion
(photo courtesy of Dr. James Surrell).

hoping to force him to leave town (the paper implied that Fanny Rosenthal had a rather vindictive temperament).[187]*

All cases were settled, though, and Max continued to live in Newberry operating a dry goods store until 1903.

His teaching replacement was a Mr. Brody of Sault Ste. Marie, who traveled down for special occasions. For holiday ceremonies, Newberry's Jewish citizens would rent a room in the schoolhouse, and order kosher food over the railway when they couldn't get it locally.[188]

In the more sparsely settled areas, congregations were served by traveling preachers "riding the circuit" from village to village to village in turn. The Catholic priest stationed in Newberry, for example, also served in Seney and Naubinway, as needed. In 1890, the Methodist minister Rev. A. Wood preached regularly in Seney. In 1892, Rev. Beshgetoor (Presbyterian) and Rev. Kishpaugh (Methodist) alternated riding every other Sunday to preach in Dollarville (though they occasionally squabbled over unconverted young people).[189]

Other ministers were sponsored and supported by "home missionary societies" from downstate in more populous and wealthier areas. J. Payson Mills was one such Presbyterian minister who preached (at various times) in Lakefield, McMillan, Corinne, Germfask, Rapinville, Scott's Point, Helmer, the Marks Settlement, and other places. He snowshoed, walked or rowed to his appointments, sometimes sleeping in a tent, while his family lived in a house in Lakefield.[190]

Frank L. Leonard was another Methodist missionary, based in Naubinway, who traveled 100 miles on foot every two weeks, visiting nine different locations. Even so, he was paid very little, sleeping on benches and lacking even the twenty cents it would cost to take the train. In 1890, the Ladies' Aid of Naubinway tried to rectify the situation with a strawberry and ice cream social, which raised $68 to help with his travel and other out-of-pocket expenses. Rev. Leonard, though, refused to accept the money because the younger attendees had left the ice cream social and formed an impromptu dancing party, which lasted until well past midnight. Rev. Leonard disapproved—strongly—of dancing, and interpreted their actions as an insult. The overwrought and exhausted minister declared his intention of never again preaching in Naubinway, declaring "I am done with Naubinway church matters now and forever."[191]

The people of Naubinway felt that Rev. Leonard was overreacting, judging by an anonymous letter to the editor, which explained:

> *Had Mr. Leonard asked the dancing party to desist, as it was against his wishes, they would have done so, but instead he rushed at them more like a roaring lion than a preacher of the gospel and a gentleman and ordered them to stop dancing and threatening to stop the mill from running nights unless they did. Such a course might have been all right for an orthodox preacher of the fourteenth century, but the people of this age are not to be driven into religion or to church....With the knowledge that Mr. Leonard is to leave us to our fate I cannot say with what feelings of regret the news has been received, but I can say that he has the good*

---

* Fanny's daughter-in-law, Hattie, later sued the elder Mrs. Rosenthal over (among other things) sabotaging her marriage. Their legal wrangling eventually ended up in the Michigan Supreme Court in 1909.

The Swedish Lutheran Church (also known as the Messiah Lutheran Church) on West John Street, at the edge of town, in "Swede Town" (photo courtesy of Dr. James A. Surrell).

The Finnish Lutheran Church, also known as the Bethlehem Lutheran Church (photo courtesy of Jerry Stimac).

Newberry's Episcopal Church (photo courtesy of Dr. James A. Surrell).

Charles Rosenthal in 1892 (courtesy of *The Newberry News*).

Advertisement from *The Newberry News* of December 7, 1906.

wishes of Naubinway's good people, and hope the world at large will not judge him too harsh, for he is only a poor innocent who knows not what he does.[192] ("Communicated," Newberry Independent, *August 7, 1890)*

Lacking a church, many of the smaller communities would hold services in schoolhouses, stores, and private homes. Raising enough money to build a church took a long time, but when accomplished, was a sign of prosperity and permanence.

By 1920 Newberry was home to six churches: Presbyterian, Methodist, Catholic, Finnish Lutheran, Swedish Lutheran, and Episcopalian. All six churches (along with many newer congregations) remain active to this day, although many have moved or rebuilt their churches over the years, and the Finnish Lutherans merged with the Swedish Lutherans in 1966.

Above: Advertisement from *The Newberry* News of September 1, 1887.

This postcard (dated 1909) shows the Methodist church built in McMillan a year earlier, after two years of fundraising. Prior to its construction, services were held in the schoolhouse or the town hall.

Above: Advertisements from *The Newberry News* of December 7, 1906 and November 18, 1890.

NEW YORK CASH STORE

Headquarters for

Groceries,
Teas,
Coffee,
Syrups,
California Canned and Evaporated
Fruits, Berries, &c.

Just Received

Two Original Crates, of Best English Crockery, Elite Pattern, Handsome new style Lamps and Glassware.

New Spring Styles

Of O. P. Hazards
Celebrated Never-Rip
work pants
Smith & Herrick's
Fine Shoes for Ladies.
Red School House
Shoes for Children.
Full French calf high-
cut sewed-edge Drive
Shoes, and other goods
of equal merit, all for
the lowest possible
Cash Price.

Present Liberal Patronage is an incentive to constant effort to merit a continuance of the same.

J. A. Shattuck.

Advertisement from *The Newberry News* of March 16, 1889

American House

E. J. Hamilton, Prop.
A 1 in every respect.
Good rooms and an Excellent table.
Sample rooms for commercial men.
Livery stable in connection. Rigs furnished to parties at reasonable rates. E. J. HAMILTON.

V. C. KEITHEN

— DEALER IN —

Watches, Clocks Jewelry, Etc., Etc.

Keeps on hand a nice line of goods and invites the public to look over stock.

Repairing of all kinds.

Done in a workmanlike manner. Give me a call when in want of jewelry. Located in Jones & Holt's store

Advertisements from *The Newberry News* of June 24, 1886 and September 1, 1887

My stock of

✳SPECTACLES✳

— AND —

✳EYEGLASSES✳

Cannot be excelled. Can suit any eye and will

GuaranteeSatisfaction

Repairing a Specialty

YOUNG LOVE !

JOHN DUCEY

Register No. 681

Veterinary Surgeon

Graduate of Ontario Veterinary College. Calls answered day or night. Office at Surrell's Livery,

Advertisements from *The Newberry News* of February 1, 1890 and February 23, 1917.

Chapter Seven
School Bells

"To allow children to grow up in ignorance is a crime and is so regarded by our courts. Schoolbooks and all come to him without money and without price. All that is asked of him is to come to school and to have him behave himself while here. This we intend that every child of school age in this district shall do."

— "School Notes," *Newberry News*, October 25, 1901

A SCHOOL BUILDING WAS ANOTHER MARK of prosperity and permanence, necessary not only for the proper education of the children, but also for the future prosperity of the region.

Luce County's first school was probably established in Lakefield Township, not long after the initial pioneers settled in. Lakefield's first nine families, as listed on the 1880 census, had about ten school-aged children among them, all illiterate (and about half of them belonging to Robert Bryers). These families may well have hired a schoolteacher. Robert Bryers, Sr. later remembered that he himself had hired the first teacher and paid that person $15 per month. It seems likely that the first schoolhouse was the Bryers School, probably located on or near Robert Bryers's farm, around the year 1881.[193]

Newberry's first school was built about 1883 out of one of the Vulcan Furnace Company homes on East John Street, near the old Village Hall, south of the railroad tracks. Although it was a one-room, one-teacher school at first, it soon expanded to two rooms with two teachers. Miss Libby handled the smaller children and Mr. Calhain the older ones. Enrollment grew so quickly, though, that an addition was built onto the house. After a third teacher was hired, the school board resorted to renting rooms in vacant buildings across town. By 1886, the school had 110 children enrolled, although only about seventy-five of them attended on any given day.[194]

The oldest, most sophisticated children were gathered in the "academic room." In the 1886–1887 school year, this room had twenty-two scholars, ranging in age from ten to seventeen. Under the direction of Ambro Bettes, principal, the pupils studied reading, spelling, writing, arithmetic, grammar, and geography. The most advanced children added history and physiology as well. A child's standing in school was an average of four factors: recitation (whether or not you could get up in class and recite your lessons), attendance, punctuality, and deportment (behavior). These four scores would be averaged to determine the student's class standing.

More than a quarter of these academic students later would become teachers in Newberry themselves.[195]

Because the "little old gray schoolhouse" was bursting at the seams, in June 1886, construction began on a new, wood-frame school building on a knoll on West John Street. When finished, the "John Street School" had three rooms ready for occupancy, three teachers, and more than 200 children, double the previous year's enrollment.[196]

School closed for a Christmas break, summer break, and whenever there was an outbreak of any serious disease.

In those days, school only lasted until the tenth grade. After completing the tenth grade, a student could choose to take a "teacher's examination" and qualify to become a teacher, if that's what he or she wanted. This was the closest thing to "graduating" that one could do then. This certificate was a prerequisite, not only for teachers, but also for those tenth graders who hoped to continue their education. Edith and Estelle Jenney, for example, earned their certificates in 1889, along with four other members of the academic room. Being too young to teach (Estelle was only fifteen), the sisters then traveled downstate to attend the Detroit High School and later Alma College. Only after graduating in 1893 did Estelle go into teaching.[197]

By 1894, the John Street School had doubled to six rooms and six teachers and the building could finally be said to have been completed. *The News* boasted on September 6, 1895, that this school was the "best and neatest of its kind in the upper peninsula." The outside was painted wood and inside the "large, airy, pleasant" rooms had plastered walls, surrounded by "woodwork inside finished in hard oil and the walls and ceilings kalsomined" (whitewashed). Each room had single seats and desks, a teacher's desk and chair, and two recitation seats, "all of the newest and best makes." They were stocked with "a most liberal supply of school apparatus, natural slate blackboards, maps, charts, globes, numeral frames, etc." This modern school even featured running water and "new water closets for the female departments." In 1897, the old coal stoves were replaced with a hot water heater and radiators, much reducing the risk of fire and increasing the students' comfort.[198]

The school's library served a dual purpose; besides 1,000-plus schoolbooks, it included hundreds of other volumes ("standard works on history, biography, poetry, etc.") that the public could peruse. Newberry's school ran from September to June, in three terms of ten weeks each. In addition, beginning in 1892, the curriculum was overhauled and Newberry schools transformed into a "graded course."[199]

A new child entering Newberry Schools in the fall of 1894 would be placed into Miss Clementina Somerville's "first primary" room. Clemmie Somerville, the daughter of Scottish-Canadian parents, had moved to Newberry at the age of nine and attended the Newberry schools herself. She completed the tenth grade, as far as she could go at the time. In October 1893, Clemmie took and passed the teacher's examinations, receiving a third-grade certificate.[200]

Clemmie had taught school for one term each in Pentland and Lakefield Township, and for one year in the three-teacher Mackinaw City School. In 1894, at age twenty, she returned home to take up the duties as Newberry's "first primary" teacher. This was the "first grade" of its day, meant for the youngest and least educated students.[201]

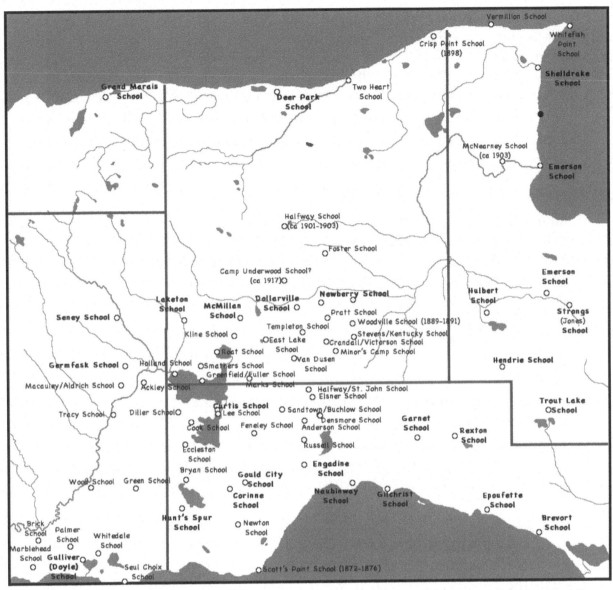

This map shows the approximate locations of the area's many schools. **Bold** indicates that the school was located in a village, town, or named hamlet.

This picture is thought to be the first school building in Lakefield Township; as such, it was probably the Bryers Schoolhouse, near to the Smathers Schoolhouse on the map above (photo courtesy of the Luce County Historical Society).

Clemmie's "first primary" pupils ranged in age from four to twelve years of age. Often, siblings of different ages would start school together. Their parents' backgrounds varied and the school became a melting pot of children, rich and poor, from a variety of lands, practicing various religions, and speaking many different languages, including German, Swedish, Finnish, French, and Yiddish. The language barrier must have been a terrible burden on Clemmie and her students. She dutifully recorded down their names as they sounded to her.

Clemmie struggled with Matt and John Jacobson,* Percy and Millie Duval, and Mamie Bijou, listing them under the surnames Yencison, Yonieson, De Volve, and Bishue. She listed little Rudolph Sicard as "Ludolph" for months. Not only did these children have to master the first grade, they had to conquer English as well.[202]

Children who had mastered the basics were "promoted when qualified," regardless of when it occurred during a school year. In December of 1893, for example, twelve students moved from the sixth to the seventh grade; nine moved from fourth to fifth, and eleven from second to third. In January, Lottie Devine was promoted from the eighth grade to the ninth, as was Maggie McLean in February. Also in February, Alta Ladner advanced from seventh to eighth, and two girls moved up to the tenth grade.[203]

On the other hand, promotion also could be a slow process, sometimes taking years. Fred Beaudin, for example, was a French-Canadian boy who entered the first primary in February of 1894 when he was five and a half and stayed there for the next three and a half years. John Nolan Cooper, who at ten was one of the oldest of Miss Somerville's first primers, did not reach the third grade until he was sixteen.

Thus, this was the largest of the classrooms, and at one time, Miss Somerville had more than 100 children under her care, although only about seventy usually attended each day. Her students included all the children just starting school, and all who had not yet managed to be "promoted."[204]

When first primary students *were* promoted, they entered the second primary room, taught by eighteen-year-old Edith Bettes in 1894. Edith was the daughter of Ambro Bettes, the first "principal." (He had quit teaching to go into politics.) A scholar, she had joined the "academic room" before she was twelve years old. By the time she was seventeen, she had passed the tenth grade, earned a "third grade" certificate, and joined the ranks of Newberry teachers. Her room was slightly smaller than Miss Somerville's, with only fifty children. Under her guidance, they studied "spelling, reading, numbers, language, geography, and writing," and about half the children were "promoted" each year.[205]

After second primary came the "intermediate room," a combination room including grades three through five. This room had about forty children. They continued their studies from the primary department, but focused more on grammar and arithmetic. Another veteran of the academic room, twenty-year-old Sara A. Campbell, served as the intermediate room's teacher. In the spring of 1893, when she was still in the tenth grade herself, she had been drafted to substitute for the fifth and sixth grades when the grammar teacher abruptly resigned.

---

* Matt (12) and John (10) Jacobson were among the oldest of the first-primary students. They had just arrived from Finland with their mother, joining their father, who had been working in United States for the last seven years. A difficult journey, seeing as how their mother could not read, write, or speak English. Matt left school at fifth grade and John at sixth.

An early picture of the Newberry School (later called the John Street School).

(Right) Professor Angus D. Chisholm in 1894, principal of the Newberry Schools, and teacher of the high school from 1892–1901.

Newberry's roster of schoolteachers in 1894. They are, from left to right, Miss Clemmie Somerville (1st primary, age twenty), Miss Sara Campbell (intermediate, age twenty), Miss Estelle Jenney (grammar, age twenty-one) and Miss Edith Bettes (2nd primary, age eighteen).
(Courtesy of *The Newberry News.*)

After a replacement teacher was hired, Sara had returned to her lessons, passed the tenth grade, earned a third grade certificate, and started teaching the next year.[206]

The next higher academic tier was the grammar department, for grades six through eight. New subjects included US history, composition, geography, physiology, and hygiene. Interestingly, Newberry teachers were instructed to give "especial attention" to "the subject of stimulants and narcotics and their injurious effects on the system." The grammar teacher in the fall of 1894 was none other than twenty-one-year-old Estelle Jenney, graduate of Alma College, and veteran teacher of the Dollarville school.[207]

The grammar department was where most scholars ended their academic career. Most children left school around the age of fourteen or so, regardless of whether or not they had managed to pass the eighth grade. Girls began to assist their mothers at home or took jobs working for other families. Boys went to work alongside their fathers, in the wood camps or clerking at the hotels or stores in town. George Roatch, for example, left high school right before graduating to take a job as a bookkeeper in a lumber company, making $50 a month (a salary higher than most of his teachers.)* George Olsen's father insisted he either go back to school or get a job, so the sixteen-year-old George went to work at the furnace. Louis Labombard left school after the eighth grade to work as a laborer, later moving to Flint, where he became a mail carrier. Joe Pelletier was still in the first primary at the age of ten. He never made it past the fourth grade, and at age fifteen, was working in a cigar shop. He lived in Newberry all his life, and as an adult ran the popular Pelletier's Restaurant.[208]

Some parents chose to send their children away to continue their schooling. Early on, Edmund Burrell sent his three children (ages nineteen, twenty, and twenty-three) to Ann Arbor, with their aunt as chaperone, in order to "attend the high school and other seminaries of learning." Seventeen-year-old Clarence Shattuck was sent to the Michigan Military Academy in 1907. Clifford Surrell headed for the St. Thomas Military Academy in St. Paul, Minnesota, although he returned to graduate from Newberry in 1914. Lula Hubbert and Cora McLeod graduated from the Catholic Loretto Academy in the Soo.[209]

However, for those interested, the John Street School of 1894 boasted a "high school" room where the principal teacher taught the oldest and most intellectual children. Some of these went on to college. Others got married, took jobs in shops, or became teachers themselves. Professor Angus D. Chisholm taught this first "High School," which initially covered only the ninth and a tenth grade. Soon it expanded to eleventh and twelfth grades, which culminated in the first graduating class of 1895. The dedicated high school students studied such advanced subjects as natural philosophy (science), rhetoric, composition, ancient history, physical geography, higher algebra, and political science. Later, the school added astronomy, geometry, arithmetic, general history, composition, English history, botany, philosophy, American and English literature, political economy, bookkeeping, and physical training. Newberry schools were indeed becoming quite sophisticated.[210]

In its first commencement year of 1895, Newberry High School held its first graduation. The class of 1895 was three students large, and included Pearl Jenney (16), Elmer McPhee (19), and Harry Nicholson (17). Pearl Jenney later attended college and moved with her family to

---

* George Roatch had already earned his own teaching certificate, and, in fact, interrupted high school once to teach a term in Lakefield.

A postcard showing the Newberry School, later called the "John Street School" (courtesy of Sterling McGinn).

Graduating Class, 1903. Top Row, left to right: Frank Gormely (15), John Metcalf (19), Chester Holt (17); bottom row, Tina Jensen (18), Elizabeth Hall (19), Rachael Brown (18) (photo courtesy Dr. James A. Surrell). Chester, class president, died of typhoid fever four months later.

Ann Arbor, where she married Byron F. Ott, a druggist; the couple then moved to Utah. Harry Nicholson attended college, got a job as a printer's assistant at *The Newberry News*, married Ina Ingalls, and later moved with her family when they removed to Minnesota, where he eventually became a village clerk. Elmer McPhee had previously attended the Bay City Business College, but had returned to graduate from the Newberry High School, worked in the lumber camps for a time, then went downstate and entered into the Ann Arbor High School (his mother and sister accompanied him), where he graduated in June 1899 with high honors. He later became a bookkeeper.[211]

Newberry graduates furthering their education by attending *other* high schools was not uncommon. The line between high school and college was still a bit blurry in those days. Neil McLeod and John Mackey both graduated from Newberry in 1901. John went on to attend the Ann Arbor High School and Neil attended both Ann Arbor and Marquette high schools.[212]

Outside the village there were the country schools, where the educational experience could be quite different. McMillan Township ran another school in Dollarville from the early 1880s until 1926, when the first school bus was purchased and the students could more easily get to Newberry. The Dollarville School had two to three rooms and, at times, more than 100 students. The Foster School, located at Four Mile Corner, instructed children north of town. Deer Park, isolated up at the far, northern, frosty end of Luce County, waxed and waned in population. At its peak, around 1895, it boasted a two-room schoolhouse with classes from primary school through the tenth grade.[213]

As the situation called for it, McMillan Township also ran one-room schools at the Two Hearted Life Saving Station for the children of the lighthouse keepers and surfmen, as well as tiny schools near the wood camps for the children of the lumberjacks. In 1898, there was the "Crisp Point School" at the Crisp Point Life Saving Station. At the "McNearney School," near the McNearney farm on the Tahquamenon River, Fanny Whitby taught five children for one month in August 1902. And halfway between Newberry and Deer Park, the "Halfway School" existed from 1903–1905.[214]

To the west, Columbus Township ran its own schools: one at McMillan and a smaller one at Laketon (a few miles further west). In 1893, the township built a two-story, wooden school that was replaced in 1912 with a large, brick schoolhouse with four (later six) classrooms. This school still stands today as one whizzes by on Route M-28.[215]

Lakefield Township and Pentland Township were farming communities, and their scattered populations had no real center. Thus, they maintained a handful of one-room schoolhouses dispersed about, most named after the residents themselves. Their early schools were organized by the early settlers, the farmers who pre-dated the railroad, especially those with young children. The first three schools in Lakefield Township have been the (previously mentioned) Bryers School (west of Round Lake), the Fuller School (north of Big Manistique Lake), and the Mark School (east of Big Manistique Lake). It is probably no coincidence that Robert Bryers, Riley Fuller, and Wesley Mark all had lots of school-age children in the 1880s.[216]

By the turn of the century, the Bryers schoolhouses had ceased to be because the Bryers children had grown up. They were replaced by dozens of new families with young children, and several new schools were erected, including the Holland/Richards School, the Smathers School, and the Roat School. Pentland Township operated the McGrath School and the Pratt

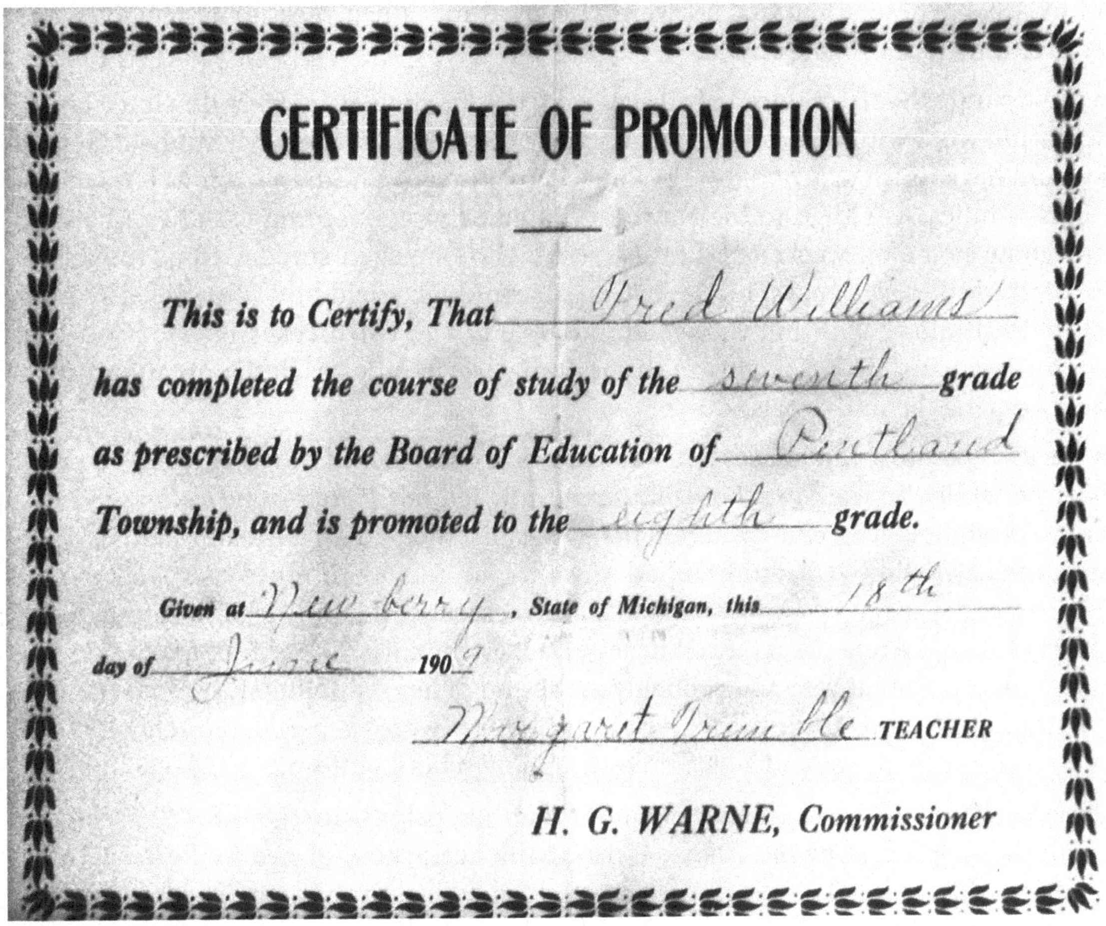

CERTIFICATE OF PROMOTION

This is to Certify, That _Fred Williams_

has completed the course of study of the _seventh_ grade

as prescribed by the Board of Education of _Portland_

Township, and is promoted to the _eighth_ grade.

Given at _Newberry_, State of Michigan, this _18th_

day of _June_ 190_9_

Margaret Trimble TEACHER

H. G. WARNE, Commissioner

This certificate from June 1909 certifies that young Fred Williams completed the seventh grade at the Stevens School. Because he was seventeen years old by this point, he did not return for the eighth grade (courtesy of the Tahquamenon Logging Museum).

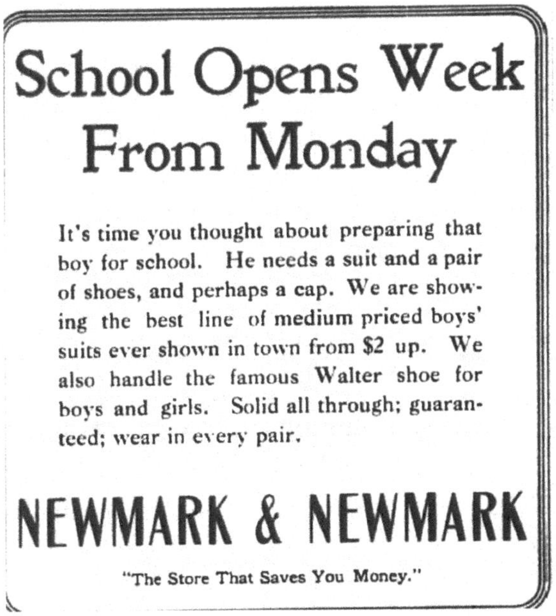

Above: Advertisements from *The Newberry News* circa 1917.

School by 1894. These schoolhouses were also used for "town meetings," religious services, concerts, and the occasional funeral.[217]

In these rural schools, children of all ages were taught, divided up by ability into classes. The teacher would work with each class in turn, while the other classes quietly studied. Generally, a pupil would have finished school by age fourteen or fifteen. Children from wealthier, or more ambitious families, would go to the Newberry High School, boarding with town families and perhaps going home on weekends. Lottie French was one such student who "took a course" in 1898. Jesse Miller was another, a seventeen-year-old Lakefield boy who took a year of high school in 1901, along with his younger brother, Ira. The two Becker boys of Soo Junction (Philip, fourteen, and Harry, eight) took the train twelve miles each day to attend school in Newberry during the mid-1890s.[218]

In the days before school buses and snowplows, a child's ability to attend classes depended on his or her ability to walk to school. This naturally led to the many one-room schoolhouses scattered throughout the county. Even then, the distance could be daunting. In 1906, for example, the Lakefield Fyvie children had to walk four and a half miles every day to the Roat School, where they made up almost half of its fourteen-scholar enrollment. Lizzie (13), Charles (12), John (10), and Anna (8) achieved near perfect attendance. The oldest, Mary (15), was not in school much at all that year and probably at the end of her schooling. Roy Fyvie (6) attended about a third of the time. Children under the age of nine were excused from school attendance if they lived more than two and a half miles from any school building.[219]

These rural schools were often little more than log cabins. In 1953, E. W. Kiebler, in his book *The Old Log School by the Lake*, described the Lee School of nearby Portage Township, which operated from 1893 to 1907, referring to it as typical of the area. The log building was 16x18 feet with a small woodshed on the rear and two outhouses out back. It was warmed by a woodstove in the center, lit by two windows, and watered by a dipper and pail. One teacher faced nine desks in three rows, which could hold about a dozen children of all ages. The rural schools of McMillan, Lakefield, and Pentland were likely very similar. They were a far cry from the whitewashed, two-story, city school of Newberry with its steam heating plant and indoor female water closets.[220]

Even so, all children in Luce County were provided with free textbooks, and each rural school was "supplied with maps, dictionaries, reading charts, geographical portfolios," and other equipment. Moreover, rural school boards were careful to only hire qualified teachers with a "legal certificate." By the 1890s, most of these turned out to be young ladies from Newberry who had passed the tenth or eleventh grades and also earned a third-grade teaching certificate.

Even in a country school, by 1903 a teacher with a third-grade certificate could make between $35 and $40 dollars per month.[221]

To earn that certificate, these young ladies had to pass examinations in reading, orthography (spelling), arithmetic, grammar, civil gov't, US history, geography, penmanship, physiology, hygiene, and the lofty subject called "Theory and Art of Teaching and School Law." If passed with an average of 75 percent (50 percent minimum for any one subject), the applicant would receive a Third Grade Teaching Certificate, which would allow her to teach in one of the rural schools.[222]

Teachers' Examinations

April 26-28, 1917.
August 9-11, 1917.
Held in the court house at Newberry, Mich.
The examination in reading for all grades is in the April and August, 1917, teachers' examination will be based on the outline in reading as given in the Manuel and Course of Study for County Normal Training Classes and in the Manuel and Course of Study for Elementary Schools.

No credit will be given on examination for reading circle work, but questions will be based on the reading circle books, selected for the year. Five of the examination questions in physiology and hygiene for all grades in the April and August examinations will be based on "Health Work in the schools" by Hoag and Terman; three of the questions in grammar will be based on "Stories and Story Telling" by Keyes.

EIGHTH GRADE

May 10 and 11, 1917.
The reading for eighth grade examination will be based on the poem, "Tuba Cain," by Charles Mackay.

ANNA I. AUTEN,
31-tf   County School Comm'r

GLASSES FITTED

CONSULT

J. LEAHY

Optometrist

Expert on Eye Strain

—

Headache, Dizziness, Nervousness, and all other symptoms of Eye Strain cured.

Crossed Eyes Straightened Without an Operation.

Fitting Children's Eyes a Specialty.

Difficult Cases Solicited.

Glasses Guaranteed to Fit.

Office at Drs. Ahrens & Mead.
Date, Tuesday, March 6.
Will remain three days.

No more of this!

Rubber Shoes unless worn uncomfortably tight, generally slip off the feet.

THE "COLCHESTER" RUBBER CO.

make all their shoes with inside of heel lined with rubber. This clings to the shoe and prevents the rubber from slipping off.

Call for the "Colchester"

"ADHESIVE COUNTERS."

· · · ·

R. H. WELER,
J. A. SHATTUCK,
ROSENTHAL & GOLDMAN,
G. ROSENTHAL
HENDERSON BROS.

Above: Advertisement from *The Newberry News* of December 19, 1890.

Left: Advertisements from *The Newberry News* of February 23, 1917.

After teaching for seven months with "ability and success," a teacher was eligible for a second-class certificate; that is, if she also passed algebra and natural philosophy (with an 80 percent average, 70 percent minimum). A second grade certificate let her teach in a town school.

After teaching for one year, an applicant would be eligible to try for a first-grade teaching certificate, which (in addition to previous requirements) upped the passing level to a 90 percent average (80 percent minimum) and added geometry, general history, and botany to the subject list required.[223]

Teachers furthered their education by attending "Teacher Institutes," which were held regularly. These were daylong symposiums, where all teachers from Luce County and beyond were welcomed to hear traveling lecturers, discuss school problems, and pursue their own studies. In 1899, the Northern State Normal School (now Northern Michigan University) opened in Marquette as a college specifically meant to train teachers. "Taking a course" became an option of which many ambitious teachers took advantage.

***

The weather was no idle threat. Luce County had no tragedies in this area, but it did have a few close calls, such as when a blizzard struck in February 1899. Miss Maggie Main, a brand-new teacher at the Pratt School in Pentland Township, dismissed classes early, but many of the children were frostbitten before they reached home.

The two worst off were Herbert (10) and Leland Bell (7), who missed the sleigh their father had sent for them in the driving snow. Lost, they wandered off the road. The boys might have frozen to death, but for the fact they had brought their dog to school with them that day. The dog kept them going in the right direction until they stumbled into a neighbor's house, the "face and hands of both...quite severely frozen." Fortunately, both boys recovered.[224]*

Like everything else in Luce County, the school system grew rapidly over the first few decades. In Lakefield Township, the Smathers School opened, replacing the Fuller School. The Templeton School, Stevens School, and Van Dusen School opened in Pentland Township and the Laketon School in Columbus Township. Up north, the Deer Park School, which had been discontinued in 1899, reopened the next year.

In Newberry, the John Street School was soon overwhelmed and the school board had to rent unoccupied buildings all over town to take care of the overflow, including the "old post office." More and more teachers were added.[225] By 1905, the school in Newberry became a completely "graded school" with classrooms devoted to one grade apiece (except for a combined seventh/eighth grade room). There were eight grades in all, plus high school with three teachers. The school now had a basement with "modern and improved" water closets, fire escapes, cement walks, and an enclosed schoolyard. Meanwhile, all rooms were repainted and a new flag was purchased. It still, however, did not have electric lights. In 1902, an addition was built to the west, adding eight new classrooms for the primary grades.[226]

---

* The fancy town schools were not immune to weather worries. As late as 1920, during a January cold snap, the overwhelmed radiators simply could not keep up and the schoolrooms were too frigid to work in.
The youngest children were sent home, alone, out into the cold. Station Agent Nichols reported rescuing one little boy, walking down the railroad tracks towards his home, "crying bitterly from the cold and with his hands and face frostbitten." (see *Newberry News*, January 23, 1920)

Left: Miss Maggie Main, 1898 graduate of Newberry High School and teacher of the Pratt School 1898–1899 (photo courtesy of Ned M. Barker).

Right: The Pratt School, formerly in Pentland Township, has been moved several miles to the north, where it is on display at the Tahquamenon Logging Museum. The Pratt School remained in regular use until the 1950s.

Left: A school in West Lakefield Township (photo courtesy of the Luce County Historical Society).

Right: The Templeton School, about the year 1900. The boys in the wagon are Blaine, Archie, and Dan Pentland (photo courtesy of Roxanna Pentland Transit).

The hot new trend in education was "Nature Study" and the Newberry schools participated eagerly. The smaller children collected autumn leaves, raised caterpillars, and examined snowflakes. Third graders collected birds' nests. Older children studied trees and fossils. Music and drawing lessons were added to the curriculum. The teachers formed the Luce County Teachers' Organization and held meetings where they heard lectures on topics like "Habit and Its Relation to Attention" and studied the plays of Shakespeare. Most town teachers were no longer merely girls who had passed the tenth grade. Almost all were high school graduates, and many had "taken a course" at "the Normal" in Marquette.[227]

Standards for school buildings also rose. By 1916, the Department of Public Instructions had codified a set of standards for rural schools "concerning lighting, heating, ventilating and decorating, seats, blackboards, outbuildings, walks and general school equipment." Schools that met these stringent requirements were dubbed "Standard Schools" and given the right to affix a commemorative metal plaque on their walls. Meanwhile, in many districts, old log schoolhouses were torn down and replaced with modern frame buildings. In larger settlements (like McMillan and Newberry), frame buildings were replaced with brick.[228]

Yet, education in the country could still be a spotty affair. Newberry schools ran for ten months out of the year, for example, but the nearby Pentland schools only operated for eight months. In Lakefield Township, the Greenfield School only ran for five months over the summer of 1889.* The Roat School closed in January 1898 and did not reopen for four months, skipping the worst of the snow. The Germfask School did likewise in January 1900.[229]

High school, then as now, was the ninth through the twelfth grade, capped with a graduation. In 1904, its thirty-eight scholars studied algebra, geometry, physiology, physics, and botany. English classes studied Shakespeare, Chaucer, and Tennyson. History classes examined American, ancient, and medieval history. Also offered were classes in Latin and German, civil government, bookkeeping, and astronomy. Every month or so, there was a program of "rhetoricals," where each high school student was expected to give a "recitation" of poems or read an original essay on subjects like, "the True American," "The Fairy Land of California," "How Bananas Grow," and other topics.** Programs were advertised in the newspaper, and parents and the public were encouraged to attend.[230]

Sports began to become a part of school life, and a football team and baseball team were organized by 1904. Sometimes these teams played other schools, and sometimes they played other community teams—most often, football and baseball teams made up of the attendants at the State Hospital (whose employees were barely older than the students themselves).

Though the 1902 addition had helped somewhat, classrooms were still overflowing. A new school building was desperately needed. In 1908, a modern, brick building was erected on the southwest corner of Newberry Avenue and McMillan Avenue, at that time considered the edge of town. The entire school (344 pupils) moved into these spacious new accommodations, consisting of fourteen classrooms, an auditorium with stage, steam heating plant, and a gymnasium in the basement.[231]

---

* The Greenfield School is possibly the same as the Fuller School, under a different name.
** For example: "Alexander the Great," "The Panama Canal," "The Girls of Japan," "Manufacture of Charcoal," "What Russia Does for Her Children," "The Society of Books," "Our Alaskan Eskimo." I could go on.

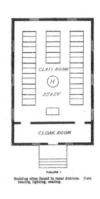

A drawing and floor plan of a typical one-room schoolhouse in rural Michigan. The illustration is of the Oakwood School in Kalamazoo County, but Luce County schools would have looked very similar (from Michigan Standard Schools, Bulletin No 9, 1915. Published by Fred L. Keeler, Superintendent of Public Instruction).

The children of the Stevens School, about 1910. The seven children pictured here belonged to the Grefvin, Williams, and Stevens families. Because the Stevens and Williams families were from Kentucky, the Stevens School also was known as the Kentucky School (photo courtesy of the Tahquamenon Logging Museum).

The spaciousness was fleeting. By 1912, with 459 students enrolled, the new building was again at over-capacity. Fortunately, the old John Street School had not been sold and was pressed back into service as the "primary school," while the new school became the Junior-Senior High. The high school of 1915 was up to nine teachers and offered a variety of subjects, including "commercial" courses (bookkeeping, shorthand, typewriting), domestic science (home economics), music, science, Latin, German, and English. With the building of the new school, Newberry now had the space to include another popular innovation: a kindergarten. A kindergarten class had been added before in 1898, but by 1901 was dropped. Now, it would be a permanent feature.[232]

Social norms and educational ideals also were changing. Now the practice of leaving school at thirteen and fourteen increasingly was seen as a bad thing. In 1913, state law required all children under the age of sixteen to be either enrolled in school or "regularly employed at some lawful work if physically able to do so." To make this palatable, in 1914 the "six and six" plan came into vogue in Michigan schools. In this plan, grades one to six were the "elementary" and seven to twelve were the "high," consisting of junior and senior high. In addition, seventh to twelfth grades were to be guided along "Four distinct lines; college preparatory, agricultural, domestic arts and commercial."[233]

"It is believed," reported the *News* in a 1914 article, "that the large number of children who now leave school in the seventh and eighth grades will be held in school by giving them work which meets specially with their needs." Although Newberry School soon would be reorganized along these lines, many country schools continued to end at the eighth grade. A "legal high school" was required to have at least two teachers dedicated solely and only to the ninth to twelfth grades. Maintaining one teacher for eight grades was hard enough for most rural school boards. Instead, rural students who wished to go on to high school still had to enroll someplace else, and their country school boards were required by state law to pay for them to do so. At least, they had to pay tuition to the high school ($1 per month per out-of-town student in 1895). Students and their families, though, were responsible for the child's room and board. Some (like McMillan's Bohn Musgrave) took part-time jobs to help alleviate the cost. Many others were not able to arrange it. Despite the expense, enrollment in the Newberry High School doubled and doubled again.[234]

Indeed, the entire school population was mushrooming. In 1885, Newberry schools had 143 pupils and three teachers. By 1915, they had quintupled to more than 750 students (about 100 in the high school). Nine teachers taught the upper grades, while the first eight grades were divided up among fifteen more.[235]

Both schools, the brand-new, spacious high school and the old John Street School, again were overcrowded. The school board began to talk of building an even bigger, better school for its 350 seventh through twelfth graders.

In 1927, a grand, elegantly proportioned, three-story brick building opened, designed by Escanaba architect Gothard Arntzen. The pride of the county, this school featured marble floors, intricate woodwork, and a grand auditorium. It reportedly made "visitors to our little city gasp with amazement on viewing the beautiful structure."[236]

While Newberry was building its bigger, better accommodations, the rural schools were poised at the brink of seismic changes, little as the people may have realized it.

A GIRL'S ESSAY ON BOYS

The following is the opinion of a Newberry school girl on this subject:

Boys are men that have not got as big as their papas, and girls are women that will be young ladies by and by. man was made befor woman. when God looked at Adam he said to himself, well I think can do better if I try again. and then he made eve. God liked eve so much better than Adam that there have been more women than men. Boys are a trouble. they wear out everything but soap. if I had my way half the Boys in the world would be Girls; and the rest would be dolls. our school master is so nice. I think he must have been a little Girl when he was a little Boy.

REPORT

FOR

Month Ending *Feb 23* 191 *7*

Deportment - *G*	Care of Books	
Industry - -	Days Absent -	
Neatness - -	Times Tardy -	
Spelling - - *Eg*	Composition -	
Reading - - *G*	Algebra - -	
Writing - - *M+*	Rhetoric - -	
Arithmetic - *G+*	Latin - -	
Lang. or Gram. - *G*	Literature - -	
Geography -	German - -	
History -	Geometry - -	
Physiology -	Bookkeeping -	
Civil Gov't -	Physics - -	
Music - - *M+*	Botany - -	
Drawing - -	Physiography -	
Monthly Average	Term Average	

Mrs WH Krempel
Signature of Parent

A SITUATION

at a good salary awaits every graduate of the Detroit Business University. Experience proves this positively. Catalogue free. Enter any time. Write R. J. Bennett, C.P.A., Principal, or W. F. Jewell, President, 15 Wilcox Street, Detroit, Michigan.

SOO BUSINESS COLLEGE

SOO, MICHIGAN.

Our new term of school opened April 1st.

Six students were placed in positions last week

One lady who had been here but two months and a half took dictation in shorthand and wrote a perfect business letter without assistance.

One student who has been here but three months was placed in a position this week writing one hundred words shorthand dictation, new matter, and one hundred and twelve words per minute on the machine.

Come to our school and get shorthand.

J J GINSTE, Prop.

Our Lady of the Straits.

URSULINE ACADEMY

ST. IGNACE, MICHIGAN

Boarding and day school for young ladies. Healthful location. Terms moderate. Complete Academic, Musical and Commercial courses. Special advantages for Modern Languages For catalogue write to MOTHER SUPERIOR.   18 4t

Left: This essay was printed in *The Newberry News* in its November 6, 1891 issue.

This report card, from the Dollarville School, was presented to third grader Lewis Krempel in 1917, to give to his mother for signing (courtesy of Jeff Chown).

Right: An advertisement that appeared in *The Newberry News* on September 13, 1907, May 9, 1913, and August 25, 1916.

As early as 1912, the beginning of the end for rural, one-room schools had begun. In that year, Columbus Township built itself a large, new, brick school and closed its little Laketon School. Laketon students now had to travel several miles to attend school, so the township borrowed an innovation introduced by the Stephenson schools (located in the western UP) and arranged for a "bus" in the form of a hay wagon driven by Herman Shufelt (which became a canvas-covered sleigh in winter time). Dollarville did the same for its older students in January 1920, arranging for a "covered rig" to transport them to the high school at Newberry. Finally a bona fide "bus" was introduced 1926, "a specially built Chevrolet, all vital parts being of extra-heavy construction." The march toward consolidation had begun. One by one, the small, one- and two-room schoolhouses began to close. None are left today.237

A McMillan school bus, dating from the 1930s
(photo courtesy of Sterling McGinn).

This postcard shows Newberry's new school, built in 1906 and meant to hold the entire student body. By 1912, however, the elementary students were transferred back to the old John Street School and this building became the high school. In 1927, a new high school was built, and this building became the Newberry Grade School, which was torn down in the 1960s (author's collection).

This postcard shows Newberry's new high school, completed in 1927, designed by Escanaba architect Gothard Arntzen with a great deal of flourish and flair (author's collection).

An advertisement that appeared in
The Newberry News on August 28, 1906.

Chapter Eight
Taking Care of Business

"There are three church buildings in Newberry, a large, two-story school house, six hotels and eight saloons and nearly all kinds of business, trades and professions represented in like proportion.... In considering the amount of labor required to keep all these industries moving...the reader can form some idea of the importance of the little village of Newberry and the magnitude of the work being accomplished here.... Newberry is but a small dot on the map of probabilities of the future greatness of this part of Michigan."

— "No Noodles in Newberry," Manistique Sunday Sun, republished in
The Newberry News September 6, 1888

WHILE THE CHILDREN WERE OCCUPIED with reading, 'riting, and 'rithmetic, what were their parents doing? Working, mostly.

The wood camps provided work for hundreds of people, of course, as did the State Hospital. Farmers took on farm hands. Schools engaged schoolteachers. Many families employed "hired girls" to help with the cooking and cleaning. Many women (single, married, or widowed) took up dressmaking or millinery work.

The railroads employed lots of people, not only train engineers, porters, and the like, but at each station, there would be a station agent (to run the office and the telegraph) and a handful of section hands. The hands performed routine maintenance on the tracks and the "sidings" (cleared areas by the side of the tracks where freight could be loaded and unloaded). By 1894, four trains left Newberry each day. Two rattled off to the east (one to the Sault, one to Mackinaw City). Two others went west: one that ended its run in Houghton; and the *Duluth Express*, an evening train, or "sleeper," that arrived in Duluth at 9:20 a.m. the next day. Freight trains carried ore and other cargo, and logging trains ran back and forth, too. The station was a busy place.[238]

The Vulcan Furnace Company was one of the mainstays of Newberry's industry for decades, in spite of the fact that it kept closing, burning, reopening, going bankrupt, being sold, and closing again. In the 1880s, it employed almost 600 men between its wood camps and factories. The wood camp workers provided hardwood, which was shipped from the camps to Newberry via narrow-gauge railroad. The wood then was turned into charcoal at the kilns.

Meanwhile, the factory also was receiving raw iron ore from out west and shipments of crushed limestone from the quarries to the south. When this unholy mixture was heated to the melting point, the limestone would rise to the top in a colorful orange and white froth ("slag"), taking with it any impurities and leaving a better, more pure iron underneath. The froth was skimmed off and the molten iron poured into molds ("pigs"). Once cool enough, another crew of men came by with sledgehammers and whacked the mold apart into fifty-pound bars of "pig iron." By 1888, the output had increased to fifty tons daily. Most of this was shipped to factories making railroad wheels.[239]

As can be imagined, the work was very physical, with all the hauling of wood, charcoal, iron ore, and iron bars. Even in the 1930s, as former employee Louis Gooseberry said in an interview in 1984, the furnace was still considered "a primitive, hard place to work."[240]

It was also extremely hot…and extremely dirty, with the men emerging from their labor stained black with charcoal dust or red with iron dust. Even washing could not always remove this dust from a worker's eyelashes and skin. On the brighter side, furnace employees sometimes had their own baseball team and boxing society. In the early days, the factory laborers were paid a munificent $1.75 per nine-hour day, and for a brief period, they even had a furnace pet, a dog called "Joe Donaldson." Besides the laborers, the furnace also employed foremen, clerks, supervisors, blacksmiths and farriers, railroad workers, engineers, and electricians.[241]

Connected with the furnace was the chemical works, "an extensive plant for utilizing the smoke from kilns, etc., for manufacturing or extracting the many valuable ingredients it possesses." The Newberry plant manufactured such important items as wood alcohol, acetate of lime, and "mordants and dyes of all kinds," among others. This auxiliary company was originally built alongside the furnace, but by 1888, "the old machinery" was "practically worthless" and a new plant was built under the direction of Elbert J. Burrell, who had made a career out of setting up such chemical plants. E. J. himself was one of the major investors in this new business, alongside Lee Burt and Joseph Berry (a Detroit manufacturer of paint). By 1889, they were producing 200 gallons of wood alcohol a day, along with other chemicals, and employing thirty men.[242]

Like all big businesses, the Newberry furnace ran into big problems. Various economic depressions, recessions, and slowdowns of the 1890s hit the industry hard, with iron prices plummeting. Production slowed to a crawl. By 1893, the Vulcan Furnace Company had reorganized itself into the Newberry Furnace Company, owned solely by James McMillan and Mrs. John Newberry. They were not able to keep it afloat. By 1894, the furnace was "out of blast."[243]

Without the charcoal from the furnace, the chemical works had little to do, and E. J. Burrell closed up shop about the same time. After a few years, he gave up waiting, dismantled his plant, and shipped the whole kit and caboodle to Manistique, where he reopened.[244]

Newberry's furnace remained idle for the next five years, until it was purchased by the International Car Wheel Company, which intended on forming the Michigan Iron Company and getting itself a better supply of iron. Newberry waited. And waited. Finally, in the winter of 1900, the village council handed James Somerville, village president, $100 and ordered him to Buffalo, New York, to confront Mr. P. H. Griffin of the ICWC and not come back without answers.

This postcard gives a nice view of the furance
(photo courtesy of Sterling McGinn).

This postcard shows the kilns at the furnace, dated 1907
(photo courtesy of Sterling McGinn).

"President Somerville," reported the paper, "arriving on the scene of action, gathered all his reserve forces and made a gallant and successful attack on Spion Kop,* and the enemy, seeing the uselessness of further resistance, gracefully capitulated." The company official assured the village president that the furnace would indeed run again, which opinion Somerville reported back to his pleased (but somewhat skeptical) compatriots. Mr. Griffin, however, kept his word, and by 1902, the furnace once again was hiring and the building was renovated and modernized.[245]

This new company did not last long.

In 1907, the furnace was sold again, this time to Joseph Berry of Detroit, an owner of Berry Bros., a paint and varnish firm that was more interested in the chemical byproducts than the iron (it had long been a customer and shareholder of the Burrell Chemical Works). Now Berry Bros. was in the iron industry, but it also had constructed a new chemical works, and hereafter both industries would be run under one company. The new company was the Lake Superior Iron & Chemical Company, and during this period, it bought and renovated pig iron plants and chemical works all over Michigan, including outfits in Marquette, Boyne City, Manistique, Elk Rapids, Chocolay, and one in Ashland, Wisconsin. But Joseph Berry died almost immediately thereafter, and in 1910, his estate sold the entire company to a group of investors from Canada, New York, and England.[246]

By 1913, the iron market again fell flat on its face and the company was looking at foreclosure. The furnace closed down, and most of the employees were let go. The enterprise was saved in 1915 when it was purchased by the Charcoal Iron Company of America, which managed to last until 1926. Then the Newberry facility became the Newberry Lumber and Chemical Company until it closed for good in the 1940s.[247]

While the charcoal iron industry was proving an unstable beast, the lumber industry chugged steadily onward. Besides the lumber camps and charcoal plants, timber also supported quite a number of sawmills and woodenware factories. The most extensive of the lumber mills was located in Dollarville.

At that time, working at the Dollarville mill was considered a good job. Initially, management paid a high wage ($1.65 to $4.50 per day) to honest men who worked a ten-hour day in one of the safest workplaces in the Upper Peninsula. During its down time, when lumber was not being cut, employees were put to work repairing, inspecting, and improving the machinery. During its first decade, people boasted that the Dollarville mill had no serious accidents. (By contrast, the Furnace had a handful of deaths and twice as many serious accidents during the same period, including broken limbs, burns, and accidental gas inhalations). Additionally, very early on, Dollarville was rigged with an extensive fire prevention system, including nineteen hydrants and 1,300 feet of hose.[248]

By the 1890s, the mill had amassed vast log piles of more than 10,000,000 feet. Besides the sawmill, it also ran a planing mill, shingle mill, lath mill, and picket mill. Indeed, the entire "village" was owned by various lumber companies, including the stores and homes.[249]

Dollarville might have been the largest mill community, but it wasn't the only one. Surrounding Newberry like a circle were all sorts of planing mills, shingle mills, stave mills,

---

* The Battle of Spion Kop, part of the Boer War in South Africa, was in the news at the time.

Newberry Furnace, circa 1911 (photo courtesy of Dr. James A. Surrell).

Cars full of pig iron leaving the Newberry furnace
(photo courtesy of Dr. James A. Surrell).

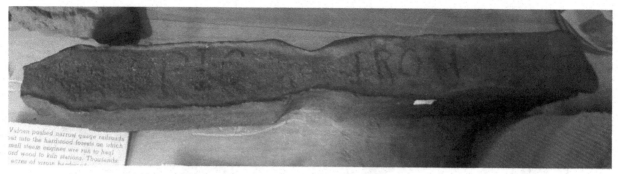

A piece of pig iron on display at the Tahquamenon Logging Museum.

and the like. Each one would form the nucleus of a small community at places such as Deer Park, Shelldrake, Emerson, Hulbert, Engadine, Black River, Curtis, and others. Some of these mills, such as at Deer Park, had electric lights, railroads, and telephones. Most had post offices and schoolhouses.

Also surrounding Newberry to the west, south, and east were the farmers. Most farms were family-run affairs, small forty-acre parcels claimed by the original homesteaders. Larger agricultural operations usually were confined to the farm at the State Hospital and the famous Newberry Celery Gardens.

One of the many associated companies formed by the original railroad executives was the Peninsular Land Company. Its purpose was to sell land and make money. To sell land, it needed to attract buyers. To attract buyers, it did many different things, including building roads, constructing sawmills, clearing farmland, draining swamps, and sending out "agents" to lure farmers to the area (mostly from Ontario and "the Thumb" region of Michigan).[250]

Additionally, the Peninsular Land Company established an "experimental farm" where its employees would endeavor to discover which crops grew best in Luce County's swampy soil. The answer to this turned out to be celery.

The Peninsular Land Company began its celery garden in the summer of 1886 with two and a half acres and 38,000 celery plants, just to the east of Newberry. By 1888, this garden had detached itself from the Peninsular Land Company and became the Newberry Celery and Improvement Company. It now boasted more than eight and a half acres and 120,000 plants. In 1892, now owned by Henry L. Harris, the company had thirty-five acres and 800,000 plants. A second farm, O. K. Celery, was started by John Van Tuyl, a former employee, and it, too, flourished. Newberry Celery or "Superior Celery" was of the Golden Plume variety, yellowish in color, and was prized for its crisp and solid state and fine, nutty flavor. It was shipped all over the country and served on the Soo Line railroads and in several plush hotels in Chicago and New York City.[251]

The Peninsular Land Company, in the business of selling land, maintained an office in Newberry for years—at least until 1894, when the company shut down, transferring all of its remaining unsold lands located in Luce, Mackinac, Chippewa, and Schoolcraft counties to the last shareholder, the Estate of Francis Palms;* thereupon, the Palms Estate took over the business of selling off the lingering land.[252]

---

* The deed was eighty-six pages long.

Broom Handle Factory in Newberry, 1892 (photo courtesy of Sterling McGinn).

Dollarville Mill, 1885 (photo courtesy of Dr. James A. Surrell).

To serve the factories, camps, and railroads, Newberry had quite a bustling business community. The abovementioned Henry L. Harris is a good example of a company employee who came with the corporations and stayed to become his own man. Another such person was Matt Surrell, who arrived in the area as early as 1880 to work at Grant's Camp as a supply hauler, driving a wagon back and forth to Naubinway. Later, he owned a livery stable, renting horses and wagons, which eventually turned into an automobile dealership. Joseph Liberty, who also had come with the furnace, began his own business cutting and hauling ice in the winter and selling it in the summer. A fourth example was Charles E. Carlson. He was a fifteen-year-old "waterboy" in 1881 when he first came to Newberry, working for DM&M crews. He evidently liked what he saw because he returned to stay in 1885, working as a lumberman and carpenter.[253]

New towns always attracted energetic entrepreneurs, and Newberry had dozens of small businesses lining its main street almost from the beginning. An 1893 map drawn up by the Sanford Fire Insurance Company shows a town with two barbers, livery stable, bank, cigar dealer, newspaper office, post office, three blacksmiths, tailor, shoemaker, painter, photographer, two laundry facilities, nine saloons, and four hotel/saloons. In addition, Newberry also enjoyed a hardware store, two jewelry stores, two drug stores, a millinery, a bakery, a meat market, a candy kitchen, a flour and feed store, and eleven stores that sold either groceries, clothing, and/or furnishings. Each store supported its owner or manager and a handful of clerks and bookkeepers. Many rented upstairs offices to doctors, attorneys, and other professional men.[254]

Shattuck's (officially named the New York Cash Store) was perhaps Newberry's largest and most well-known general store in the 1890s, featuring a wide variety of goods, furnishings, and groceries. Throughout the year, depending on the season, it advertised, among other things:

> Men's and boys' rubber boots, high-cut storm slippers, men's shoes, Smith & Herrick's fine shoes for ladies, high-cut snow protector rubbers for ladies, Royal Blue Shoes, Russet shoes, Red School House shoes for children, genuine kangaroo hand-sueded shoes, warm felt shoes, women's sandals, river-driving shoes, double-knit German socks, gloves, hand-knit mittens, "scarfs," rubber goods;

> tailor-made suits, boys' knee pants, worsted pants, workingmen's pants, celebrated Never-Rip work pants, Jexen pants, cottonade pants, Mackinaws, men's and boys' cotton shirts, straw hats, wool and fur hats, neckties, Gordon hats and caps, $14 Rochester suits, ladies' waists, ladies' lightweight vests, high-grade underwear, extra fine underwear, Camel's Hair underwear, children's black seamless hose, ladies' spring hosiery, overcoats, pea jackets, spring neckwear, children's handkerchiefs, ladies' hemstich or embroidered handkerchiefs, Harrison and Marton cigars;

> crockery, glassware, engraved water sets, wine sets, lemonade sets, imported dinner sets, French and Austrian china, painted china cups, saucers, fancy mugs for children, banquet lamps, piano lamps, extension hanging lamps, asbestos or unbreakable lamp chimneys, willow clothesbaskets, hand baskets, lunch baskets, berry-picking baskets, books, linen or Turkish towels, pound bars of soap for 5¢;

Line drawing from *The Newberry Independent* of November 17, 1892.

Cleared Lands For Sale!

The Peninsular Land company offer for sale several section of cleared lands near Newberry at

$4.00 PER ACRE,

On easy terms.   Now is the time to secure a farm.   Apply to

H. L. HARRIS, Supt.

Left: An advertisement that appeared in *The Newberry News* of January 8, 1892. Right: The photograph appeared in *The Newberry Enterprise*'s Trade Edition of October 1894.

Left: Harry L. Harris in 1894. Right: Michael Hammes in 1894. Both were heavily involved with the Newberry Celery Company.

Parlor Pride stove enamel, men's furnishing goods, Virginia smoking or Buckthorn tobacco, plug tobacco, cob pipes, stone milk pans, patent washtubs;

Beet, carrot, rutabaga seeds, field peas, garden peas, Sweet Vernal, Kentucky Blue Grass, millet, white clover, timothy seeds;

Fresh eggs, cream cheese, choice dairy butter, fresh roll butter, new full cream, teas, Japan teas, coffees, catsup;

Spy and Baldwin apples, Tallman sweet apples, ripe bananas, strawberries, black raspberries, luscious Florida oranges, pineapples, Messina lemons, grated pineapple, Damson plums, apricots, coconuts, nectarines, muskmelons, cherries, pitted cherries, gooseberries, Niagara grapes, peaches, "the largest watermelons ever seen," California dried grapes, Valencia raisins, Smyrna figs in sacks, new golden dates, Cape Cod cranberries, Vostizza currents, California prunes, California walnuts and almonds, Sicily filberts;

Strawberry, peach, and cranberry preserves, "pails of jelly," evaporated apricots, plums, apples, pears and raspberries, jell-cured apricots, new canned tomatoes, canned goods of all kinds, pint, quart and half-gallon Mason fruit cans and extra rubbers;

Beets, potatoes, new cabbage, Louisiana cabbage, carrots, celery, home-grown cucumbers, eggplant, California onions, green onions, parsnips, green peas, pie plant, Jersey sweet potatoes, Siberian crab apples, ripe and green tomatoes, turnips, peppers for pickling, citrons for pickling, Evergreen corn, dry popcorn, mixed pickles, sauerkraut, horseradish;

12-pound smoked hams in light canvas and smoked breakfast bacon, choice ham at 10¢ per pound, potted ham, No. 1 boneless barrel beef, picnic hams, tongue and chicken, barrels of boneless beef, fresh canned salmon and mackerel, kipped herring, frozen herring, finnan haddies, codfish, salt whitefish, fresh-packed salmon and lobsters, pickled pigs feet, oysters;

Lakefield maple syrup and maple sugar, white clover honey, brown sugar, Gold Medal flour, rice, pure patent-hulled buckwheat flour, graham flour, kiln-dried yellow bolted meal, Schumacher's Akron Oatmeal, rolled oats, rolled wheat, Pettijohns Celebrated Breakfast Food, oyster crackers, Zephyr crackers, Battle Creek Butter Crackers, Nudavene Flakes, Dr. Price's baking powder, rock candy;

Pure kettle-rendered leaf lard, pork lard, Pure cider vinegar, Crystal Spray water, white Pennsylvania oil, kerosene oil, firecrackers, cannon-crackers, torpedoes, balloons, flags for the Fourth of July, one ton of candies for Christmas, and Easter Eggs.

John A. Shattuck was not a young man when he came to town. He had left behind a successful store in Sand Lake, operated by his grown-up son. He prospered in Newberry, built himself a large house, and retired in 1912, selling the business to A. Westin & Company.[255]

Manhard's Hardware was probably the second most prominent store. M. R. Manhard was a successful Marquette merchant who sensed an opportunity to expand and opened a branch in Newberry in the mid-1880s. In 1889, M. R. sent his nephew to take charge, James C. Foster,

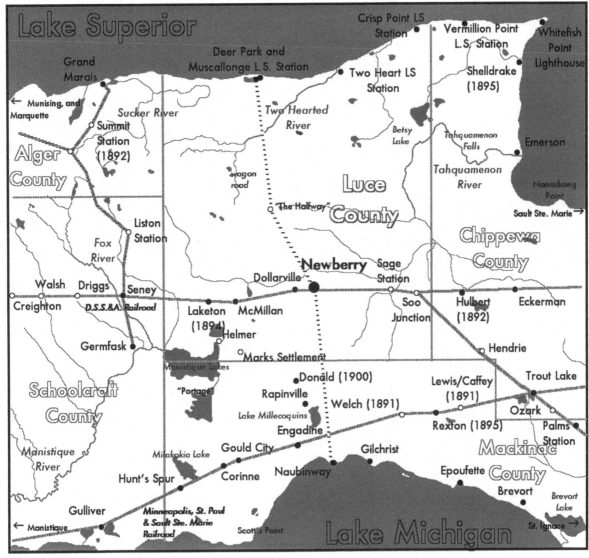

Luce County and vicinity, circa 1900.

Advertisements of November 18, 1892, in *The Newberry News.*

a twenty-year-old go-getter. Young James thrived in his new post. He eventually bought out his uncle's interest, renaming it Foster's Hardware. Besides the main store building (at various addresses over the years), Foster's also maintained four warehouses about town, stuffed with furniture, building supplies, sporting goods, garden supplies, heavy equipment, and tools of all kinds. J. C. Foster quickly became one of Newberry's most prominent citizens, rearing a large family and fully participating in village life.[256]

Rosenthal's, or the People's One Price Store, was another Newberry institution. Gustave and Fanny Rosenthal opened their store in the mid-1880s, selling dry goods and clothing, later branching out into furniture and home furnishings. "One price" referred to an early slogan, "honest dealing and one price to all," which meant that it wouldn't quote different prices to different customers. Gus was described as a man of "simple tastes who lived a quiet life devoted to his family and his religion." Their advertisements alternated between invitations like "Come and see G. Rosenthal" and "Big sale at F. Rosenthal's." The Rosenthals and their children initially lived in ten rooms above the store, but later built themselves a large house on Newberry Avenue. They also owned and rented buildings all over town.[257]

By 1910, the Rosenthal children were grown and gone, and the couple was preparing to leave town. The newspaper reported:

> "By strict attention to business, he has amassed a considerable fortune, and last year when he announced his intention of closing out his business and retiring, our people could hardly believe that he was really in earnest."[258]

Of course, Gus had been trying to get out of the business for years. Numerous reports over the last decade had him turning over control to his son, or his nephew, or announcing a "going out of business sale." This time, though, he meant it.

The business was sold to Fanny's brother, Samuel Newmark. They then sold another building to another brother, Isaac Newmark, and the Rosenthals moved to California. The town threw them a going-away party, and all the schoolchildren assembled at the depot to give them a send-off.[259]

There were dozens of other stores that came and went: Ingalls' Drugs, Sherman's Drugs, the Newberry Drug Store, Fred Fuller's City Drug Store, Stafford's Drug Store, Central Pharmacy, Boston Store, Murney's Cheap Cash Store, Walter Smith's Newberry Grocery Store, Henderson Bros. Right House, Emory Barr's People's Cash Store, H. E. Smith Flour & Feed, Vulcan Store, Richardson Shoes, Mrs. Tyler's, Miss Fretz' Millinery Parlors, Bailey's, Noble's, Leighton's, Sheer's, J. Trueman & Company, Sundstrom's, Krempel & Taylor, Host & Mertes, and many, many others. Some lasted decades. Others only hung on for a few months.

The drug stores not only made up prescriptions, but sold patent medicines, beauty supplies, perfumes, tobacco, stationery, school supplies, candy, books, musical instruments, small gifts, and sometimes ice cream sodas. The meat markets sold freshly butchered cuts of meat, as well as seafood and canned goods. Jewelry stores also sold watches, clocks, silverware, spectacles, and (in the case of L. N. Forbes) coffins and undertaking supplies. "Dry goods" meant clothes, cloth, and sewing notions, and general stores sold groceries and a bit of everything else.

Perhaps the splashiest and most noticeable businesses in town were the hotels, of which Newberry usually had four or five. They played home to all kinds of guests, from celebrating

A Business Section, Newberry, Mich.

This postcard (which dates between 1907 and 1913) shows the J. A. Shattuck's New York Cash Store, H. E. Smith's Flour and Feed, a saloon/ cobbler shop and the Johnson House, as well as an early automobile. Shattuck's was probably the most prominent of early Newberry stores (author's collection).

Manhard's Hardware (later called Foster's Hardware) was the next most important retail establishment in town (photo courtesy of the Tahquamenon Logging Museum).

woodsmen and traveling salesmen to company executives from Detroit or Chicago and the occasional tourist. Medical specialists like Dr. J. Leahy, the optician, would come and stay at a hotel for a few days, treating patients. Judges, court reporters, lawyers, and witnesses crowded into town whenever circuit court was in session. Longer-term lodgers might stay at a boarding house instead of the hotel, and it was the odd family that didn't have one or two boarders living in a spare room in their homes. In spring 1890, the newspaper reported that Newberry was playing host to 426 out-of-town visitors, between five hotels and four boarding houses. The most crowded was the McLeod House, stuffed with 135 guests.[260]

The White House was Newberry's first and grandest hotel, erected by the Peninsular Land Company. In fact, the Peninsular Land Company erected three hotels—each called "The White House"—at Marquette, Seney, and Newberry, though the one in Newberry was nearly always referred to as the Newberry Hotel. It was a large, wood-frame building complete with saloon and dining room. Over the years, it hosted dances and community meetings. In 1894, it was given extensive remodeling. Now the hotel offered a basement with the saloon and billiard rooms. The first floor was dedicated to offices, entry halls, parlors, and reading rooms. Sleeping chambers dominated the second floor, along with *two* bathrooms "supplied with all the latest improvements in plumbing." In addition, the hotel offered steam heating, electric lights, and a grand veranda and balcony. In 1895, its current manager, Frank L. Harris, installed a fine new, fireproof safe.[261]

Good thing he did. Three months later, the building burned completely to the ground. It was the middle of the night, and a defective flue smoldered for several hours before anyone was aware. The fire department turned out, but it was unable to do anything other than keep the flames from spreading. Guests jumped from the second story in their nightgowns, one young lady breaking her window open with a water pitcher. The Peninsular Land Company, then at the end of its life, chose not to rebuild.[262]

The McLeod House also had a good reputation. It opened in 1886 as the Clayton House when Donald N. McLeod purchased and renovated the old Vulcan Furnace boarding house.

McLeod was an energetic fellow who was always making improvements and additions. His saloon sported a marble-top bar, hardwood floors, and a dining room that could seat fifty. He had a barn and livery stable for his guests, a verandah along the northeast side, and electric lights as early as 1889, making his house "shine forth in dazzling splendor." Unlike the Newberry Hotel, which was a $2 a day joint, the McLeod House only charged $1 per day. Dan McLeod sold out in 1896 to better concentrate on his burgeoning career as a lumber baron. The subsequent owners kept up the name of McLeod House, as well as its stellar reputation.[263]

It burned to the ground in 1914.[264]

Of course, not all of Newberry's hotels burned to the ground.

The first-ever building in Newberry was a small boarding house built by W. H. Kaye, the DM&M's telegraph operator. In 1884, this building was acquired by Philip S. Hamilton, a former Canadian policeman and current farmer. He replaced the boarding house with a hotel and saloon—the American House—"The Home for the Lumbermen," where a nickel procured you the largest glass of beer in town.

Left to Right: Fred Fuller (druggist), C. B. Noble (merchant) in 1892, Philip S. Hamilton (farmer, hotelier, politician), and Matt Surrell (transportation mogul)

Left: Stafford's Drug Store and Bailey's Grocery, 1894.
Right: Newberry Avenue, circa 1912 (photo courtesy of Dr. James Surrell).

PEOPLE'S
Cash Store!

cor Newberry ave and Helen st.
—Always keeps in stock —

Fresh fruits in season,
Canned goods,
Confectionery,
Oysters, Cakes,&c

Which are selling at Bottom prices.

In connection we run a first-class

REsTAURANT

Suppers furnished and a special discount given to parties of ten couple or more.

Our latch string is always cut and we invite all to come and see us.

E. BARR & Co.

THE NEW
MILLINERY
STORE

IS STILL BOOMING.

LATEST STYLES

AND REASONABLE PRICES

Is bound to take the lead. Thanking the people of Newberry for their past patronage, I solicit a continuance of the same.

Respectfully Yours,
MRS L. N. FORBES.

Helen Street   -   -   Newberry.

TO THE PUBLIC

Thanking the public for the very liberal patronage that I have received in the past, I would respectfully announce that I have lately added to my stock as fine a line of

GROCERIES,

As can be found in the village. I have also a

MEAT MARKET,

In connection, and keep all kinds of fresh and salt meats. I still invite a continuance of your patronage.

WALTER SMITH.

Above: Advertisements from *The Newberry News* of September 1, 1887, February 1, 1890, and May 12, 1887.

Phil soon lost interest in being a hotelier, yet also had a hard time finding someone to run his hotel for him. Among his many managers were Charles Hall, Harry Abbott, Matt Surrell, Fin Clark, Jim Craig, "Mr. Kennedy of Bothwell, Ontario," N. H. Hill (absconded on the early morning train), and a man named W. J. Scott, who "suddenly disappeared," abandoning his small son who had to be sent to an orphanage. After Phil's death, his widow sold the business.[265]

By 1919, the "old American House" had devolved into a mere restaurant, and was so dilapidated that it was condemned by the state. The building was salvaged, however, eventually becoming Edgar's Bar, Johnny's Bar, and Spence's Tavern. It no longer exists.[266]

At the Nelson House, run by Price Nelson and located near the depot, accommodations could be had for $1 per day. A guest later reminisced that "the good old Nelson House was often crowded from cellar to attic, and when the beds were filled, the guests got leave to sleep on the bar room floor; but you were carefully reminded not to sleep on the pool table, unless you first removed your calked boots." Price Nelson sold his hotel to Frances P. Gormely and his brother-in-law, William T. Murphy, in the late 1880s. Now called the Hotel Murphy, it was renovated and improved, painted a clean white on the outside, with a fifty-person dining room, at least twelve bedrooms, a saloon, a parlor, fancy cocktails, cigars, and feather beds. It had room for almost 100 guests. It continued being the Hotel Murphy for years, even after John Quinlan bought it in 1907, and after Liel McLean bought it in 1930. Eventually, the Murphy Hotel became the Long Branch Tavern and then a parking lot.[267]

A more modest establishment was the Clifton House (renamed the Club House), which was "a favorite stopping place for commercial men." It did, however, boast "large, well-ventilated" rooms, a "first-class bar" and an "unsurpassed table." It passed through the hands of many managers and owners, and was only active for a few years in the late 1880s and early 1890s. Then the building became a shoe store.[268]

The Harris House opened in 1897 with twenty rooms, created out of a former hardware store. The *News* assured its readers that Frank Harris "knows how to cater to the traveling public," especially as "the new hotel will be very convenient to the trains, being less than a minute's walk from the depot." The Harris House became the Hunt House in 1907. It was almost destroyed in 1911 when a piece of flaming wood fell out of a fireplace and ignited the wooden floor, but a convenient garden hose managed to put it out just as the firemen were arriving. This, however, did not stop the guests from "tumbling and rushing down the stairs in dishabille, carrying their clothing in their arms and careless of appearances and formalities." Hunt House lasted until the 1930s.[269]

The Scandinavian House, established by August Hanson, was located near the depot. It catered (as per its name) to guests from Sweden, Finland, and Norway and was advertised as "one of the cleanest places in town." Hanson didn't stay in the hotel business long, though. By 1907, his building hosted a saloon and a cobbler shop, and it was torn down soon after. August Hanson went into farming.[270]

The Scandinavian House's spiritual successor was the Johnson House, erected in 1899 just south of the railroad tracks, which planned to "cater to the Swedish and lumbering class of trade." A more modest hotel, with only twelve rooms, saloon, and dining room, it nevertheless was "a money-maker from the start." The Johnson House was renamed the Hotel Luce in 1918 when new owners took over, and it continued as a bar and boarding house for decades. Today, it is a restaurant.[271]

The Newberry Hotel, in a drawing from 1894 (*Newberry Enterprise).*
Overnight guests paid $2 a day here.

This postcard, dated 1906, shows part of the Dollar house (on the right edge). The
left edge shows the vacant lot where the old Newberry Hotel burned to the ground
and where the new Newberry Hotel would be built.

For almost twenty years, the site of the late, lamented Newberry Hotel lay empty. Duncan Campbell had been the owner of the nearby McLeod House when it burned in 1914, and instead of rebuilding on the spot, he chose to build on Newberry Avenue over the decaying remains of the other, old hotel. There he built himself an impressive, three-story, brick hotel—the new Newberry Hotel. The "modern and up-to-date building" was revealed to the public on January 12, 1915 with a grand dancing party. It featured steam heat, cold storage, reading rooms, a ladies' parlor, servants' quarters, and toilet rooms. Several bedrooms even had their own baths. "Nothing," reported the newspaper, "has been overlooked that will add to the comfort or convenience of the guests." The Newberry Hotel (later called the Falls Hotel) continued as Newberry's preeminent and fanciest hotel for decades.[272]

The hotels were often the first businesses in town to equip themselves with the new, modern technologies: electric lights, steam heat, and indoor plumbing. They gave their guests a taste of the high life, a glimpse into the luxuries of the future.

An advertisement for the Clayton House from 1887. It was later renamed
The McLeod House (drawing from 1894).

The Nelson House (advertisement, 1890) was later named the Hotel Murphy
(photo courtesy of the Tahquamenon Logging Museum).

Scandinavian House!

Newberry Avenue, Near Railroad Depot.

BOARD BY THE DAY OR WEEK.

Good Sleeping Accommodations.

Bar Stocked with Wines, Liquors and Cigars

FIRST CLASS POOL TABLE.

August Hanson, Prop.

Advertisement for the Scandinavian House, from *The Newberry News* of November 18, 1892.

AMERICAN ✶ ✶ HOUSE!

W. H. HILL, Prop.

First-Class Accommodation
To the Traveling Public.

House Neatly Furnished
and lighted throughout
by Electricity.

Bar stocked with the choicest brands of Wines, Liquors and Cigars.

---THE---

CLUB HOUSE,

D. CAMPBELL, PROP'R.

Headquarters for lumbermen and traveling public.

First-class bar in connection with hotel.

TABLE UNSURPASSED!

Your patronage solicited

DOUGALD CAMPBELL,
Proprietor.

The NEWBERRY HOTEL

D. CAMPBELL, Proprietor
CON J MAHONEY, Manager

SUNDAY DINNER MENU

Hot Tomato Bouillon

Green Onions   Celery   Chow Chow

Broiled Superior Trout, Drawn Butter

Roast Loin of Pork, Apple Sauce

Mashed Potatoes   Steamed Potatoes

Baked Young Chicken, Stuffed

Stewed Tomatoes   Stewed Peas

Dressed Lettuce with Egg

Apple Pie   Banana Pie

Fruit   Layer Raisins   Sherbet

American Cheese   Water Crackers

Tea   Coffee

Dinner Served from 12:30 to 3:00

Advertisements from *The Newberry News* of November 18, 1892, February 1, 1890, and May 21, 1915.

The new "Newberry Hotel," built in 1915, was Newberry's fanciest and most luxurious and modern hotel. See menu above. This postcard shows the building in its first winter (author's collection)

Chapter Nine
Newberry Nuthouse

"It is my opinion that as these persons are insane, and must be detained under observation, that it is better to attempt to care for them in this institution, even though overtaxed for room, than allow them to be confined in the county jails and county houses."

— Dr. Earl H. Campbell, Superintendent,
Report of the Board of Trustees of the Newberry State Hospital, 1911

"The state of Michigan is famed throughout the United States for the splendid care accorded the insane, both in point of housing, food and clothing, but especially is she noted for the splendid men whom she attaches to the staffs of resident officers.... I say without reservation that in the Newberry hospital of the insane, as it stands complete in all details today, the state has an institution that the whole people may well be proud of."

— Dr. James H. Dawson, MD, "Letter to the Mining Journal," August 28, 1914

THE FIFTH PILLAR OF LUCE County's economy was the "insane asylum," known first as Upper Peninsula Hospital for the Insane, and then after 1911, the more euphemistic Newberry State Hospital.

In 1893, the State of Michigan declared its intention of building an asylum specifically for the insane residents of its northern peninsula. The State Board of Corrections and Charities formed a committee to search for a suitable site to place it. Specifically, they were looking for land "in a healthy, easily accessible part of the Upper Peninsula of the state, as a site for the asylum, a tract of land containing not less than four hundred acres, which shall be capable of being easily supplied with a sufficient quantity of living water for all the purposes of such institution, and also to furnish proper facilities for drainage," as well as "400 acres of farming land for the institution." This committee then sent out invitations to various Upper Peninsula communities, asking them to make offers.[273]

Claude W. Case, a manager at the furnace, immediately formed a committee to arrange for Newberry's bid. Soon it chose an appropriate site: a piece of land on a hill in Pentland Township, boasting "a fine southeastern exposure, good soil, unsurpassed drainage facilities and...within five minutes' drive of the railway station." Then the committee submitted a long and glowing application, especially touting the bracing air, pure water, and restful setting of the asylum. *The Newberry News* further described the offer as follows:

> The asylum gets a cash bonus of $6,000, a 560-acre site of good farming land, 350 acres of which is cleared, the balance being timbered land and a twenty-acre lake of pure spring water. The site selected is less than one mile from town, situated on the crest of a hill nearly 200 feet higher than the town site and commands an extensive view of the surrounding country. It is a beautiful location and seemed planned by nature to carry some public institution.[274]

The $6,000 was raised by a subscription list, and 160 businesses and individuals of the county gave liberally, from as little as $5 to as much as $455 and $500 (from Mrs. Fanny Rosenthal and the Dollarville Lumber Company, respectively). Robert Dollar, now a California resident, pledged $50. Even James A. Demarest, the scandalous saloonist who had skipped town in 1887, heard about the project and sent $31.25 for its support.[275]

As other towns also put in bids—Marquette, L'Anse, Escanaba, Ontonagon, Menominee, St. Ignace, and Sault Ste. Marie—the competition was fierce. A group of state officials arrived on August 10, 1893, to inspect the proposed site. They were taken to the finest hotel in town (the Newberry Hotel) for a meal and driven out to Pentland Township in carriages.[276]

On November 2, 1893, the committee received word that Newberry had won. Several citizens set off firecrackers, others guns, and some banged anvils. When Claude W. Case arrived back in town, he was greeted with a forty-gun salute.[277]

The choice had been unanimous. Newberry was picked, not only because of its "unsurpassed drainage," but also because it was an inland town, which was thought to have better weather, far from the "fierce winds...from the lakes." This is not to mention the free 560 acres of farmland and "valuable woodlands," twenty-acre spring-fed lake, $6,000 cash bonus, and the free pumping station the town promised to build. The townsfolk were thrilled. The win represented "a new era of prosperity to the town and a considerable addition to the wealth and population of the county."[278]

The losing towns submitted, fairly ungraciously. Rather regretfully, the Soo stated that "all join in congratulating Newberry in its good fortune," even if "it has not the traveling facilities of the Soo." "Whatever we may think of the State Board's choice of location," said St. Ignace, "we of St. Ignace will hustle for the next plum."

Marquette, the most bitter and waspish, referred to Newberry as a "little village buried in a swamp" full of "somnolent people." For generations, the other towns took their revenge by snidely calling Newberry the place "where all the crazy people go" and "the Nuthouse."[279]

Floods of contractors, stonemasons, electricians, and other workmen took the train to Newberry. Some even brought their families with them because the project was to take months.

Construction began in 1894 on the first five buildings, the state expending in total upwards of $500,000 for the initial construction. Nineteen more buildings were planned to ultimately form a large quadrangle. The Newberry asylum was to be built on the "cottage plan," which "provides for the distribution of the patients throughout a group of pleasant cottages and permits the different classes of patients to be quartered, where those who are convalescent, or

CLAUDE WILLARD CASE.

Left: Claude W. Case. He led the campaign to bring the state asylum to Luce County.

Right: Dr. George Chamberlain, an early superintendent of the insane asylum.

Both images taken from the book *Men of Progress: Embracing Biographical Sketches of Representative Michigan Men*, a kind of old-timey *Who's Who*.

Building the hospital, 1893, in the Italianate style (photo courtesy of the Luce County Historical Society).

whose condition gives promise of recovery, will not be brought into undesirable contact with the hopeless and violent inmates." Each building would be connected with sheltered promenades.

"Cottage" was something of a misnomer, as each freestanding building—"in the style of the Italian renaissance"—was built to house fifty patients. "Dormitory" would be closer to the truth, even if it didn't sound quite so homey. Still, each brick and sandstone cottage was to have steam radiators, running water, tiled bathrooms, and modern ventilation systems "sufficient to assure a constant and abundant supply of fresh air for each patient."[280]

By November of 1895, the first sixty-eight patients had moved in. Within a year, the asylum consisted of two large main "cottages," a female ward and a male ward, with more to come. Each had a day room below and a sleeping room above with "a few small rooms partitioned off at one end in which the more refractory patients are kept." Further, the asylum had its own laundry buildings, electricians, carpenters, and farmers. This was only the beginning, and as the institution grew, more and more buildings would appear.[281]

A newspaper reporter toured the facility in 1896 and came away quite impressed, pronouncing the institutions "neat, clean and comfortable."

He rather condescendingly described the women's ward as follows:

> All the patients were congregated, some walking about ceaselessly, others sitting in all kinds of postures on chairs and benches, others reclining at full length or couched into corners with heads bowed over hands as if buried in the deepest of sorrow. A few were busy sewing, and one or two were taking care of a young child, whose mother is an inmate. Nearly all were jabbering incoherently, and but few noticed or seemed to notice the little bevy of visitors who were critically examining them. There were 51 patients in the female ward at the time of our visit. They are sad wrecks of humanity but they have comfortable quarters where they now are and everything possible is being done to bring relief or effect a cure.[282]

The reporter (probably Charles Brebner, the editor at the time) then was taken to visit the men, where he observed: "The restless ones pace the floor with hanging head and aimless tread, but they have not the eternal jibber-jabber of their unfortunate sisters in affliction. As a rule they are more cheerful. There are a few good-looking men, but the greater part are like the women, poor wrecks of humanity."[283]

He then spoke at length with one inmate, Henry Van Dallen, a forty-year-old Dutch immigrant, a farmer from Menominee, and a "well educated man, conversant in several languages." Henry was absorbed in polishing small stones and carving his name into them with a needle, for doing so (as he readily explained) was the best way to preserve his name for future generations. "It is really interesting to meet and study such characters," marveled the reporter. Henry lived out the rest of his life in the asylum, dying there in 1920 of pneumonia at age sixty-four.[284]

The causes of "insanity" were not understood very well. Doctors blamed heredity and alcoholism. Bustling city dwellers were said to go insane by the "overstimulation" of city life, while farmer's wives went insane by living monotonously and working too hard. Immigrants were thought to be especially vulnerable. More than half of the patients admitted had been born elsewhere. The doctors found this very interesting.[285]

"Many of them have lived under despotic forms of government and have been used to the most frugal mode of living," explained an article from 1910. It continued:

> The great change in their environment proves too much for them. Liberty becomes license to do as they please, regardless of the laws of God or man. Liberal wages that seem a fortune to their simple minds induces dissipation. Many of them soon become wrecks both bodily and mentally, and then the

Convalescent Home for Women (from the Report of the Board of Trustees of the Upper Peninsula Hospital for the Insane for the Period Ending June 30, 1906).

Women's Cottage Day Room (from the Report of the Board of Trustees of the Newberry State Hospital for the Period Ending June 30, 1916).

sheriff turns them over to the state to be cared for. Thus ends their dreams of fortune and home in the new world. It paints a sad and gloomy picture.[286]

Finns, being the "most oppressed nationality on earth," were thought to be especially susceptible to insanity. Nearly 29 percent of the asylum patients were Finnish. The language barrier between the patients and the doctors made for a heavy burden, hampering cooperation on both sides.[287]

Some immigrants were deported back to their country of origin, the justification being that "the authorities do not feel like furnishing asylum accommodations for the insane of other countries." Carl Carlson was one such inmate. He was sent back to Finland in the winter of 1904, and after returning, murdered his mother and sister and was killed while resisting arrest.[288]

The asylum treated a wide variety of psychological maladies, including: "Manic Depressive Insanity" (bi-polar disorder), "Maniacal Insanity," "Delusional Insanity," "Dementia Precox" (schizophrenia), "Melancholia" (depression), etc.

Not all patients were actually insane. Neurological disorders were treated there as well. A distressing number of patients were elderly people, either alone in the world or whose families could not or would not take care of them. Most suffered from either "Senile Dementia" (Alzheimer's) or "Apoplexy" (stroke).

The asylum also cared for a large number of epileptic patients, as well as those with Huntington's disease, multiple sclerosis, alcoholism, "morphinism," brain tumors or head injuries. A seven-year-old girl was committed in 1895 for being deaf and dumb, but later transferred to the Michigan School for the Deaf in Flint, a more specialized institution, as Dr. Bell had "observed signs of intelligence" and thought that a more specialized environment would be better for her.[289]

A very common ailment (and cause of death) was called "general paresis of the insane," a paralytic brain disease caused by syphilis. Nearly 40 percent of those who died at the asylum from 1895 to 1920 were victims of this disease. There was no treatment. Those suffering from this kind of "insanity" lived an average of one year after being admitted.

Most patients were ignored by the newspaper, but occasionally, one would be committed who had a bit of an interesting story, and a news item would appear about "the unfortunate." Some examples follow:

> John Carey, a deputy sheriff from Rexton, was discovered October 10, 1904, with his "memory gone, mind a blank and walking power virtually gone." Suspecting a brain tumor, he was sent to the asylum a week later, where he died October 21, 1904.[290]

> Julian Coulette of Nadeau was "insane on the subject of religion" and had an "irresistible impulse to hang himself" and also to "kill his 17-year-old daughter and throw her body into the creek."[291]

> The "demented Hungarian" Kose Kasimir (also spelled Kase, Kazo, Kasimer, Kazimer, Kozimer and any variation thereof) went insane and attacked eight Catholic cemeteries across the Upper Peninsula and Wisconsin, destroying more than 200 tombstones before being caught in 1905 and committed. He died in the asylum in 1918.[292]

The covered walkways, in which patients may promenade (from the Report of the Board of Trustees of the Upper Peninsula Hospital for the Insane for the Period Ending June 30, 1896).

The asylum in 1902, showing the quadrangle (from the Report of the Board of Trustees of the Upper Peninsula Hospital for the Insane for the Period Ending June 30, 1902).

Michael Hill, a Finnish immigrant, told people he was both the president of the United States and richer than Rockefeller.[293]

Frank Wolf was a "crazed socialist" who had terrorized his community.[294]

Mike Nyhacka, committed after beating his wife, was obsessed with building a perpetual motion device.[295]

Mrs. Eli King of Rapinville, "a lady of great worth," went insane due to "physical suffering." [296]

Mrs. Anthony Robinson went insane through grief over her sister, who was also insane.[297]

Seventeen years after opening the asylum had grown exponentially, suffering from near constant overcrowding. As early as 1898, it was reported that "nearly every upper peninsula county has insane persons detained in the jails," waiting and waiting for new "cottages" to be built so they could be transferred to the hospital. By 1907, the asylum was already caring for 100 more patients than it had room for and was "compelled to release a number of patients before they had become entirely cured." Superintendent Earl H. Campbell begged judges to "urge friends of insane patients to furnish them when possible with the private care and treatment, and instances where the mania appears to be only temporary to commit the patient to the county jail," commenting that "the situation is serious."[298]

Nothing seemed to help, and by 1911, the asylum was still 135 patients over capacity and the state had run out of money to build more buildings. Nearly 100 residents waited in county jails and poorhouses for a transfer, and this number does not include any whose families were still trying to care for them at home.[299]

The original two wards had grown in to fourteen "cottages" (eight for men, six for women) surrounding a large yard of "green grass and flower beds" and holding almost 800 patients. Chronic cases, "for whom there is little or no hope of recovery," were mostly kept separate from the "acute" cases, but the overcrowding made this difficult.[300]

The nurses and attendants, in their blue uniforms, were said to be underpaid (originally $16 to $26 a month) and overworked, yet devoted to their jobs, "directing, subduing, placating, soothing, controlling by kindness rather than force." They were not averse, however, to using straightjackets or locking patients up in small rooms. "Striking an inmate," on the other hand, was strictly forbidden, and any "attendant guilty of such an act is immediately fired without being given an opportunity to resign." Whether or not this rule was followed in practice is hard to tell. Especially early on, most attendants and nurses lived and slept in the same buildings as their charges. They were together almost twenty-four hours a day.[301]

The hours were long and the work could be dangerous as well, as when Superintendent Campbell was "struck over the head with an iron bar by an insane man." The inmate, "a trusty," was "suddenly seized with a homicidal mania, and sneaking up behind Dr. Campbell struck him a vicious blow over the head with a heavy hydrant wrench." Luckily, Dr. Campbell recovered.[302]

In another instance, a board member named Charles J. Byrns sat down next to an inmate (the aforementioned Kose Kasimir). The tiny Kasimir took exception to being crowded by the large Byrns and "struck at him." Byrns interpreted this as a "vicious attack" and hit back, giving the little inmate "a sledge-hammer blow delivered straight from the shoulder." Although "striking an inmate is one of the most serious offenses against the rules of the institution," the rest of the board members decided that Byrns deserved a vote of confidence, as he had a right to defend himself, and Kasimir was, in the end, unharmed.[303]

It was difficult to get good help. "One of the most arduous duties a young woman can assume is caring for the insane," admitted the Board of Trustees in 1914. "The hours of service are long and there is ever-present a mental strain." The Board went to beg the state for more money to build a private dormitory for the nurses, further admitting that "it is difficult, at times, to retain efficient help." This request was eventually granted. To further alleviate the shortage, the hospital then established its own training school for nurses, both male and female. The course lasted two and a half years, which included six months of study in a Chicago hospital.[304]

The day room in Cottage A (from the *Report of the Board of Trustees of the Upper Peninsula Hospital for the Insane for the Period Ending June 30, 1902*).

The industrial-sized laundry room at the asylum (from the *Report of the Board of Trustees of the Upper Peninsula Hospital for the Insane for the Period Ending June 30, 1906*).

ROSS LEIGHTON, PUB.   *This is the female infirmary and one of the cottages*
ASYLUM FOR INSANE, NEWBERRY, MICH.

Another postcard, this one postmarked 1908, showing the "Asylum for the Insane." By 1911, the institution had been renamed the "Newberry State Hospital" (author's collection).

The general kitchen for the asylum
(from the *Report of the Board of Trustees of the Upper Peninsula Hospital for the Insane for the Period Ending June 30, 1902*).

Left: Nurses at the asylum, circa 1910, having fun
(photo courtesy of Dr. James Surrell).

Center: Dr. Earl Campbell, long-time superintendent
(photo courtesy of Dr. James Surrell).

Right: Charles Byrns, a prominent Upper Peninsula businessman, and at one
time a trustee of the Newberry State Hospital
(photo from the *Escanaba Daily Press* in 1936).

The Hospital Band, made up of attendants and employees, in 1906. They
were in great demand, not only at the asylum, but in town as well (from
the *Report of the Board of Trustees of the Upper Peninsula Hospital for the
Insane for the Period Ending June 30, 1904*).

Besides the staff, who worked directly with the insane, there was also a large force of other employees working in the large administration building, laundry, kitchens, light and heat plants, and on the hospital's large farm, which grew vegetables and hay. They also kept a prize-winning herd of Holstein cows and a "rove of hogs."

The asylum was considered a "model institution" and far from a Dickensian madhouse. A sincere effort was made to keep the inmates comfortable.[305]

During fine weather, patients were allowed to walk around the grounds, "which are planted with rose bushes, hedges, plants and shrubbery." In inclement weather, they could stroll down the large porches that connected the cottages to one another, which could be glassed in during the winter. A little "deer park" on the grounds was a "source of great delight to the patients."

Fresh flowers decorated the wards whenever possible.[306]

Indoor amusements were not neglected. The men were given billiard tables and checkerboards, while the women received phonographs and music boxes. The hospital sponsored weekly orchestra concerts and brought in theatrical troupes to give performances or rolls of film for "motion picture plays." Every week, a dance was held as well. There were sleigh rides, picnics, card parties, and sewing circles for those who could participate.[307]

Ambulatory patients could work in the laundry, barns, and farm, or in the conservatory, growing carnations and chrysanthemums. Others "give evidence of their sanity by shirking all the labor possible." Religious services were provided by a variety of chaplains of different faiths. Christmas, Easter, and the Fourth of July were all celebrated.[308]

Still, it can't have been a pleasant place to live. Some committed suicide, and many patients did try to escape. Most were recaptured. Some died in the attempt.

Paul Messenger escaped in 1900. "He was regarded as 'trusty' and was allowed to go to a ball game one day and never returned." His bleaching bones were discovered two years later by a hunter under a rotten rope hanging from a tree branch.[309]

John Wojciechowski, an illiterate Polish immigrant and father of six, began to hear voices in the winter of 1902 and became paranoid, believing that someone was trying to kill him. He was sent to the asylum, but escaped the next summer and walked more than 200 miles to his home in Menominee. He arrived "thin and emaciated, with his shoes and clothing nearly in tatters, and his mind still deranged," and asked after his family. He was eventually sent back the asylum (though not before leaving his wife with a seventh child), where he died of pneumonia in 1917.[310]

Paul Renauld escaped during a particularly cold winter in 1906. Although "without hat or top coat," he made it as far as Escanaba before being recaptured. John Boleg escaped in 1911, walking more than 200 miles back to his home in Calumet, eating bread when he could get it and tree bark when he couldn't.[311]

Nora Sweeney, a forty-two-year-old schoolteacher from Calumet, picked the lock of the room in which she was confined. Within an hour, the staff realized she was missing, but she had already disappeared into the swamps east of town. She had escaped September 29, 1918, and the search for her was kept up until winter. Traces of her were found, but the woman herself seemed to have vanished. The search resumed again in the spring, and in June of 1919, her body was discovered, huddled under the roots of an upturned tree.[312]

The Assembly Hall at the insane asylum, where patients might be entertained (from the *Report of the Board of Trustees of the Upper Peninsula Hospital for the Insane for the Period Ending June 30, 1906*).

A "men's room" (from the *Report of the Board of Trustees of the Upper Peninsula Hospital for the Insane for the Period Ending June 30, 1906*).

NEW ADMINISTRATION BUILDING, U. P. H., NEWBERRY, MICH.

This postcard (postmarked 1916) shows the grand Administration Building of the Hospital. Quite an impressive sight for the middle of the north woods! (author's collection).

The physicians and attendants may have dearly hoped to "effect a cure," but for most, this was not possible. For those who were discharged, a relapse was always a risk. During the years 1910-1912, a report to the state explained that 228 patients were released, but ninety-six "readmitted or returned." In the same report, Dr. Campbell complained that "the State is doing practically nothing along the line of prevention and after care and that the "percentage of readmissions appears too large."[313]

In its first twenty years, the Newberry facility treated 3,006 patients. A few were transferred to other facilities, while 499 were eventually considered "recovered," and another 801 "improved."

Yet most would die there.[314]

Nurses at the State Hospital. The ladies are: Maude Snodden, Julia Quinlan Detzler, Ethel Burns King, Bessie Collins, Estella Candy, and Margaret Burt (photo courtesy of Sterling McGinn).

Chapter Ten
A Tale of Two Newspapers

*"In those days anybody with a shirttail full of type and a political idea could
start a newspaper, and many did."*

— *Newberry News*, July 2, 1986, Centennial Edition, We're 100 Years old!

*"One man has just as good a right as another to start any kind of business he
has a mind to, and if the people of Newberry want another newspaper and print
shop, it is not for us to gainsay them."*

— Charles Brebner, Editor, *Newberry News*, November19, 1897

MOST OF THE MATERIAL FOR this book comes from the archives of *The Newberry News*, the town's newspaper, founded three years after Newberry sprung into being. The newspaper had a rocky first decade.

Clyde Hecox, of Sault Sainte Marie, was the first editor, working out of a small office with a pedal-powered printing press, setting type by hand, one letter at time. His opening issue debuted June 10, 1886, two pages stuffed with ads, local news items, and a history of the town (so far), as well as two more pages of "boilerplate" for state, national, and general interest stories. This paper, declared Mr. Hecox, was meant to promote the new town and to be "essentially independent politically" and would "rather preserve the middle course and place public interest always before that of party."[315]

Clyde sold his interest in the paper (as well as all the printing equipment) to Royal A. Jenney in December 1888. Jenney was the superintendent of the furnace, and a very important man. In later years, it was stated that Royal A. Jenney had had a financial interest in *The Newberry News* from the very beginning, and that Hecox had been forced out due to his political views. The true details are unclear. In any case, Jenney was now in charge and everybody knew it. Even though he hired E. T. McGraw, formerly of the *Alger County Republican*, to be the nominal editor, it was common knowledge that Royal himself was the power behind the throne.[316]

Jenney, with his friends, formed *The Newberry News* Publishing Company and vowed to continue Hecox's policy of political neutrality. He promised "to defend the weak and to show up any evils existing in the community, no matter on whom the blow may fall." But this approach proved too hard for Jenney, a stalwart Republican, to bear. Within four months, the paper had changed its slogan from "a progressive independent paper" to a "progressive republican paper." An editorial whined that neutrality was a "heavy load to carry" and that "it has required so much labor to let politics alone that we have been able to do but little else."[317]

This seems to have outraged Clyde Hecox, who almost immediately started his own, new, rival newspaper, with a young journalist named Bob Wright, who had been working in newspapers since he was twelve while taking high school courses at night. Hecox and Wright called their new publication, a trifle smugly, the *Newberry Independent*. It was not independent at all, however, but as Democratic as Jenney's paper was Republican.[318]

At first, relations between the two papers were cordial, with the *News* welcoming the *Independent* "to our table" and declaring it a "bright, newsy sheet." The *Independent*, for its part, encouraged the *News* to keep up the good work. With an election approaching, however, a nasty little game of name-calling began almost immediately. The bosses loathed each other and were not afraid to express it.[319]

The *Independent* accused the *News* of plagiarism and being "inclined to be a little reckless in handling the truth." The upstart newspaper further claimed that E. T. McGraw, nominal editor, was "afflicted with a peculiar mania to run off with other people's hats" and that manager Royal A. Jenney was a drunkard. It charged that that the *News* was playing a game of "freeze out" against the *Independent* by artificially lowering its prices and other such "contemptible and sneak methods." *The Independent* now called the *News* an "unreliable sheet" and the "little one on Helen Street." The *News* retaliated, referring to the *Independent* as "young'un," "dirty rag," and "odious animal," as well as the bad puns "try weakly Independent" or "in Dependent."[320]

Village clerk Ambro Bettes, a Democrat and supporter of the *Independent*, declared in a letter to the *Independent* that Jenney, "in his fit of malice, has tried and is trying to malign my character." Jenney indignantly denied this, declaring that "The *News* bears no malice nor have we any personal quarrel" with Bettes. This may or may not have been true, but past articles certainly *had* implied that Bettes was overly ambitious, as well as lazy, and more recent articles suggested he had embezzled $32 from the county. But, of course, such reporting was only done in the public's interest. Naturally.[321]

It's difficult to judge more than a century later. Ambro Bettes was a former schoolteacher and current politician, family man and, by all accounts, a good and decent soul with the good of the town at heart. Royal Jenney was one of the oldest residents of town, a manager at the furnace, village trustee, family man, loyal friend, and also a strong and committed believer in his town. However, he also did seem to be rather…heavy-handed…as he antagonized people left and right. His enemies were all too happy to complain about him to the *Independent*. And the *Independent* was only too happy to print their complaints.

George Jones, who dared to defend Bettes in a letter to the *Independent*, was relentlessly mocked for it in the *News*. George W. Sickles, Dollarville's schoolteacher, began by urging the two papers to get along, pleading that political animosities had no business in local politics. He finished by being the *Independent's* Dollarville correspondent, trading barbs with the *News'* Dollarville correspondent and declaring himself a Democrat.[322]

An unnamed subscriber, who stopped his subscription due to the controversy, was ridiculed. The "true reason" the *News* opined, "is he wanted to sponge his reading matter… he will read this item before the man who pays for the paper he reads it in has had time to look it over."[323]

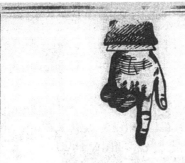

Come To The

NEWS JOB ROOMS!

···FOR YOUR···

COMMERCIAL PRINTING,

—We Carry a Full Line of—

Note Heads, Letter Heads, Bill Heads, Statements, Etc.

Fine Wedding Stationery!

Ball Programmes and Invitations.

—A Nice Line of—

CALLING CARDS.

OUR PRICES ARE RIGHT,

And we Guarantee that our work will please you.

JUST RECEIVED!

—A Large Stock of—

BUSINESS -:- STATIONERY,

All Orders promptly attended to at the

Newberry News Office.

Left: An advertisement from *The Newberry News* of November 25, 1890 (Note the typo!).

Right: Clyde W. Hecox in 1905 (from *A Bunch of Optimists: Some Stories of Endeavor and Achievement by the Men Who Have Made the Soo*), and an advertisement from *The Newberry News* of December 19, 1890.

Royal Jenney also infuriated the Knights of the Maccabees, one of the many fraternal organizations, when he reported that the organization was on its last legs, in financial difficulty and hemorrhaging members. *The Independent* said that this was because he had been kicked out for failing to pay dues. Incidentally, the Knights of the Maccabees lasted longer in Luce County than Royal Jenney did.[324]

Even other newspaper editors seemed to dislike Jenney. When he dubbed *The St. Ignace Watchman* "the worst-looking paper that it has ever been our misfortune to see" and an "apology for a newspaper," the *Watchman* returned the compliment by calling the *News* "the worst looking rag ever turned out of a newspaper office."[325]

The *Alger County Republican*, when referring to Jenney as "editor and manager," added "(a miserable poor one, too)." Jenney also had poor relations with the *Mining Journal* (accusing it of plagiarism) and *The Rock River Republican* (also calling it an "apology of a newspaper"). The back and forth is exhausting to read about a century later. It must have been even more exhausting to live through. Before too long, both papers soon experienced major changes.[326]

After only a few months, Clyde Hecox left town, returning to Sault Ste. Marie. There, he started yet another new paper, the *Soo Democrat*. Bob Wright was left at the helm in Newberry. E. T. McGraw, nominal editor of the *News*, quit in January 1890 to go and work for the *Independent*. Four months later, he quit the *Independent* to work as a hotel clerk. The next month, The Newberry News Publishing Company sold out completely to Charles Brebner, a former furnace employee and grocer who had no newspaper experience whatsoever.[327]

Without Royal Jenney's polarizing presence, the fighting died down quite a bit. The *Independent* even wished Brebner success at his new job; however, Brebner was as Republican as Jenney had been, and the quarrelling quickly resumed, though it lacked something of the personal animosity of before. Then, in 1891, Bob Wright and his new partner, W. H. Crowe, retooled the *Newberry Independent* into the more appropriately named *Luce County Democrat*.

The renamed paper lasted another year before Bob Wright's interest in Newberry began to wane. A few months after the *Luce County Democrat* appeared, the *Alger County Democrat* opened for business, with Wright & Crowe listed as publishers. The partners then planned to open a second paper in Harbor Springs. This was too much work for the two men to handle. *The Luce County Democrat* closed up shop in January 1892.[328*]

All was quiet for the next three years, but by 1894, the economy was in terrible shape. In Newberry, the furnace and chemical works had closed down. Many families were collecting food supplies from the poor house, and the situation wasn't expected to get better anytime soon. Besides which, it was an election year. Political parties were willing and eager to blame each other, and Newberry's Democrats were becoming increasingly annoyed by Brebner's Republican slanted editorials.

So attorney Frank H. Peters (a committed Democrat) organized a new rival paper, the *Newberry Enterprise*, and Ed Jones from Manistique was brought in to edit it. The debut issue appeared in February of 1894.

---

* Bob Wright later created the *Munising News* (1896), the *Lake Superior Pilot* (1901), the *Cloverland Farmer* (1915), *Wright's Illustrated Weekly* (1923), and the *Munising News* (1928). He also wrote several non-fiction books, and in 1940, it was claimed he had popularized the term "lumberjack."

A sketch of Robert H. Wright that appeared in the *Detroit Free Press* of April 30, 1892.

Attractiveness

Is the most important requisite of good printing. It is the quality which compels attention and makes a lasting impression. It doubles the efficiency and insures results. Its production requires not only a modern equipment mechanically but it demands the constant and careful attention of competent, experienced workmen. A trial order is all we ask.

The Newberry News
Phone No. 11.

Advertisement from
The Newberry News
of December 19, 1890.

THE NEWBERRY NEWS.

THE NEWBERRY NEWS.

The Newberry News.

THE NEWBERRY NEWS

Various versions of the masthead for *The Newberry News*, over the early years -- iterations from 1886, 1890, 1892, and 1898.

As almost his first act, Editor Jones called on Editor Brebner, announcing the new venture. There he received an (understandably) subdued welcome that Jones complained was "cold." Jones then launched his newspaper, insisting in his welcoming paragraphs that they were not out to "run any rival out of the business." No, no. Their motto was to "live and let live."[329]

Those lofty ideals lasted all of two articles before he launched into a series of complaints about the *News*'s recent editorial over a current scandal. As the weeks went by, it became clear that Ed Jones not only hated all Republicans, but especially hated Claude W. Case (who was on the village council) and Charles Brebner, whom he insisted was Case's puppet.

As the November elections approached, Jones' jibs and jabs, snipping and snapping increased both in volume and shrillness. It was an odd week where Ed Jones didn't hurl some kind of insult at Charles Brebner. In the early stages, Jones referred to the *News* sarcastically as "old reliable" and its editor as "our more or less esteemed contemporary" and "Brother Brebner." Later, he grew angrier. The *News* was now the "Screwdriver" and its editor was "Prince Charlie" and "Lickspital." His aggressive volleys included slurs, inside jokes, subtle innuendos, deliberate misunderstandings, mockery, and accusations of everything from prevarication to plagiarism, hypocrisy to toadyism.[330]

Jones made fun of Brebner's Scottish accent (calling it "vile"), education, and ancestry. He taunted Brebner for being a sycophant and also for not *acting* like a sycophant. He railed at him for fighting back and laughed at him when he didn't. He pointed out every typo and mistake—unavoidable in any newspaper (as Jones really ought to have understood, being himself guilty of using words like determental, swoolen, and ligitimate).[331]

Charles Brebner mostly ignored the abuse, but not always. Sometimes he would reply in kind, always referring to his rival as "the buzzsaw" and once calling Jones a "poor brainless whiffet."[332]

In October 1894, the *Newberry Enterprise* produced a massive "trade edition," an illustrated magnum opus describing the town and many of its prominent inhabitants, stores, schools, and industries. Its flattering portraits and gushing prose were refreshingly apolitical and respectful to all.[333]

Not so its regular issues. The rivalry grew more intense as the November election closed in. Both papers were now openly mocking each other's candidates, conventions, and campaign tactics, while simultaneously claiming to be holier than thou. Ed Jones claimed that the glitches in the Republican campaigns were "none of our affair" after several weeks of discussing and criticizing said glitches. Charles Brebner said "The NEWS does not deem it necessary to decry or belittle the democratic candidates for county office" after weeks of doing just that. *The Enterprise* dropped all pretense of polite riposte, baldly stating that "*The Newberry News* really makes our stomach ache. Its editor must surely be off his base." Both editors quite emphatically (and frequently) stated that they hated a hypocrite.[334]

The November election came and went. The dust cleared and the verdict was in. Ed Jones, Atty. Peters, and the Democrats had lost nearly every single race. A jubilant Charles Brebner was not able to resist needling his fallen foe with the following nonsensical paragraph, inserted among "local and county news."

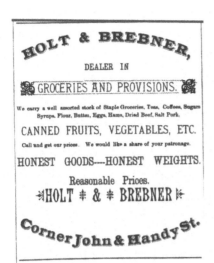

Before becoming editor, Charles Brebner was a groceryman. This ad appeared in *The Newberry News* of October 25, 1889.

Charles Brebner and wife, in later years (*The Spokesman-Review*, August 13, 1933). Merle Fretz later described Brebner as "a small but fearless and fiery Scotch Presbyterian."

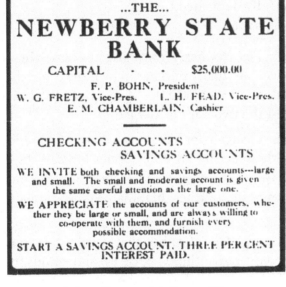

Advertisement from *The Newberry News* of August 28, 1908.

The Newberry Enterprise.

The masthead for the *Newberry Enterprise* of 1894.

Frank H. Peters, from the October 1894 Trade Edition of *The Newberry Enterprise*.

Buzz!

Buzzsaw!

Buzzsaw buzzing!

Buzzsaw buzzing candidates!

"Don't monkey with the buzzsaw."

Buzzed candidates dead!

Buzzing ceased!

Buzzing!

Buzz!

B'z! whiff! Bang! "buzzsaw"
dead as a door nail.[335]

The Newberry Enterprise lasted only a few weeks after the election. Ed Jones packed up his entire plant and announced his intention of moving his Democratic paper to St. Ignace (which already had two newspapers) and regrouping.[336]

In November of that year, *The Newberry News* ran a small, black-bordered obituary reading:

Sacred to the memory of The Newberry Enterprise,
established February 8th, 1894, departed this life
Nov. 21st, 1894. Aged 9 months and 2 weeks.
This corner is respectfully dedicated to
the memory of the departed.[337]

Meanwhile, Ed Jones made good on his word. *The Newberry Enterprise* became the *St. Ignace Enterprise*, which managed to flourish and was eventually purchased by none other than Clyde Hecox. Ironically enough, after Hecox retired in 1933, he sold the *St. Ignace Enterprise* to one of its rivals, the *St. Ignace Republican News*, and the two papers merged.[338]

In November 1897, proving that those who do not learn from history are doomed to repeat it, *The Newberry Journal* appeared, created as a "side issue" by Ed Jones. Jones himself stayed in St. Ignace, but arranged for his new newspaper to be edited by W. W. Ashley, not the most reliable of employees, the *News* once describing him as in "a rather dilapidated condition after a two-week's toot."[339]

In the spring, Ed Jones replaced Ashley with George Connley, but that April a fire broke out at the offices. The crowds that gathered managed to save the type, cases, and stands, but the printing press was too heavy to be moved and was destroyed. Nevertheless, *The Newberry Journal* soldiered on until July 1898 when George Connley vanished "just ahead of a Mackinac county officer," later joining the army to escape his creditors. Ed Jones then turned the paper over to Charles Custer Metcalf, son of one of Newberry's more prominent Democrats, Cyrus Metcalf. Charles was all of seventeen years old and had just graduated from high school. By September 1899, *The Newberry Journal* ceased production.[340]

In the same year, Brebner sold his business to his employee, William G. Fretz, who had been with the company since almost the very beginning, having been hired by Clyde Hecox. *The Newberry News* stayed in the Fretz family for the next ninety years.[341]

Left: Editor Ed Jones, from the October 1894 Trade Edition of
The Newberry Enterprise.

Right: William G. Fretz in later years
(photo courtesy of Sterling McGinn and Avis Fretz)

Left: An advertisement from *The Newberry News* of December 19, 1890. Ida
Fretz was the first Fretz to settle in Newberry.

Right: William G. Fretz, again in later years (photo courtesy of *The Newberry
News*, identification courtesy of Sterling McGinn).

In 1918, *The Newberry News* purchased this Mergenthaler Linotype machine. This state-of-the-art piece of machinery revolutionized the process of setting type by creating "lines o' type." These lines then could be arranged into articles. It was much faster than the old way of assembling letters, one by one. With this purchase, the newspaper left behind its own wild and woolly days and entered the modern era.

Chapter Eleven
Fun and Games

"Isn't it about time that some of the numerous societies here gave another dance, or what would be better still, form a club? Amusements have been few and far between so far this winter, and it is time to make up or spring will cut short the time when tripping the light fantastic will be more work than play."

— Clyde W. Hecox, *Newberry News*, January 12, 1888

"A jolly, jingling, merry, mirthful mélange of music, song and laughter..."

— Bank Opera House Advertisements, June 5, 1903

ALL WORK AND NO PLAY makes Jack a dull, sad boy.

The need for recreation and entertainment was a concept that the late nineteenth century was beginning to embrace. So what did the early residents do for fun? Options were varied.

During the summer, hot air balloons, street fairs, and circuses set up shop on occasion. Traveling entertainers often stopped in Newberry for a few days. So, too, did actors, singers, and the like. Sometimes, they would perform in the Village Hall. Other times, they would rent one of the many other "halls" across town, where "hall" was the generic term for the unused open space on the top floor of a store building.

After 1890, Newberry had its very own "opera house" in the form of a stage built into the second floor of the bank. There, lecturers lectured, singers sang, and traveling players put on shows.

Not a week went by without some sort of entertainment or another. Traveling theater troupes put on plays like *The Temple of Fame* (1893), *Peck's Bad Boy* (1896), *The Missouri Girl* (1904), and the musical farce comedy *Who Is Who?* (1903). Alternatively booked were minstrel shows or traveling singers. The Blunders Comedy Company and Pete Baker German Comedy troupe both made stops in 1893. A local ordinance passed in 1894 required a license fee of $10 per day, which was meant to keep out the "bum shows," "medicine troupes," "street fakers," and other "undesirable barnstormers." City fathers wanted their entertainment to be at a high level of quality.[342]

The opera house stage also was rented for school graduations (both high school and eighth grade), school entertainments full of songs, skits, and speeches and church events.

Canadian Jubilee Singers.

BANK OPERA HOUSE—FRIDAY JUNE 13
ADMISSION 25, 35 and 50 CENTS

Bank Opera House

S. N. DUTCHER, Mgr.

Coming Attractions.

The following attractions are booked for the future:

April 27

Mahara's Minstrels

Above: Louis Cyr, the Strongest Man in the World (Bibliothèque et Archives Canada / C-086343)

Right: advertisements from *The Newberry News* of June 6, 1902 and April 21, 1905.

Lecturers came to both educate and edify on such subjects as "Canadian Annexation," "Electricity," "The Southern Negro," and "Marriage" (the last advertised as being for men only).[343]

The Bank Opera House held balls, masquerades, Christmas parties, "social hops," card game tournaments, harvest suppers, Japanese teas, and once a "Poverty Soshul." In 1893, residents could come and see Louis Cyr, "the strongest man in the world," who lifted weights and held his own against horses. In 1911, the bank hall sponsored a wrestling match between Frank Burns and Perry Schad for the middleweight championship of Michigan. Drama, music, documentaries, comedy, sports—the Bank Opera House was the cable TV of its day.[344]

As mentioned, there were other "halls" scattered throughout town, located on the second floor of many store buildings where lodges and social clubs held their meetings. Men could choose (at various times) from the Masons, Oddfellows, Knights of the Maccabees, Knights of Pythias, Good Templars, Ancient Order of Hercules, Ancient Order of Foresters, Modern

Woodmen, Gleaners, and Scandinavian Aid and Fellowship Society of America, among others. Eventually, the Masons even built their own temple on a corner of Newberry Avenue and John Street.

Women were served by the Lady Maccabees, Helpful Circle of the King's Daughters, Order of the Eastern Star (Masons), or Rebekahs (Oddfellows), as well as church committees. The Women's Christian Temperance Union was also an important organization that lobbied hard against the saloons, as did the Band of Hope (a similar organization for the youngsters). Ladies often entertained their friends at pedro parties* or fudge parties.

Newberry also supported its religious clubs, Shakespeare clubs, and garden clubs. There was the Newberry Study Club, Newberry Lyceum, Bay View Reading Circle, and Epworth League. Every Sunday there was church, where families would dress in their best and see all the neighbors. The churches also sponsored concerts, plays, lecturers, and ice cream socials. The various Sunday Schools held picnics and Children's Days. There also were young people's organizations and Ladies Aid societies, all with their own meetings, dinners, and amusements.

In December 1898, a new type of entertainment made its Newberry debut when a traveling entertainer—the New York Biograph Company—promised to give a moving picture exhibition with one of "Edison's latest machines." They promised to "show all the battles participated in by the army and navy in the Spanish-American war." Instead, they showed up with "an old rattle trap" featuring "about a dozen different scenes." The operator soon gave up "and dismissed his audience amid the jeers of the small boys and gallery gods."[345]

About a year later, a more professional and well-regarded entertainer, T. B. Barry, came to town with a "large assortment of moving pictures...including the Jeffries Fitzsimmons prize fight and Yanko-Spanko war scenes." He charged 25¢ for adults and 10¢ for children.

Advertisement from *The Newberry News* of August 28, 1908.

* Pedro was a type of card game very popular in Newberry's early days.

This second movie house went over much better. Over the next ten years, other movie exhibitors came and went, setting up shows in the village hall and opera house.[346]

J. F. Husted and Pat Haley opened Newberry's first permanent moving picture theater, the Gem, in 1908, which lasted for about a year. Movies were a modern and popular new industry, and many other theaters operated in Newberry over the next few years.

The Vaudette Theatre opened around 1909, booking traveling vaudeville acts, "illustrated songs," and some films. In March 1911, the Circle Light Theater debuted with admission costs of 5¢ and 10¢. The venture promised such exciting films as footage of the New York shirtwaist factory fire, "where so many unfortunate souls went to their doom."[347]

By 1913, the Vaudette had dropped the live acts and transitioned into a purely moving picture venue, advertising its modernity (including "electric fans," "opera chairs," and

Oscar M. Anderson, owner of the Vaudette. He risked his life in a bad fire rescuing his projector (photo courtesy of Larry Johnson).

"electric orchestra," as well as a "No. 6A Powers motion picture machine...one of the best and most modern machines on the market"). Owned by Oscar Anderson, the theater was struck by fire in January 1916. Mr. Anderson risked his own life, plunging through a burning window and then retreating with his very valuable "picture machine" strapped to his back. It was a good thing he did so, for with it, he was able to rebuild and reopen within a few months. The Family Theater on Helen Street opened in 1914, promising to "cater especially to the ladies and children, and will show only the best five-reel productions." The Grand also opened in 1914, with a seating capacity of 200 people and "one of the best machines manufactured," which was used to screen "only the best films."[348]

Movies were popular in Newberry, as they were all over the country. Being silent, they could be enjoyed by everyone, regardless of one's mastery of the English language. And they were cheap, ticket prices ranging from a nickel to a quarter. The advent of movies, though, sounded the death knell for the opera house over the bank. Small opera houses and vaudeville theaters were closing throughout the nation, and talented acts were disappearing along with them. Newberry's opera house closed in December 1914, and the space was rented to Charles Beaulieu for a furniture display room.[349*]

Alongside the need for amusement, the concept of "physical fitness" also was beginning to evolve in the late nineteenth century. In Newberry, as it was across the country, outdoor activities and indoor sports were held in high esteem. Many such activities were held in the

---

* Still, like all new technologies, movie theaters were a chancy business. Of Newberry's first four motion picture palaces, only the Grand survived into the 1920s.

"The Fall of a Nation"

*The World's Mightiest Motion Picture Spectacle,
Dealing With the Origin and Destiny of Our Republic.*

**America Attacked!
Big Guns in Action!
A Foreign Viceroy!**

Union Rescued by the Boys in
Khaki Led by Modern
Joan of Arc.

See *Thos. Dixon's Thrilling Epic
of Love and Patriotism.*

Accompanied by the Original
Victor Herbert Music.

AT THE

Grand Theater

Friday and Saturday

JULY 20 and 21, 1917

Matinee at 2:30 p. m.   Evening Show at 7:30

ADMISSION -:- 25 and 50 Cents

Vaudette Theater
Saturday
10 and 20 cents

Vaudeville

Madson Sisters
Age 10 and 16 years

Len Phillips,
The "Irish Swede"

H. Parkhurst,
The Book Agent

In addition to the above
program the usual 2,000
feet of film and songs
will be given.

Right: An advertisement for the Vaudette appears below from before it converted completely into a movie house (*The Newberry News*, June 25, 1909).

Left: The Grand Theater was its main rival (*The Newberry News* of March 3, 1917).

"central park," which was presented to the town by the Peninsular Land Department in 1890. It was a popular place for picnics, festivals, sports, and other outdoor celebrations.[350]

Bicycles became popular around 1899, being sold by Manhard's Hardware, Shattuck's, and Stafford's Drug Store from $25 to $50 each. The "enthusiastic wheelmen" took up a subscription and built a biking trail, running from town out to the State Hospital. This was supposed to be an eight-foot trail of fine, packed gravel. Unfortunately, almost immediately, teamsters began driving their heavy wagons over the path, ruining it and causing much bitterness among the bicyclists.[351]

In the early 1890s, "base ball" was very popular, with clubs springing up sponsoring games between towns during the summer months. Newberry, McMillan, Dollarville, the State

Hospital, St. Ignace, Sault Ste. Marie (Michigan), and Sault Ste. Marie (Canada) all had their "nine."

Exhibition games also were organized in town between the "East End Businessmen and West End Businessmen," single men vs. married men, Boy Scouts vs. Businessmen, and Hospital vs. High School. The furnace sometimes had its own team, as did some of the larger sawmills. A Fourth of July baseball game was an annual tradition. Even "indoor baseball" could be found during some winters.

Newberry's very first game of "foot ball" was played in October 1902 between the Soo High squad and a team composed of employees from the State Hospital. Since Newberry schools wanted their own football team, in 1904, a paperhanger and painter named J. D. Parker began to organize one, promising to act as coach. He had raised quite a considerable sum before he absconded with the money in October. A warrant was issued and Sheriff Cyr hotfooted it after him. It's just possible that this was all a misunderstanding, as no legal action was ever brought against Parker. But, in any case, he never coached.[352]

Instead, Coach Patterson of the "hill team" (hospital employees) took over Parker's coaching duties and Newberry's initial high school football team played its first game against Munising in November 1904, winning 16—6 in two twenty-minute halves. The team had eleven players, ranging from fourteen to twenty years of age. The football team was disbanded in 1905 due to lack of funds, but it would be back.[353]

During the winter, the cold, snow, and ice restricted residents to indoor activities, but many would also get out anytime weather permitted. Ice-skating was popular on cleared spaces on the rivers, lakes, ponds and—after the turn of the century—outdoor rinks. Children even took to skating on the icy sidewalks, which annoyed their elders. Sledding, both on ordinary hills with ordinary sleds and on man-made "toboggan slides," was another common activity.

Nevertheless, the region's long winters made indoor sports very desirable. Nearly every saloon and hotel had a "pool room," as unrespectable as they were popular. Bowling alleys connected with pool rooms opened in Newberry and McMillan in1915, with teams named the Privates, the Fords, the Gold Medals, the Meal Tickets, the Counter Hoppers, and the Allies. Girls bowled themselves in two alleys in the school's basement, since they weren't allowed in the regular clubs.[354]

Around the same time, the young ladies of Newberry organized a "basket ball club," playing in the village hall. Two unlucky young men thought it would be fun to ogle the bloomer-clad girls by peeping through a knothole under the stage, but the girls discovered their scheme, plugged the peephole, locked the door, finished the game, and then left the fellows overnight in the unheated February basement.[355] Soon thereafter, basketball was taken up by the schools, with official teams for both boy and girl students.

Excursions were another form of entertainment. Sunday school picnics in summer, hunting camps in fall, sleighing parties in winter: the people of Luce County would take any excuse to go and play out of doors.

Newberry's beloved early sheriff, Adam G. Louks (incidentally, he was said to be so strong that he could crush a potato one-handed), also was known as Captain Louks, for he owned a boat, the *Edna*, a little steam-powered launch that he kept on the Tahquamenon River.

Baseball team, 1914 (Courtesy of the Luce County Historical Society).

Girls' Basketball Team, 1914 (Photo courtesy Luce County Historical Society). The girls include, back row, left to right: Dorothy Campbell, May Young, "Big" Esther Johnson, Marie Johnson, Miss Irma Hurlbert, coach. The two seated are Martha Hutton and Effie McKinnon.

Throughout the summer, sometimes almost every weekend, he would take sightseers upriver to the Falls. Generally, Sheriff Louks and his tourists would leave early in the morning at the bridge just north of town.

Captain Louks and the *Edna* could make the fifty-seven-mile trip in seven hours. The party would camp overnight and return the next day. Many Newberry residents took advantage of the opportunity.[356]

In July 1894, Editor Jones of the *Newberry Enterprise* took a break from his usual tasks of belittling his enemies, promoting his politicians, and tooting his own horn to take a trip down to see the Falls. With him went thirteen other men, and they had a grand time. They stopped to fish, eat, explore an empty trapper's cabin, and take potshots at passing birds. The group steamed upriver until 1:00 a.m., finally stopping in the "inky blackness" to sleep for a few hours. After awaking, they hiked the few remaining steps to the Falls, where Percy G. Teeple, "the Kodak fiend," took photographs. They arrived back in town at 9:00 p.m. "a tired but happy crowd." Several other residents also owned these little steamships, and were more than happy to organize adventures for their friends. Similar trips occurred throughout the 1890s.[357]

The modern motorboat with a gasoline engine was developed in the late nineteenth century, and around the turn of the century, "gasoline launches" became popular on both the rivers and lakes, replacing the "steamers." (Although Edward Johnson used a "naptha launch" instead).[358]

Many local businessmen purchased a gasoline launch with which to play. They formed a Boat Club late in 1915, holding races on the Tahquamenon River. The earliest of these could travel up to eight miles per hour. Later models, such as the 12-horsepower, twenty-seven-footer built by Bror Stark and Basil Hunter in 1915, reached the unheard of speed of twenty miles per hour (until they crashed into a deadhead and capsized).

This was new, exciting, technology and sometimes not quite understood. Years later, Merle Fretz recalled his father bringing in his boat to Frank Seymour to repair a gas leak. Holding a lighted candle, Frank peered over the engine and its leaking fumes. The subsequent explosion rocked the shop and blew out its windows.

"Bill," said Frank, "I found that gas leak."

"I see you did," replied Editor Fretz. "Now, you chump, see if you can find me a new boat."[359]

James C. Foster bought land and built a cottage on the shores of Round Lake, and S. N. Dutcher did the same on Big Manistique Lake. On South Manistique Lake, a number of Newberry people (including Dr. Bohn and Ross Leighton) clubbed together to build a cottage of their own. In these cottages, they and their families could enjoy their summers, swimming, boating, and fishing.

The Foster children stayed there all summer, with their father visiting on weekends. The other families visited for weekends or even weeks at a time, often hosting other friends and relations.[360]

For those who wanted to go a little farther from home, the railroads often issued promotional fares for one-time deals, reducing their rates and ordering extra passenger cars to encourage residents to travel, visiting Marquette, Sault Ste. Marie, and Munising. Advertisements encouraged the residents to go and see the "encampment of Michigan State troops" on Mackinac Island, the Ringling Bros. circus at Marquette ($2 round trip), the Firemen's Tournament in

Advertisement *Newberry News*, April 4, 1902 and December 23, 1904. Sometime between these two dates, Manhard's Hardware became Foster's Hardware.

The McCloskey children of Dollarville enjoying the snow. This picture was probably taken in the winter of 1899–1900. The children are: John Martin (11), Wilbert (9), James (4), Hugh (3), Mary Ellen (6 mos.), Margaret (14), and Patrick (6). (photo courtesy of Patricia Proebstel).

Houghton ($4), and the Chicago World's Fair ($15 round trip). Often, special rates were issued for holiday traveling.[361]

Christmas was the most important holiday, but it was a family holiday, spent at church and at home with relatives. Still, there was shopping to do, cards to send, baking to accomplish, community dances, school recitals, and sleigh rides.

Independence Day celebrations were looked forward to each year, and the holiday was easily the second-most important. Picnics, balls, baseball games, bicycle races, and fireworks abounded.

A typical celebration is represented by that of July 4, 1899. The day began at 10:00 a.m. with a "grand parade." Led by the Newberry Band, a large procession of people marched from the Village Hall on East John. The parade included groups from the "secret societies" (like the Masons), fire department, "city officials in carriages," other organizations, and "thirty young ladies dressed in red, white and blue to represent 'Old Glory.'"

The parade tramped all around town and finally settled at the village park, where a minister offered a prayer, the Declaration of Independence was read, and Newberry's prosecuting attorney, Sanford N. Dutcher, "delivered a sound and logical oration."

After a break for lunch, it was time for the games, most for cash prizes. There were foot races for men and boys, bicycle races for men, boys and girls, a wheelbarrow race, potato race, "putting the shot," a tug of war, jumping contests, and "catching a greased pig," the prize for which was listed simply as "pig."

The contests were followed by a baseball game and horse race in the evening. At dusk, the people were treated to a "grand display of fireworks," followed by dancing parties all over town that "were in a full swing until a late hour."[362]

Later, parades would add "business floats" to the mix. For example, J. A. Shattuck's 1907 float depicted "the nations of the world grouped about the feet of the Goddess of Liberty." Another example is Krempel & Taylor's float, described as "very tasteful and appropriate, containing an orchestra which discoursed patriotic airs on the line of march."[363]

Youngsters enjoyed Halloween every year by stealing gates off fences (sometime reattaching them upside down), smearing soap on windows, and knocking over outhouses and woodpiles.

Their greatest triumph may have occurred October 31, 1905. When their parents awoke the next day, they found Newberry Avenue blocked by a mountain of dray wheels, wagons, and crates, "towering as high as the second stories," a-topped by a fluttering American flag. Adults turned an indulgent eye to this "innocent amusement" as long as there was no property damage.[364]

Indeed, the grown-ups were quite fond of Halloween themselves and often celebrated with "masquerade balls." In 1902, the Tahquamenaw Club sponsored one such event, the "most unique ever given." It was described as follows:

> The electric lights were shaded with green cloth and jack lanterns placed about the rooms. Black cats, wolves' and bears' heads peered forth from darkened corners, the whole presenting a gruesome effect indeed. The dancers, arrayed in white sheets from head to foot and all masked, presented a ghostly appearance,

but they were the liveliest bunch of ghosts ever assembled in one crowd and vied with each other in making the evening pass pleasantly.[365]

This seemed to inspire the young employees at the State Hospital, for the next year they held their own Halloween party, which became an annual tradition, including "figures of the Evil One, black cats, grinning pumpkin lanterns and ghostly blue lights, as well as the shrouded figures dressed in sheets and pillow cases." There, they had "a true ghost dance and passed the evening hours playing pranks."[366]

Newberry 4th of July Float, circa 1904 (photo courtesy of Dr. James Surrell).

LETTER TO SANTA CLAUS.

A Lakefield Youngster Writes Letter to Santa Telling His Wants.

A letter directed to Santa Claus,, North Pole, was among the mail arriving at the Newberry postoffice Tuesday, and found its way into THE NEWS box. The youngster makes known his wants as follows:

DEAR SANTA CLAUS:

Will you please bring me a drum and a pair of mits. Ray wants a gun and a pair of mits. Annie wants a doll and a sleigh. Lizzie wants a broom.

JOHNNIE FYVIE

From *The Newberry News* of December 23, 1904. Johnnie Fyvie was nine years old when he wrote this letter. Roy was four, Annie seven, and the practical Lizzie twelve. Several other siblings were not mentioned.

"Captain" Louks (courtesy of
The Newberry News).

This postcard (postmarked 1913) shows the Tahquamenon Falls, as they existed in
the wild and woolly days (author's collection).

**FRANK S.
SEYMOUR**

**PLUMBING
A N
HEATING**
x

ESTIMATES FURNISHED
ON APPLICATION. ALL
KINDS OF SHEET IRON
AND METAL WORK
x

Gun and Bicycle Repair-
ing a Specialty

**NEWBERRY
MICH.**

Advertisement from *The Newberry
News* of November 30, 1906.

This boat was used for an expedition
to the Tahquamenon Falls in 1919
(*Cloverland Magazine*).

THE DAY WE CELEBRATE

Sat., July 3rd

—AT—

NEWBERRY, MICH.

PROGRAM OF EVENTS

Civic Parade will form at the village hall at nine o'clock and headed by the Newberry band will proceed to the Village Park where the exercises of the day will be held

Games and Sports

Water battle between two companies from Fire Department	$15.00	$10.00
100 Yard Dash, for men	2.00	1.00
100 Yard Dash, for boys under 15	2.00	1.00
75 Yard Dash, for boys under 10	2.00	1.00
50 Yard Dash, for girls	2.00	1.00
Sack Race	2.00	1.00
Wheelbarrow Race	2.00	1.00
Bicycle Race, for boys under 15	2.00	1.00
Running Broad Jump	2.00	1.00
Running Broad Jump, for boys under 15	2.00	1.00
Standing Broad Jump	2.00	1.00
Standing Broad Jump, for boys under 15	2.00	1.00
Men's Three-Legged Race	2.00	1.00
Boys' Three-Legged Race	2.00	1.00
Calithumpians	5.00	3.00
Best Business Float	12.00	8.00

JUDGES—Ross Leighton, Nels Anderson and W. H. Krempel

Blue Rock Shoot

U. P. Hospital vs. Rod and Gun Club

Base Ball

Grand Marais vs. U. P. Hospital at 2:00 p.m.

Firemen's Dance— Afternoon and Evening

FIREWORKS IN THE EVENING

OFFICERS OF THE DAY:

President, J. H. Hunter; Orator, Rev. Baxter Waters, Chaplain, Rev. Levi Bird; Reader, Jay Hamilton; Marshal, Dr. H. E. Perry; Secretary, W. E. Donegan; Treasurer, J. E. Quinlan.

Left: Advertisement from *The Newberry News* of June 25, 1909.

Right: Advertisement from *The Newberry News* of June 30, 1905.

Make Your Chidren Happy!

~~By buying them a~~

Handsleigh!

AT

M. R. MANHARD'S

Who carries the Largest Stock in Town
and will sell you one at a

REASONABLE PRICE.

—A FULL STOCK OF—

Heavy and Shelf Hardware.

Corner of Newberry avenue and Helen.

THE VULCAN STORE!

Ha! Ha! Ha! This is a jolly old chimney, the best in the land; I have been depositing my choicest treasures here ever since last Christmas, intending to fill the old thing to the top. But the fellows down stairs keep handing the goods out to the throng that is continually coming and going. Then I thought surely this must be the best place in this cold northern country to distribute my Wares, and kept putting them down with all my might and wondered where all the things could go to. But the mystery was solved when I came to realize that this was the chimney of the

VULCAN -:- STORE
SANTA CLAUS.

R. H. WELLER, Proprietor.

Advertisements from *Newberry News*, December 19, 1890 and
November 25, 1890 (Note the typo—the elusive, inevitable typo).

Chapter Twelve
Sportsmen and Nimrods

*"The upper peninsula will be over-run with deer hunters this season.
They are coming in twos, threes and in parties of from six to ten. They are
accompanied by dogs and are armed with all kinds of death-dealing implements.
One lonely sportsman struck Newberry on Tuesday, his outfit consisting of an old
army rifle and a sack of beans. His having the beans stamps him as a hunter of
experience."*

— *Newberry News*, October 5, 1894

AND IN FALL, THERE WAS hunting.

The late nineteenth century was a time of increased urbanization—and much angst about urbanization. As a result, there was a strong "back to nature" movement, especially among the well-educated, well-off urbanites, with the leisure time and funds with which to enjoy nature. Hunting, fishing, camping, and other wholesome outdoor activities were on the rise, and the Upper Peninsula was well-placed to capture some of that interest.

During the warmer months, many wealthy, big-city men from downstate and beyond flooded the area looking to reconnect with nature. They boarded at the hotels, rented rooms from farmers, and camped, sometimes utilizing old, abandoned lumberjack shacks. Some hired locals to guide them to the best fishing holes and deer spots.

E. O. Lancaster, a traveling salesman from Flint, was an early enthusiast who began taking annual fishing trips to Lake Manistique just as soon as the first railroad was finished. After a business trip to New York City, he would catch a train and ride more than thirty-six hours until he reached Sault Ste. Marie. He then caught another train from the Soo to McMillan, whereupon he rode by horse to Jerry Holland's farm on the northwest corner of the lake, where he rented a room. Lake Manistique, he later wrote in *Forest and Stream* magazine, was "a wild lake, and is hardly ever visited from the outside," where fish were "wonderfully plentiful, including small mouth bass, wall eyed pike, also pickerel and muskellunge—the bass averaging 4½ pounds each."

On the other end of the lake, Gaylord Helmer welcomed annual camping trips by Ohio businessmen who came every year, renting rowboats and a space to pitch their tents. "Mr. Helmer," reported Lancaster, "has a general store and a post office; also, two or three good boats." He could easily "accommodate one or two...camping out parties."[367]

Trout fishing in the rivers and streams was a favorite pastime among the locals. The Two Hearted River was an especially popular destination, and catches could be spectacular. Four men landed eighty-three trout there in 1889. In another instance, one lucky party came back with "three and four hundred of the speckled beauties" from an 1891 trip. And in 1898, a visitor named Clarence Anderson caught a brook trout sixteen-and-a-half inches long.[368]

Ice fishing was sometimes indulged in during the winter. For example, in 1888, "Doc" Hibbard Ingalls had quite a misadventure. He and five men dragged out a heavy shanty onto the ice near Deer Park, preparatory to fishing, but a heavy wind tipped the structure over, pinning the men beneath. They were apparently stuck fast, but unhurt. A passerby rushed over to the Life Saving Station, rounding up its men. The high-spirited crew raced to the rescue, using their Lyle cannon to shoot out a rope to the men (the Lyle cannon being designed, of course, to shoot rescue ropes to floundering ships at sea). They pulled the anglers, one by one, out from underneath the shanty, all while bellowing the hymn "Pull for the Shore, Sailor." The live-savers were clearly (pun intended) having a blast. Once the fishermen were safe, another neighbor came up with a horse and sleigh and toted the shanty to shore, where it was repaired and the party recommenced their fishing.[369]

The "resorter" business grew slowly but surely. In 1914, a robust seventy-six-year-old fisherman named E. S. Whitaker traveled up from Ohio to the lakes, later documenting his experiences in *Field and Stream* magazine. Like Lancaster, he traveled by train to McMillan, where he was picked up by Charles Fyvie "by his auto." The Fyvie family had purchased Gaylord Helmer's business, which now was described as "a good hotel with clean rooms, well furnished, excellent table, with well-cooked meals prepared by Mrs. F., a comfortable parlor facing the lake—and a commodious porch on two sides."

Whitaker took enthusiastically to the lake, rowing about in his "Kalamazoo canvas boat." Sometimes he was accompanied by local guide, Marion Hoig. They went pole fishing, Whitaker lovingly describing his own as an "11-foot split bamboo Wheeler fly rod with an artificial fly attached to a Hildebrant Slim Jim spinner." Hoig preferred "a steel rod and a bit of pork," and he usually brought home more fish. On their best trip, they "caught eleven small mouthed bass, a number of wall-eyed pike and ringed perch, besides a few not-wanted pickerel."

Whitaker described Round Lake as "a pretty body of water" surrounded by farms and "but one summer cottage, owned by Mr. Foster, a merchant of Newberry." Big Manistique Lake boasted "principally wooded shores…interspersed with a number of good farms and at a few favorite spots, cottages of resorters from Detroit, Toledo and Newberry."

South Manistique (Whitefish) Lake had "Gish's Hotel" and "Norton's Resort" and was "quite picturesque," although Whitaker complained that the removal of a dam had "reduced the volume of water very much and consequently the shores are not so attractive."[370]

Other visitors were unaware of any detriments, a Cheboygan visitor declaring there was "no more beautiful spot on the map" than Whitefish Lake. He praised "Englewood Beach…a delightful sandy beach where you may bathe and swim to your heart's content," and "Bohn Island," which had "a log cabin called the Club House equipped with all modern conveniences and even luxuries." Many people from Newberry had built cottages nearby, with names like "Englewood Cottage," "Idle Hours," "Birchwood," and "Log Cabin." Out-of-towners could stay at the Hotel Albany with "guests from every state in the union" and the Hotel Amalvarene, which gave a dancing party every week.[371]

Left: William H. Krempel after a successful fishing expedition. His wife kept this image in a locket after his death (photo courtesy of Jeff Chown).

Right: Young fisherman, from the Krempel family album (photo courtesy of Jeff Chown).

Advertisements from *The Michigan State Gazetteer and Business Directory* for 1906.

Alas, the rivers, which had once featured six-foot sturgeon, held them no more. One of the unforeseen consequences of the river drive was the annihilation of breeding beds. Anglers protested such destruction, but the lumber bosses, and the men who depended on them, prevailed. Fishermen were more successful in passing laws designed to restrict fishing in order protect the fish and their favorite pastime.

The fishing season, in the year 1901, as an example, lasted from May 1 to September 1. Most fish of at least six inches were lawful prey. Net fishing was forbidden. Additionally, the government arranged to plant new species of fish in Michigan's waterways to enhance the experience. "German Brown Trout" and "California Trout" (rainbow trout) were introduced to UP streams in the 1880s, joining the native brook trout.[372]

Likewise, laws restricting hunting were growing in power. By the time Newberry and Luce County came into being, Michigan already had conservation laws on the books. Various animals were allowed to be hunted at different times of the year, but the richest hunting season was in the fall. By 1901, the fall season began October 1 with the allowable killing of partridge, quail, spruce hen, woodcock, ducks, and geese. Beginning October 15, the hunter also could take fox and squirrels. By November 8, three weeks opened up when deer could be taken. The fall season ended on November 30.[373]

Protected animals—those not to be killed at all—included deer fawns, beaver, moose, elk, caribou, prairie chickens, pheasant, wild turkey, and wild pigeon. The use of dogs, lights, and motorboats was prohibited.[374]

Hunters were allowed to take three deer each year per license. Many locals (especially those with lower incomes) were irritated by the conservation laws, which restricted, punished, and cut off a cheap source of food and fun for them. They tended to see conservation laws as instruments designed for the benefit of the rich and the detriment of the poor. Additionally, hunters from downstate could be very annoying.

Luce County residents were both amused and irritated by the yearly influx of "sportsmen" and "nimrods." More than five hundred deer hunters alone entered Luce County in November 1902. Locals appreciated the business, to be sure, but often found their guests hopelessly inept.[375]

Much scorn was heaped on a Judge Whelan of Detroit, who arrived with a party in 1895. He managed to shoot just one deer, a "poor, half-starved pet fawn that belonged to a little boy in Lakefield" and "did most of his hunting in the hotel," only later arranging for someone else's kill to be delivered to his door in Detroit.[376]

Judge Whelan returned in the fall of 1897 for another try. After several fruitless days of Whelan wandering about the woods, local lumberman Cornelius D. Danaher procured a freshly shot deer, tied it to a tree, and called for the judge. When Judge Whalen saw the deer, he at once let loose with his double-barreled shotgun, letting off "several rounds of buckshot" in the rough direction of the corpse, where "only one pellet touched the deer." The judge was apparently a little confused, reportedly exclaiming "Why in Hades didn't it run?" Nevertheless, he took his prize home to Detroit, boasting that "he was the only man of the party that shot a deer." Some said that the wealthy lumberman did this because he felt sorry for the fellow, but Mr. Danaher himself admitted it was merely to win a bet.[377]

In another case, a group of out-of-state hunters arrived in town in 1916 and arranged for Emil B. Crane to ferry them up the Tahquamenon River in his little steamer, the *Mary Ann.* They would tow their supplies (several weeks' worth) in a scow behind them. Jovially, the hunters piled up all their gear into the scow until it was bobbing down low, only a few inches above the water line. Not a mile downriver, the overloaded craft dipped its nose underwater, flooding. The hunters watched helplessly as their tents, blankets, and other gear sank to the

A postcard showing the happy folk on an expedition to the falls, postmarked 1917 (photo courtesy of Sterling McGinn).

Fun on the river, circa 1908. The men are identified as Myron Chamberlain, Jim Foster, Percy Foster (no relation), Bill Fretz, and Frank Seymour. They are traveling in Bill's boat, the *Ruth*. (photo courtesy of Sterling McGinn).

bottom or floated merrily away. Each man lost about $100 worth of equipment, as well as their good humor. Packing up what they had left, they boarded the train for home. Wet blankets, indeed.[378]

Once, in 1914, an unexpected cold snap stranded hundreds of hunters out in the woods. Many had rented boats to take them up the Tahquamenon River, which was now "filled several feet deep with slush snow." A lucky few were within easy reach of the logging railroads and could catch rides, but others had to hike up to eighteen or twenty miles through the snow, abandoning their supplies, their camping gear, and their kills. Several exhausted men, within four miles of the mill town of Eckerman, paid a passing sleigh $10 each to ride the rest of the way. Eventually, it was reported, seventeen boats had become stuck in the ice in that storm, their owners having to wait for a thaw in order to retrieve them, some resorting to axes and saws.[379]

Many visitors had accidents with their guns. Year after year, the locals lost cows and horses by misdirected bullets. Year after year, they groused about it. Sometimes, the visitors shot themselves. In 1913, a hunter named Charles Erickson, who worked at Sage Station, was climbing into a rowboat with his companions. He then used his loaded shotgun to push the boat out from shore. The gun went off, and Erickson's right arm was shattered. In a "stern race against death," his friends had to carry him eleven miles through the woods to Sage Station, then onto a handcar down the railroad tracks to Newberry. Erickson was "maimed for life."[380]

Sometimes, they shot each other, mistaking their cohorts for deer. Every year, the paper ran a short story, usually titled something macabre, like "This Season's Death Toll," and listed as many as thirty to forty names from hunting accidents all over the UP, many fatal. Joseph Sanders, of Calhoun County, was one such fellow. The old gentleman supposed he was shooting at the hindquarters of a deer, but actually shot and killed his nephew, John.[381]

Other city slickers vanished in the woods, never to be seen again. For instance, take Robert Shattock, a "motor-cycle dealer" from Detroit who disappeared in November 1914. He was last seen entering a one-mile stretch of woods between a creek and a road and never reappeared. Mr. Shattock had previously expressed doubts about his survival skills, reportedly warning friends that he'd commit suicide if he ever became lost. Sure enough, the next year a fisherman found his body, bullet hole through his skull, lying gently on a bed of cedar boughs. He was only one mile from the railroad tracks.[382]

The most famous case of a missing hunter was that of Harry Brownell, twenty-three, of St. Charles, Michigan. During the hunting season of 1909, he traveled up from St. Charles with a pal, leaving his new bride at home. The friends intended on doing a little hunting in the forests about six miles south of Newberry. One night, Harry sauntered out of camp and did not come back. His worried friend alerted the locals, who formed a "searching party" the next day.[383]

The searching party grew to include more than thirty "woodsmen," the sheriff's department, a trained bloodhound, Harry's father, all of the Masons in town, and all the other hunting parties in the area (save one, whose members were not interested in helping and were thus ordered to "get out" by infuriated local officials). Hundreds of men combed the woods for two weeks, forming human chains through the woods.[384]

Left: Advertisements from *The Newberry News* of November 4, 1892 and November 3, 1905.

William Henry Krempel, Newberry and Dollarville merchant and outdoor enthusiast, with a brace of pheasants (photo courtesy of Jeff Chown).

Lakefield bear hunters from around 1905 - 1910. They are identified as Edith Fuller, Louis Fuller, Jessie Smathers, Lawrence Horner, Alfred Fuller, Lena Fuller, and Riley Fuller, Jr. (photo courtesy of Joanne Jessee).

The weather was "extremely mild," reported *The Newberry News*, so it "would be impossible to travel for any great length of time in any direction before he would come to a road that would take him to some settlement." Thus, they feared Henry Brownell had been killed in some accident.[385]

The weather turned colder. "It is now believed," stated the paper, "that the missing man has become crazed from the exposure and fear, and this makes the work of the rescue doubly difficult." Then, a "blinding snow storm" hit, "effectually obliterating the trail and making it impossible for the dog to longer follow the scent." The reports of "an apparently crazy man" who "had come out of the woods and shot at Miss Smythe" turned out to be nothing.[386]

The authorities gave up on November 26, 1909, leaving only the Masons and Harry's distraught father to continue the search, but even they had to stop before long. "Had the earth opened and swallowed him up," mused the newspaper, "Brownell could not have more completely or mysteriously disappeared."[387]

He was almost certainly dead, but his bride refused to accept it. "No, no," she cried, "Harry is not dead. If he were dead I should know it in some way. He may be in awful trouble somewhere, but he isn't dead." When the census taker came through a few months later, she reported herself as still married, with Harry living with her and her parents, and working as a freight clerk.

Four years later, "while attending a picture show," she fainted when she thought she recognized her husband in a film taken in Chicago. She gathered a group of family and friends "and all agreed it was Harry Brownell or a most remarkable double."

"Perhaps he was lost and the hardships he underwent caused his mind to become blank," she was quoted as saying. "Such things have happened. Perhaps he has forgotten all about us, but maybe some shock will cause him to remember and then he'll come back home."

"He may be deranged," concluded the *News*. "It is possible he has lost all memory of his wife and the tiny garments which she was so busy fashioning for the 'wee little mannie' they were planning for, but whatever his condition, she hopes and prays to find him soon."[388]

But the man in the film was not Harry after all, and the mystery was solved for good ten months later. Two employees of the State Hospital, Irving Weber and J. A. Baetz, were out hunting. Weber sat down on a log to rest and "looking down noticed the remains of a skeleton at his feet." Among the "handful of bleaching bones" were personal items, including a rifle and a diamond ring marked with a "B." Harry's father was called up, and he confirmed that the items had indeed belonged to Harry. "He was shot in the back," reported the paper "and probably instantly killed, the body pitching forward where it was found." The coroner's verdict read "came to his death by being shot by parties unknown."

Harry Brownell, as he looked in 1909.

Whether by terrible design or terrible accident, Harry Brownell had been shot to death, his body covered with leaves to keep it hidden. "And thus endeth another grim tragedy of the north woods," remarked *The Newberry News* sadly.[389]

The Masonic Temple, built in 1915. Brown & Turnbull rented the first floor as a grocery store. The Presbyterian church can be seen in the background (photo courtesy of Sterling McGinn).

Above: Several fraternal order advertisements that appeared in *The Newberry News* of December 19, 1890.

Chapter Thirteen
Accidents, Fires, and Other Disasters

"The matter of fire protection was discussed at the last two meetings of the village board.... We are glad to see action taken in this matter, as the recent fires have proved conclusively that some means should be at once adopted to insure our citizens fire protection, as we know not at what moment the dread destroyer of property may come upon us."

— *Newberry News,* June 17, 1886

LIFE IN THE EARLY DAYS was fraught with danger. Accidental death was lurking around every corner. Horses kicked; blizzards struck. Calamities happened, even if a body was stone cold sober.

In 1888, John Rosin, a fifty-year-old Lakefield farmer, walked into town and was unable to start back due to the bad weather. He "lingered around the hotels and was seen at the Nelson House at 3 o'clock a.m.," after which he went to visit his friend, John Patterson, who was running the night shift at the furnace. While leaving, Rosin slipped beneath a wheel of the great engine, got caught on its spokes, and then became pinned "in an incredibly small space between the wheel and floor." He was not found for twenty minutes, when Patterson heard him moaning, "Oh, Johnny, stop her, stop her!" This he did immediately, but Rosin, being "a mass of broken bones," only lived for twenty minutes more, his last words being about his children and asking Patterson to write them.[390]

Three years later, a "fearful explosion" blew out two walls of the furnace stack, which fell down, collapsing the roof of the casting house below. John Labombard, who had been laboring in the stack itself, was "literally cooked to death." Six other men, working down in the casting house, were badly injured, one man having his feet burned by molten iron. Dozens of men were thrown out of work while the furnace made the necessary repairs—that cost upwards of $5,000. The townsfolk organized a subscription committee, which raised $110 for John Labombard's widow and small son.[391]

In 1899, sixty-year-old James Devine, one of Newberry's oldest citizens and current manager of the American House hotel, was repairing the steam engine at the shingle mill in Dollarville. His clothing caught in the shaft, "drawing him in and crushing the life out of him." His arms, legs, and ribs were all broken and he died within a few hours.[392]

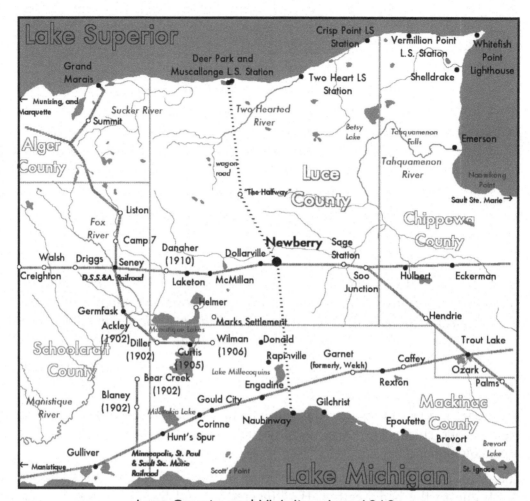

Luce County and Vicinity, circa 1910.
This was the pinnacle of railroads. Within the next decade, tracks would begin to be pulled up, stations would close, and the state highway system would grow.

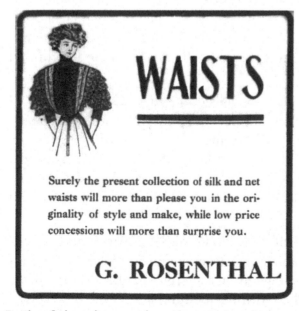

WAISTS

Surely the present collection of silk and net waists will more than please you in the originality of style and make, while low price concessions will more than surprise you.

G. ROSENTHAL

FALL SUITS...

of incomparable make and style. It will do you good to see the swellest styles in town. Prices reasonable.

The life of clothes is lengthened when they're built right. Hershfield Clothes are hand built—the shape stays.

G. ROSENTHAL

Both of the above advertisements appeared in *The Newberry News* of August 28, 1908.

Left: Advertisements that appeared in *The Newberry News* of August 28, 1908.

Below: Advertisements that appeared in *The Newberry News* February 23, 1917 and October 7, 1904.

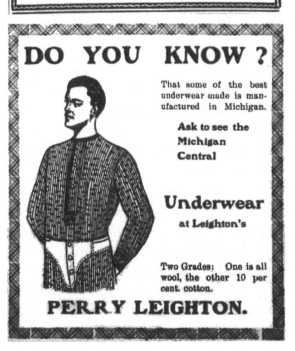

On May 31, 1913, Robert Milne stopped at the drugstore in McMillan to pick up a bottle of carbolic acid for his employer's cattle and a bottle of whiskey for himself. Unfortunately (and contrary to state law), Dr. Leland Moss had packaged both bottles almost identically. Robert Milne "swallowed a huge draught and died within 20 minutes." Dr. Moss was arrested and pled guilty to "a charge of selling poisons in a manner contrary to law." The poor doctor had, explained *The Newberry News*, "been a victim of the drug habit for years and had taken the cure several times." This time, the judge waived imprisonment, and in return, Dr. Moss would make a "final effort to straighten up." But on June 30, 1917, as the *News* sadly reported, "the habit proved too strong for his willpower to resist, and finding himself again relapsing into his evil ways, he evidently decided to end it all and sent a bullet crashing through his brain."[393]

John Tuskey of Rapinville slipped and fell into "the maw of a threshing machine" in October 1912. He broke his neck, and his body was "ground to pieces." James Mackey was struck over the head by an iron pipe when a steam valve broke at the Water & Light plant. He never regained consciousness. William and John Kak got caught in a sand slide, becoming buried under six feet of earth. Only John was rescued in time.[394]

Workplace conditions were not the only danger. Horrible accidents happened everywhere to anyone.

Sarah McPhail and a party of other women had attended a church meeting and were returning to their homes by using a small handcar on the railroad tracks. When a "gasoline speeder" rammed into them, Mrs. McPhail's chest was crushed and she died. Mrs. Albert Reitenbaugh was gored by an "ugly cow" and given very painful injuries. Mrs. R. Boulton was picking potatoes when a dead tree blew over and broke her skull. Mrs. J. C. Weller was playing Mrs. Claus in an 1887 church concert when she bent over a lighted candle and her costume caught fire. While her neighbors tried to smother the flames, Mrs. Weller panicked. She bolted for the outdoors, while the audience (mostly children) shrieked in terror. At the door, two more men caught Mrs. Weller and pounded the flames out, but all of them suffered severe burns.

Mrs. Mary Lyons was picking raspberries by the side of the railroad tracks in July 1892 with her little son. Two mail coaches thundered by, derailed at the worst possible moment, and slammed Mrs. Lyons and her child into a ditch, knocking the woman unconscious. A Marquette doctor was called down to treat her, but he paused to watch workmen trying to pull the mail coaches out of the ditch. A metal cable caught on a stump. The men kept pushing and the cable sprang free, slashing through the air and "striking Dr. Northrup on the abdomen." He almost died.[395]

Mrs. Lyons' little boy was only bruised, but he was very lucky, as childhood accidents were common and even expected. In November 1901, Marguerite Barber, then a toddler, was running and playing, blowing on a tin whistle. When she tripped and fell, the whistle jammed into her mouth, lacerating her throat. In 1911, a girl identified as "the little daughter of Mr. and Mrs. Victor Johnson," was watching a merry-go-round at a street fair, when one of the seats flew off, tumbling out riders and flying onto the child. "Her forehead struck against the cement gutter, inflicting an ugly wound." While riding the same merry-go-round, Lottie Cameron had a finger crushed so badly that it had to be amputated.[396]

Right: Advertisements from *The Newberry News* of February 12, 1904.

Below: Advertisements from *The Newberry News* of October 29, 1915.

Willie Brebner, age five, was almost killed by an enraged bull that was wandering the streets of town. Three-year-old Eddie Reed of Dollarville nearly lost an eye in a similar incident. In response, the village council hired a pound master, under orders to round up and detain stray cattle, horses, and hogs. This was a very unpopular ordinance. Someone even attempted to burn the pound down before people got used to the idea.[397]

Catherine Richardson was playing with a new sled on the sidewalk in December 1909 when a horse pulling a sleigh became frightened by the train and bolted. The animal fled up onto the sidewalk, and his sleigh caught the little girl and dragged her an entire block. That she suffered only a fractured shoulder was considered a miracle. Thirteen-year-old Clarence Zenker dropped his gun while hunting in 1907. The gun discharged, damaging the muscles in his arm, and he was reported "crippled for life." His cousin, Carl Zenker, was nine years old in 1914 when he brought a stick of dynamite to school, lit it, and blasted off part of his hand. Little Lillian Ackley of nearby Germfask was "maimed for life" at the age of five after her young siblings played with a loaded hunting gun. Part of her foot had to be amputated.[398]

They were the lucky ones. In 1905, ten-year-old Royal Clyde McDurmon was watching a Fourth of July hot air balloon when a heavy pole holding the balloon down slipped and fell, "striking the unfortunate little fellow on the head" and killing him instantly.[399] Two-year-old Victor Campbell strangled himself to death in his own yard while playing with a rope and a gate door.

John Shelson, a "surfman" (live saver) at Deer Park, lost two children on two separate occasions to accidental gunshots. The first, eight-year-old James, was killed when Surfman Graves of the Life Saving Station took a shot at a flock of geese that turned out to be a group of children playing by the pond. Two years later, the teenage son of the captain of the Life Saving Station was doing a little target practice. He missed his target, and the bullet sailed through a small woods and hit twelve-year-old Alta Shelson, who was attending a bonfire on the shore with her friends. Two different doctors agreed there was nothing that could be done, and she died two days later.[400]

Teenagers took stupid chances back then, too, often with fatal consequences. In 1898, a group of young men had taken to hitching rides on the trains, and then jumping off before they reached the station. Sixteen-year-old James Nichols was one such boy. Unfortunately, in the dark he jumped off the train and into a culvert, knocking himself unconscious. More unfortunate still, he was now bleeding internally, which he unsuccessfully tried to hide from his mother. By the time she summoned a doctor, there was nothing to be done, and he died a few days later.[401]

Yet the most feared disaster was fire.

In a world built of pine, powered by coal, and lit by kerosene, fire was always an ever-present threat. The people of Luce County lived one little mistake—one dropped match, one unwatched stove—away from catastrophe. There's a reason that electric lights and steam radiators were considered luxuries.

The Hamilton family of Pentland Township knew this well. Philip Hamilton and his wife, Emma, ran the American Hotel in town and the forty-acre Maple Leaf Farm in Pentland Township, where their hired men raised "numerous cows and horses" as well as "green corn, string beans, radishes, turnips and lettuce" for his hotel. Phil was a successful and prosperous

The William H. Ackley family, in 1905. Lillian is the little girl in the center.
Front Row: William (7), Lillian (5), Edward (12)
Middle Row: Emma (27), William (47), Phoebe (42), Margaret (23)
Back Row: Charles (23), Emogene (14), Thomas (20)
(photo courtesy of Brandy Walsh).

Left: Advertisement from *The Newberry News* of October 29, 1915.
Right: The rebuilt Maple Leaf Farm, from October 1894.

businessman, lumberman, contractor, and politician. He served as a trustee on the village council, and later as supervisor of Pentland Township.[402]

Phil was a "genial, whole souled" citizen who enjoyed life, weighed 280 pounds, and was said to have a fine singing voice. He also was once arrested for resisting an officer, held dog fights, and once kept a pet bear, which he shot when people grew bored with it. Mrs. Hamilton was an active member of the Presbyterian church and sponsored Sunday school picnics at their farm. The family had terribly bad luck when it came to fire.[403]

In December 1887, a tenant of their Pentland Township farm dropped a lamp, which exploded and destroyed the house. No one was hurt, but the two tenants and their wives lost everything they had. The Hamiltons received only $400 from their insurance policy.[404]

A few years later, tiring of the hotel business, Phil and Emma moved the family out to their farm in the fall, improving and enlarging the structure. Unfortunately, the next February, the roof caught fire and the farmhouse burned to the ground again. They rebuilt once more.[405]

Phil died in 1897 and Emma moved into a new house in town with her young children. Two years later, she accidentally knocked over a lamp, which caught the floor on fire. She was able to call the fire department, but the squad's first water hose burst under the pressure and the fire was not put out for a long while, creating considerable damage to the home.[406]

Finally, in 1901, while the family was away, the newly remodeled house caught fire from another exploded lamp. The building was completely destroyed, along with all its contents. This time there was no insurance. The Hamilton family was fortunate in one aspect, at least: No one died in any of their four fires. Countless others were not so lucky.[407]

Fred Cassady was a one-armed farmer from Reed City, whose sister Maud had worked as an attendant at the State Hospital. Maud had married John Somerville and the young couple acquired a small farm in Pentland Township that they intended to rent out. In 1902, Fred moved to the area so he could work this farm, along with his wife, Mary, and three small children.

In June 1903, Mary gave birth their fourth child, and almost immediately afterward fell ill with typhoid fever. Maud Somerville came over to help nurse her. One hot August day, around noon, the family discovered that the house was on fire and spreading quickly. Horror-stricken, they remembered that four-year-old Vernon was napping upstairs, and the staircase was now aflame. Fred wrapped himself in a wet blanket and "plunged through the flames" for his son. Meanwhile, Maud got Mary out of bed and outside, along with six-year-old Howard, two-year-old Neola May, and baby Neva. Out in the yard, frantic, they called and waited for Fred and Vernie. Neither came out. Their charred remains were discovered later.[408]

Mary, worn out from typhoid and "prostrated by the tragedy," died a week later. Then Maud Somerville came down with typhoid herself and the baby was sent downstate to be cared for by relatives. On September 13, 1903, Baby Neva died of "cholera infantum," a type of gastroenteritis thought to be caused by hot weather and bad milk, especially common in bottle-fed babies.[409]

Little Neola was taken in by a family called Taylor in Clinton County, Michigan, where she died of diphtheria in 1905 at the age of four. Only the oldest boy, Howard, lived to grow up. He was raised by the Somervilles, eventually moving with them to Munising, and later to California, where he died in 1971.[410]

Newberry firefighters, about 1890, posing by the Village Hall which doubled as the firehouse. The men are identified as:

Front Row: John C. Patterson, Martin Skipper, Kenneth McLellan, Mike Hammes, Ed Munson, Tom Webster, Louis Liberty, John L. Brown, Neil McLean, and a Mr. Shirley.

James Holt is standing on the hose wheel.

Back Row: H. R. McInnes, Lyle Younglove, Ed Cyr, Sandy Trerice, William "Long Bill" Johnson, Mason Howlett (the six sitting on the wagon), Bob Johnson, Alex Main and William Hines (standing).[411]

(photo courtesy of the Luce County Historical Society).

Advertisements from *The Newberry News* of December 11, 1908 and November 11, 1905.

In July 1905, a similar tragedy occurred in McMillan. Daniel Long was building up the kitchen fire early one morning using a can of kerosene. He had recently moved his family up to Michigan where he had taken a job as an engineer with the Northern Cooperage Company.

That particular morning, the can did not happen to contain kerosene, but gasoline. The resulting explosion encased the house. Dan, a "living sheet of flame," ran shrieking outside and collapsed. He lived for a few hours before mercifully dying. Upstairs, a pregnant Mrs. Long found the staircase blazing and retreated to the window, intending on jumping first and catching her children. The fall, however, injured her back so badly that she was unable to stand. Ten-year-old Floyd jumped next, and was caught by Darb Tait, a neighbor who had run over to help. Four children were left inside.[412]

Seven-year-old Alpha grabbed Paul (6) and Judd (2) and forced them out the window. Alpha, however, was unable to find Coral (4) and had to leave her behind. Coral was "burned to a crisp." The community collected a "large purse" for Mrs. Long, who used it to move back home to her father's house in Ohio, where her last child, Lewis, was born in 1906.

Another horrific fire happened later that year in Laketon, the little whistle stop west of McMillan. Rudolph Wiertella was the station agent for the DSS&A there, and he and his wife, Augusta, made extra money by renting beds to railroad men in two converted boxcars near their home.

On September 12, 1905, while the men were at work, Mrs. Wiertella decided to walk to McMillan to get her mail. The baby she would take with her, but she thought she would leave three-year-old William and two-year-old Minnie at home. All of the men were working and there was no one to watch the children. Not wanting them to wander into the woods, or into an oncoming train, she locked them up in one of the box cars, after carefully removing all the matches.

She had not been careful enough. Coming home, she found both boxcars ablaze. Men working nearby had responded to the flames, but not realizing children were locked inside, had concentrated on removing furniture from the second, unlocked, less fiery car. "The bodies of the two children being burned beyond all recognition," reported the newspaper, "very little... was found to consign to the tomb." Although Augusta went on to have ten more children with Rudolph, "the Laketon horror" must have haunted her to the end of her days.[413]

In 1914, a "most spectacular fire" devastated Dollarville. Although Dollarville, when it was founded, had established one of the most complete systems of fire protection around, the years had taken its toll. Now, as the newspaper explained, "The buildings were mere shells, built of pine and...dry as timber."

Someone (unnamed in the news story) fiddling with a new "picture machine" somehow caused an explosion and "almost instantly the building was a mass of flame." Although a bucket brigade formed immediately and "worked like fiends," they were unable to check the fire. Soon "the flames leaped from one building to another with lightning-like rapidity until the whole western end of the village was a mass of flames."

The fire destroyed William Krempel's general store (and all his stock), the offices of the South Shore Cedar Company (and all its records), and the homes of twenty-two families (and all their worldly possessions).

Dollarville Fire, 1914 (photo courtesy of Sterling McGinn).

The McLeod House burns. At this time, the business was owned by Duncan Campbell, who had purchased it from William Green, who had purchased it from Dan McLeod. A snowroller can be seen in the lower left corner (photo courtesy of Sterling McGinn).

The fire spread so quickly and so ferociously that nothing could be saved. Abandoned furniture burned in the street, where it had been dropped by fleeing homeowners. When the flames finally died down, half the village was gone. County residents scrambled, trying to find space for twenty-two homeless families. Only a week later, the Dollarville Lumber and Shingle Mill closed its doors, citing "absolutely no demand for either shingles or lumber." Fifty men lost their jobs overnight.

Dollarville never really recovered.[414]

Many families left and never returned, such as the McCloskeys. James and Emily McCloskey had lived in Dollarville since the late 1880s, but now they had nothing to show for it. They and their nine children packed up and started over in Cloquet, Minnesota. Two years later, a massive forest fire ripped through the region, once again leaving the McCloskeys homeless. Sticking together, they eventually ended up in Ohio.[415]

Those devastated by illness or accident, and without the wherewithal to adapt, may well have been taken care of by the county's commission of the poor, which ran a "poor house" and "poor farm" south of Newberry. There, a caretaker looked after Luce County residents who had become elderly, impoverished, or otherwise incapacitated. Inmates of the poor farm were given food, clothing, medical treatment, and burials. The Poor Fund also provided "relief" for widows, deserted wives, and families stricken by illness, allowing them to stay in their own homes. In the 1898 fiscal year, the poor farm gave care to fifty-seven men, two women, and four children, as well as supporting six families living in town. The Newberry village council helped further by exempting all widows from village taxes.[416]

Once, during a depression in 1895, a lack of tax revenue forced the poor house to close. The sole inmate at the time was taken in personally by the supervisor of McMillan Township. By autumn, however, the county had managed to reopen the institution. Edward Cooper, who had lost the use of one arm, was appointed caretaker at a salary of $15 per month. Of course, recipients actually had to be Luce County residents to get any aid. Wandering indigents were encouraged to get out of town and not come back.[417]

Orphaned, abandoned, neglected, or delinquent children faced a similar situation. The poor house was not equipped to take care of parentless children. If lucky, orphans were taken in by their relatives. Kindhearted neighbors may have occasionally adopted them, but this was rare. Usually, orphans with no reliable relatives were "sent to Coldwater," the state's "Public School for Orphaned Children" in Coldwater, Michigan. Another option, after 1899, was the Good Will Farm, an orphanage at Houghton.[418]

Chapter Fourteen
In Sickness and Health

"At one time the idea was generally prevalent that the appearance of disease was due to the influence of evil spirits. At the present time it is demonstrated that many of the most common, as well as the most dangerous of diseases, have their origin in some specific germ, called, commonly, a disease germ, each germ producing a disease according to its kind. So we have typhoid fever, cholera, yellow fever, scarlet fever, diphtheria and other forms."

— Dr. Almon W. Nicholson, "How Householders May Ward Off Disease," *Newberry News*, March 23, 1889

A DEPRESSING ADDENDUM TO EVERY NEW town is that alongside the new schools, businesses, and homes, the people also have to build a new cemetery. Newberry's first cemetery was located at the foot of Truman, in a plot of land that later became Sherman Park. This location was quickly considered "unsuitable," so the Peninsular Land Company donated ten acres of land between Newberry and Dollarville, five acres of which were consecrated especially for Catholic burials. The Forest Home Cemetery Association formed to organize the selling of lots and upkeep of grounds. Its first burial was the infant son of Mr. and Mrs. Mackea, who died in September 1887. Later, most of the graves in the old cemetery were disinterred and reburied in the new.[419]

There is a playground legend in Newberry that passes from schoolchild to schoolchild. It says that in the cemetery there is a certain tombstone belonging to a young girl. Set in the center of the tombstone is a circle of purple glass and underneath the glass is a photograph of the deceased child. The photo is said to change, children assure one another. Every year, the girl ages or changes expression. Every year, it is different.

The "purple bubble" gravestone is worn now, and somewhat unreadable. "Beatrice" it says, "dgtr of Wm. & D (illegible, but probably Hayes). Died (illegible) 1898, Age 4 years, 4 months, 20 days." Underneath a circle of protective purple glass is a crumbling photo. The figure in the photo does not bring to mind a four-year old child; it does rather look like an old woman. The photo may have been taken after death.

William B. Heighs (also spelled Heighes and Hayes) was a millwright at Dollarville, and he and his wife, Delilah, did have a daughter who might fit this grave. This little girl does not appear to have had a birth certificate or death certificate. Her birth and death were recorded in the newspaper, which proves that she existed at least. She was born in June 1894, and died

October 27, 1898, which means she was aged four years, four months, and some days. The name of this little girl was not noted, but it could well be Beatrice. Whatever she died of was not noted either, only that it was an "illness." This tombstone, with its photograph and carved vines, must have cost a fortune.[420]

Children born into this era faced a strong possibility of an early death. Matt and Tina Jacobson had twelve children between 1903 and 1920, seven of whom died as infants.

The infamous "purple bubble grave." Poor little Beatrice: gone, but not forgotten, although probably not in the way her grieving parents meant. (author's photo).

Edward and Bertha Boggs, a Kentucky family who came north in the 1910s, had thirteen children altogether, five of which died as babies. Phil and Emma Hamilton lost five of their eight children, and David and Mary Ann Davern lost nine out of twelve.[421]

The first year was the most dangerous time. Stillbirths, inanition, and "general weakness" claimed many babies at birth and in the first week. In the winter, babies died of lung diseases, like pneumonia, bronchitis, or La Grippe (influenza). In the summer, a wide variety of digestive problems killed many infants. They died from diarrhea, colitis, gastro-enteritis, cholera infantum ("summer complaint"), indigestion, obstructed bowels, and more.

Toddlers and young children were a little more likely to survive, but dangers lurked all around them. Quite a few were scalded to death by overturned pots of boiling water. Eighteen-month-old Robert Mullen drank "a quantity of kerosene" and died.[422]

Advertisements from *The Newberry* News of
November 18 1892 and March 16, 1889.

Advertisements from *The Newberry News* of October 21, 1892,
and a health notice from the early 1900s.

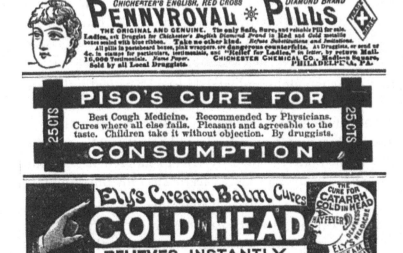

Advertisements from *The Newberry News* of
November 28, 1890 and December 19, 1890.

Many fell victim to the "childhood diseases," which included measles, diphtheria, scarlet fever, and whooping cough.

Diphtheria was a respiratory, bacterial illness that made it very difficult to breathe, choking patients to death. It was "a black threat eternally hanging over every child life," as it mostly struck children, especially younger children. Whooping cough was a similar disease, which closed the airways and made breathing difficult. Measles was generally benign, but not always, especially if it transitioned into pneumonia.

Scarlet fever was characterized by high fever, sore throat, and a red rash. Luce County had breakouts of it in 1892, 1895, 1902, 1907 (no deaths), 1908, 1919, and 1920, mostly in the spring. Even children who survived this fever were at risk of dangerous complications like heart disease, kidney disease, rheumatism, deafness, and blindness (Helen Keller is a famous victim). Cornelius "Connie" Harris developed scarlet fever in 1907 at the age of eleven. The disease led to complications that nearly killed him and was further blamed for his subsequent appendicitis, as well as an abscess that he had to travel to Bay City to get removed. That summer, he had three operations in total. He was lucky, though. He survived. The blame for scarlet fever and diphtheria was placed on dirty yards and dirty sinks. During outbreaks, residents were urged to clean their yards of rubbish, garbage, and filth to check its spread.[423]

Between 1885 and 1920, fourteen children died from diphtheria, most under ten and all under twenty years of age. Measles outbreaks caused the deaths of at least twelve children during the same period, while eight died of scarlet fever. Countless others missed school.

Older children and young adults who survived were now set for a few decades of good health…unless, of course, they came down with tonsillitis, appendicitis, meningitis, or "brain fever." Some women, of course, died in childbirth, but not as many as you would have thought. In 1904, Archie Campbell's entire family became seriously ill "by eating canned salmon." All ages died from typhoid fever and dysentery, which was spread by contaminated food and water. Emerson, the nearby sawmill village on Lake Superior, suffered from annual typhoid outbreaks during the 1890s.[424]

Twelve percent of adults developed tuberculosis and were condemned to a long, slow, inevitable death. Tuberculosis (also called consumption or phthias) was greatly feared. It was rarely referred to in the paper without the adjective "dread" hanging somewhere about. It was the dread disease, the great white plague, the insidious disease, the relentless disease.

A disease of the lungs, consumption was contagious and fatal, killing its patiently slowly—sometimes taking years. Consumption struck anyone, anywhere, rich or poor, tidy or slovenly, native born and immigrant alike, and treatments were few and mostly ineffective. Many sufferers headed west, hoping the drier air of the Rockies and the deserts would help. Sometimes it did. Mostly, it didn't. Ten percent of deaths at the State Hospital were from tuberculosis. Twenty percent of teachers were said to be sufferers. The average age at death was only thirty-two.*

After age forty, good health often began to fade. Cancer, Bright's disease (disease of the kidneys), alcoholism, apoplexy, and various kinds of heart disease took their toll. The elderly, too, had to worry about bronchitis and pneumonia, which now reared up as a deadly force once again. The highest age reached by any Luce County resident, in the early days, was believed to

---

* Those who died of tuberculosis include the following people mentioned in this book: John Cooper, Catherine Richardson, John Sherman, Tom Boulton, Fred R. Fuller, Mrs. Eli King, and J. D. Parker.

be Mrs. Lucy A. Slavan (from Kentucky), who died in 1918 at the reported age of ninety-five.[425]

The strongest and best weapon against disease was prevention. Doctors hyped cleanliness, cleanliness, and more cleanliness. "Every person should take a warm bath with soap at least once a week, and if possible, should have a cold bath every morning," they said. They urged their patients to get fresh air, keep a clean house free of dust, and also avoid whiskey.[426]

Hygiene was a topic taught in schools. School boards were assured that "proper construction, warming, ventilating and lighting of school buildings will go a great way towards remedying this situation" (referring to sickly students). In 1913, boards also

Dr. A. W. Nicholson
(courtesy of Billie Nicholson)

were urged to replace the old-fashioned, common drinking dipper and pail with a modern, hygienic drinking fountain.[427]

The modern sewer system found in town helped. The lucky houses that were connected to it were able to whisk their wastewater away through pipes, where it was dumped directly into the Tahquamenon River. The early residents had no problem with this. Out of sight, out of mind.[428]

At the first sign of any outbreak, schools and other public places were shuttered, anything to prevent the spread. Schools closed due to epidemics of measles or diphtheria, scarlet fever, smallpox, and others. In many cases, patients and their families were quarantined, forbidden to leave their homes, or receive visitors. Other times, the sick would be gathered together in a makeshift "pest house."[429]

Newberry's first physician was Dr. Hiram C. Farrand, hired by the Vulcan Furnace Company. He was already in his sixties when he came to Newberry in 1883 with his daughter. A Civil War veteran, he was especially skilled at amputations and had worked for decades as a "railroad surgeon." His partner, Dr. S. John Fraser, arrived in 1885 with a medical library of 100 volumes, and a specialty in children's diseases and midwifery. Later, Dr. Fraser fell under contract with the Peninsular Land Company to treat its employees under the "insurance principle."[430]

The year 1887 brought Dr. Almon W. Nicholson, who had formerly worked for the state government and whose main focus was disease. He had moved to Newberry hoping its northern climate would be better for his own precarious health. Dr. Nicholson was an intellectual who wrote articles for the general public and medical journals, studied meteorology, raised exotic plants, gave lectures, and wrote poetry. At his death in 1907, he owned a private library of 3,000 volumes and several microscopes.[431]

Yet most of the doctors arrived in Newberry in the early days were greenhorns, fresh out of medical school. Dr. Frederick W. Neal was one such, who arrived in Luce County in 1891 to partner with Dr. Nicholson.

Dr. F. W. Neal
(*Newberry Enterprise*, 1894)

"Of a jovial and hearty disposition," he was easily "one of the most popular and best known men in the county." He left town in 1905, "retiring" in order to go back to school, but died of cancer five years later.[432]

Dr. George B. Kelso, another newbie, arrived in town in 1886. He was a physician of the homeopathic persuasion, and he quickly became successful—marrying, building himself a large home, and attending his rounds in a horse and buggy. Though successful, he didn't stay long. Dr. Kelso left in 1888, moving to Indiana, where he eventually became the head of his own hospital.[433]

Dr. G. B. Kelso (*The Pantagraph*, Bloomington, Illinois, October 13, 1926)

Dr. F. P. Bohn (*Cloverland Magazine*, July 1916).

Dr. Frank P. Bohn graduated from medical school in 1890, and then moved to Seney, another novice with no experience. A dandy, dressed in a Prince Albert coat and silk tie, the young Dr. Bohn alighted from the train, quickly realized how out of place he was, and retreated to a "secluded spot" to change his clothes. His very first patient was "a jack who had been crushed by a falling tree" and was located at the end of a twenty-six-mile forest hike.[434]

Dr. Bohn stayed in Seney several years, and when that town declined, he transferred his practice to Grand Marais. He then moved to Newberry in 1898, hoping the inland climate would improve the health of his sickly first wife, Maud. It didn't. She died a year later. Dr. Bohn stayed in town, marrying again and becoming one of Newberry's most prominent citizens. He became part owner of a drug store and was a board member of the Newberry Bank.[435]

In later years, Dr. Bohn recalled a harrowing trip wherein a remote lumber camp sent for him during a blizzard. He and the messenger set off by handcar, using brooms to push back the snow over eight miles of tracks. Disembarking at Walsh Siding, they were dismayed to find no one there to meet them. The good doctor, already exhausted, then had to hike through ten miles of knee-deep snow to get to his patient. During another blizzard, he was called up to the Tahquamenon Falls. First, he traveled by handcar to the Sage River, then transferred to a motorboat. When the boat broke down, he switched to a canoe.[436]

Doctors traveled by any means available: horse and buggy, sleigh, railroad, railroad handcar, railroad velocipede, horseback, and dogsled. In the fall of 1888, Dr. Nicholson answered a call from Seney. He and a companion "rowed" down the railroad line by handcar, then found a horse and buggy and drove for several miles more. On his way back, a terrible rainstorm hit and the two men were "obliged to remain in the woods all night," wet and miserable.[437]

In 1912, Dr. Henry E. Perry (who had bought Dr. Neal's practice) was sleighing his way out to attend to a patient at a distant wood camp, following the narrow-gauge line, the only cleared path available. Suddenly, a wood train shot around a bend. Dr. Perry and his horse jumped for it into the drifts, but the sleigh was demolished.[438]

Dr. H. E. Perry (courtesy of Sterling McGinn)

Pineules

For the Kidneys, Bladder and Rheumatism.

RELIEVES

BACK-ACHE

30 days' treatment for $1.00.   Satisfaction guaranteed or money refunded.

FOR SALE BY CENTRAL PHARMACY

Advertisement from *The Newberry News* of August 28, 1908.

H. D. CHAMBERLAIN,

House and Sign Painter keeps on hand

Coffins and Coffin Trimmings.

Coffins all Sizes and Prices

Advertisement that appeared in *The Newberry News* of May 12, 1887.
Besides being a house and sign painter, H. D. Chamberlain was also a
furniture dealer. In frontier towns, furniture and undertaking businesses often
went hand in hand.

MONUMENTS.

I have secured the Agency of the Monumental Bronze Co., of Bridgeport, Conn., for the sale of their celebrated White Bronze Monuments in the upper peninsula. These monuments are beautiful of design, imposing and of excellent proportions and will outlast either marble or granite. In color they resemble granite. White Bronze is the most desirable metal that has yet been discovered for monumental purposes. It is composed of pure zinc and will last for centuries without discoloring or changing in any particular.
Prices one-third less than granite or marble.
Wm. Darcy. Agt.   **Newberry, Mich.**

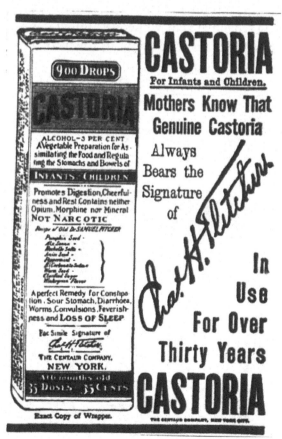

Advertisements that appeared in The Newberry News
February 12, 1904 and May 21, 1915.

Dr. French of Seney and Dr. Trueman of Munising were well known in Newberry as well. Dollarville had Dr. Morris, and McMillan was home to Dr. Moss and Dr. Prentice. A whole ream of doctors and nurses were available at the State Hospital.

Physicians were popular people and many parlayed that goodwill into politics, serving on the village council, board of education, and the various secret societies. Dr. Bohn was even elected to Congress in 1926.

Children often were named in honor of their parents' favorite physician. Mrs. Christina McKay named her youngest son Fraser McKay, around the same time that Dr. S. John Fraser saved her life. Matthew and Ellen Frasier were a little more explicit, naming one of their sons Frederick Neal Frasier, presumably after Dr. Frederick Neal. Dr. Almon T. Nicholson had namesakes in Almon T. Crocker (1894) and Almon Beaudin (1903). Bohn Musgrave (1904) sported the name of Dr. Bohn. Dr. Bohn's own beloved son Thiell (who died young) appears to have been named after Dr. A.K. Thiell, a prominent Marquette physician. Other Thiels in Luce County (albeit with a slightly different spelling) included Theil Kalnbach (1907), Theil Bryers (1909), and Theil Howald (1910). [439]

Newberry's doctors were always praising the Upper Peninsula for its healthful climate and good drainage. Still, in its first few decades, Luce County had one or two notable outbreaks of disease.

Just before Christmas in the year 1900, a woodsman named Pease and his two companions sauntered into town. Pease had only just come to the UP two weeks before to work the winter logging season at Dan McLeod's lumber camps up by the Sucker River near Lake Superior. Pease was clearly ill and had come to town to seek a doctor. Upon reaching town, his companions promptly abandoned the unfortunate fellow, who was left on his own to seek Dr. Bohn's office.

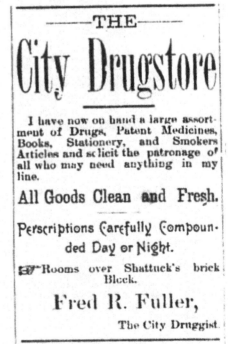

Advertisements from *The Newberry News* of
March 3, 1889 and December 19, 1890.

To the Pacific Coast—to California, Oregon, Washington—round-trip, long transit and return limits, liberal stop-over privileges.

The rate is practically on the basis of one fare for the round trip. Of course, if you wish to visit *both* California and *Oregon* or Washington, the cost is slightly more.

These reduced rates are in effect on certain dates in months of May to October, inclusive. They apply from all Eastern points via Chicago, St. Louis or Memphis gateways. The Rock Island System will take you up in either Chicago or St. Louis, or at hundreds of other Middle West points and carry you to the Coast in through Standard or Tourist Sleepers with unexcelled Dining Car service. The Rock Island also affords a choice of routes: on the "Scenic" route you can stop off in Colorado—see Salt Lake City—visit Yellowstone National Park; on the "Southern" route you can go via El Paso, thru New Mexico, then "up coast" to San Francisco and on to Portland or Seattle if desired.

In short, these Pacific Coast excursions offer an unusually good chance to see our western country in a comprehensive manner.

If you desire to go only as far as Colorado, there are excursion rates in effect to that section and return, all summer long, specially reduced June 30 to July 4, August 12 and 13, and August 30 to September 4. Extension trips to Ogden or Salt Lake and return at low cost also.

From September 15 to October 31, 1905, one-way tourist or "colonist" tickets will be on sale to California and the Pacific Northwest—about half regular fare.

If interested, send name and address on this coupon, designating which booklet wanted and to what point you plan to go. Name probable date of start also, so we can advise definitely with respect to rates, etc.

Address
JOHN SEBASTIAN,
Pass. Traf. Mgr., Rock Island System,
CHICAGO.

Send Colorado / California booklet and rates.

Name_____

Address_____

_____

Leave about_____

Destination_____

An advertisement that appeared in *The Newberry News* of June 6, 1905. Sufferers from tuberculosis often were urged to "go west" in the hopes that dry mountain air would help their symptoms. Sometimes it did; often it did not.

"His face and body being covered with eruption," Dr. Bohn at once diagnosed smallpox, locked Pease in his office, and notified Dr. Nicholson, the health officer. Dr. Nicholson traveled up to McLeod's camps and discovered "several suspicious cases." He vaccinated all the men, disinfected their living quarters, and ordered a quarantine on the camp. No one was to leave. Nearby at the Two Hearted River, John H. Hunter preemptively ordered his own men to stay put. None were allowed beyond the confines of camp on pain of losing their paychecks. Meanwhile, at Newberry, Pease's two companions were collared and quarantined with him, just in case. They hoped to contain the disease and keep it from spreading.

Of course, it already had. James Green was the son of the manager of the McLeod House hotel, and he had been feeling under the weather ever since coming back from the Sucker River camps two weeks earlier. Turns out, he had a mild form of smallpox. The McLeod House was quarantined, as was the nearby American House hotel, and then the Murphy House. The schools were shut down and the employees of the State Hospital were forbidden from coming into town. Even the newspaper office was quarantined when one of its employees (Dr. Nicholson's own son, Harry) came down with a mild case after talking to James Green.[440]

Meanwhile, Dr. Nicholson cast about for a suitable "pest house," to which victims could be gathered together—a kind of temporary hospital. He commandeered a building "about half a mile north and some distance west of town," which was none other than the "Hotel de Swamp." This building was described as "one of the lowest dives we believe that exists in this peninsula," a "disgrace to a civilized community" and a "hell hole." Nevertheless, it suited Dr. Nicholson's purpose. The residents were booted out (and given a temporary quarters in town) and "the unhappy victims of the dreaded plague" moved in.[441]

By January, the epidemic had blown over. The schools reopened, with the school board rather exasperatedly deciding "it is better to have the children at school where they can be looked after, than running around the streets." They did require that each child produce a certificate of vaccination. This "epidemic" was mild in nature. There were only about a dozen cases, including one fifty-year-old man who claimed to be sick, but really only wanted to be quarantined in the same house as the reluctant teenage girl he was trying to woo. There were no deaths.[442]

Even so, the county was out $3,000, and Dr. Nicholson had to burn all his office furniture. Because it had been so mild, some at the county claimed it was not smallpox at all, and that the doctors had overreacted. They refused to pay Dr. Nicholson and Dr. Bohn their expenses, but Judge Steere ruled in favor of the doctors. Nine years later, smallpox reappeared in the lumber camps, but no one worried much. Once again, there were no deaths.[443]

The same could not be said of the Spanish flu outbreak of 1918. People expected the flu to kill a handful of victims. They expected babies to succumb, and the elderly, and the sickly. This was a sad, normal part of life. Still, Modern Medicine was conquering mountains, and an improved grasp of sanitation and inoculation had lessened the blow of most diseases. Prompt action and modern methods could likely contain the damage of any new epidemic. But not this time.

Earlier in the year, most likely around the Fort Riley military base in Kansas, a fairly strong flu virus arose. It crossed the Atlantic with the troops bound for French trenches. Upon reaching Europe, the virus spread quickly, where it took on the name "Spanish flu" because the Spanish newspapers were the only ones reporting on its journey.

The Philip Blankinship family in 1909, before moving to Newberry. Left to right are John, Charles, Philip (holding Clarence), Mayme, Lillie May (holding Ethel), Goldie, Jenny (their hired girl), and Nettie (photo courtesy of Kathy Fitzgerald).

This postcard shows Newberry Avenue as it would have looked during the Spanish flu epidemic (author's collection).

With World War I winding down, the disease accompanied returning troops back home. By early September, it was in Boston, where it had mutated into something far more deadly. There it branched out from seaports to military bases, along the railroads to major cities, reaching the smaller venues, seeping down the lines like a poison, exploding out around the towns and railroad stations.

Friday, October 4, 1918, *The Newberry News* reported on mundane matters. Nearly three thousand had attended the Luce County Fair, drawn to its exhibits, baseball games, and horse racing. Visitors came from all over the eastern peninsula, including Seney, St. Ignace, the Soo, Marquette, and Manistique. St. Gregory's choir held a dinner party. The Red Cross organized a community singing class. Mrs. H. E. Smith gave a going-away party for Mrs. F. J. Park. Six young recruits left for the training school in Ann Arbor. The prospects of the University of Michigan's football team were weighed and found to be "anything but brilliant."

True, brief snippets of "news from around the state," mentioned the death-by-flu of three Michigan soldiers at the Great Lakes Naval Training Station outside Chicago. Such things happened in wartime. There was no other mention of the epidemic. It was, after all, nearly 400 miles away.[444]

Yet, even as the paper was going to press, that optimistic October day, death had struck Ruby Blankinship. She was a twenty-year-old widow with two small children living with her in-laws, the Philip Blankinship family. Her husband, Charles, had died in a freak accident only a few weeks previously, scalded to death at the charcoal plant.[445]

Three days earlier, both Ruby and her mother-in-law, Lillie, had sickened. Now Ruby was dead and her children were orphans. Spanish flu had arrived. Lillie Blankinship died the next day. Goldie Blankinship Stone, a five-month bride whose husband was overseas, was the third to die, along with her premature baby. Then Mrs. Grace Stoll, Philip's niece, died, too. She was twenty-three years old and had a one-year-old daughter.[446]*

Immediately, the Board of Health ordered all schools, churches, theaters, and pool halls closed. Lodge and club meetings were forbidden. It was too little, too late. Within the next six days, more than 100 additional people had fallen sick. And twenty-five more at the State Hospital.

But town residents did not yet realize the danger. Funerals were still being held, complete with out-of-town visitors, and the circuit court still planned on judging cases the following week. After the schools were ordered closed, several teachers even took up temporary positions with the Horner Flooring Company and other factories.

In any case, work at the Horner plant soon was crippled by a worker shortage. The Dollarville mill and the furnace were forced to close outright, and the flu was "raging among both the patients and attendants" in the State Hospital. Entire families were stricken, leaving no one to care for the sick "as it is impossible to secure nurses."[447]

---

* Within a month, the youngest of Phil Blankinship's sons, John, died, albeit this one of appendicitis. Phil eventually packed up his remaining children and grandchildren and left town.

Left: Advertisements from *The Newberry News* of
December 21, 1906 and November 28, 1890. It is indeed quite doubtful that
children *always* enjoyed it.

Right: Advertisement from *The Newberry News* of November 11, 1905.

By Thursday, October 17, four teenagers, an infant, and a three-year-old boy also had died and panic was spreading. The avalanche of death had begun.* "There is a profound air of sadness and depression over the city, and business of all kinds is at a practical standstill," lamented the paper.[448]

It was a sudden disease, a "swiftly spreading malady." A person could be fine at dawn and dead by dusk. And while the hale and hearty fellow was still feeling fine, before he showed any symptoms at all, he would have spread the virus to other victims. Beginning with cough, high fever, chills, and "catarrh" (a Victorian term for inflammation of the throat), this particular flu soon turned violent. Victims bled from the nose, mouth, and ears. The lungs filled with blood, and patients suffocated and choked themselves to death. Those who survived the initial run of the disease—those who seemed to be on the mend—often would then come down with pneumonia and die anyway.

One of the most frightening aspects of this particular flu was just whom it struck down. The vast majority of deaths were between the ages of fifteen and thirty-five. Young adults were not expected to die. Stolid, solid, healthy, hearty, husky souls in the prime of life were supposed to shake off illness. They had already successfully escaped the ravages of childhood disease. They were teens and twenty-somethings, newlyweds and young parents. They were popular fellows like twenty-nine-year-old Howard Reynolds, a local baseball star, a "trained athlete." He died a few days after his wife, orphaning two small sons.[449]

Young people were not supposed to die. Yet they did, by the score. The very heartiness of their immune systems betrayed them, launching such a violent counterattack against the virus that the ensuing battles literally tore the lungs apart. The disease was violent and baffling and mysterious. No one knew how to stop it. No one knew how to treat it.

Newberry at that time had several beloved doctors: Dr. Bohn, Dr. Perry, Dr. Gibson of the village, several doctors at the State Hospital, and a dozen or so trained nurses. They were all overwhelmed.

Because of World War I being fought at the time, the country as a whole suffered from a shortage of doctors and nurses. Many of the best and brightest had been enticed, drafted, and shanghaied into the army and were still serving overseas. Those left did their best. Dr. Gibson and Dr. Bandy (of the state hospital) became ill themselves. So did Mrs. Catherine McLeod, head of the local Red Cross. Professional nurses Minnie Hall, Mary Catherine Reardon, and Cora McLeod abandoned their city careers, hurrying home to help friends and family. Mary Catherine Reardon would catch flu herself and die. So did Katherine Simmet, a State Hospital nurse.[450]

The State Board of Health sent what additional doctors it could spare. Three doctors arrived from Marquette and soon were joined by six medical students from Detroit. Together, they fitted up the John Street Grade School as a temporary hospital. There, nineteen more succumbed. When the school proved inadequate, the doctors commandeered the Newberry Hotel, a new, three-story brick building, for its replacement. The new hospital held sixty beds. They were needed; Luce County racked up twenty-five more deaths over the next week.[451]

---

* They were Mary Beaudin (18), Louis Turnbull (3), Hattie Sylvia Keaner (2 mos), Wilman Ratka (19), Esilda LaCross (15), and Roy Bruseau (13).

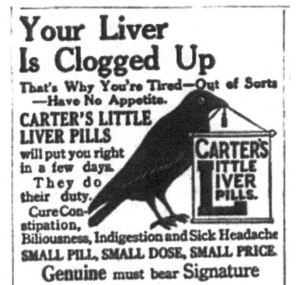
Advertisements from *The Newberry News* of May 21, 1915 and February 23, 1917.

Advertisement from *The Newberry News* of June 23, 1905.

No one knew what to do. Theories abounded, of course. A "traveling man" recommended hot lemonade, bed rest, and a concoction of Castor oil and manganese sulphate. Everyone wore a paper mask, even though "the good doctors disagree as to its effectiveness." Residents of the Soo drank up all the whiskey in town. According to family lore, Philip Blankinship, in a desperate attempt to save his remaining family, brewed up a "horrific" tasting "pine pitch tonic" that he fed to his surviving children twice a day.[452]

Meanwhile, the Board of Health printed inane rules about breathing through one's nose, keeping clothes clean and loose, and chewing food well. They urged parents to keep their children at home and ordered quarantine on homes where the influenza raged—but only after pneumonia appeared. "Why," asked the incredulous paper, "... wait until pneumonia develops before establishing a quarantine? Why not quarantine the 'Flu' at once?" Later, the Board distributed a free serum "which is claimed to be a preventative after three treatments." And yet, and yet, sighed the paper, "the doctors and health officers are all at sea" with "many divergent opinions as to its cause, and the proper treatment." By November 1, more than 250 cases were in the county.[453]

By early November, the horror began to abate. The first week saw only seven deaths. The second week had only five. The virus had moved beyond the town and was flaring in the surrounding communities, farms, townships, and lumber camps. Doctors sent their critical cases into the Newberry "hospital," which was "crowded to its capacity, new cases being brought in as fast as room is made by the departure of convalescent patients."[454]

Still, slowly, the virus declined. Churches and schools were reopened by November 18, and the emergency hospital officially closed November 29. The disease rallied in December and January and gave a parting shot of a half-dozen or so more deaths. Then it was over. It had been "a long dreary siege that depressed the spirits of the old and young alike."[455]

Dozens of men and women were widowed. Six pregnant women gave premature birth, and all six died, while none of the babies lived past a year. More than twenty-five children lost their mothers, several lost their fathers, and six were outright orphaned altogether. Three Newberry soldiers—Reamie Geoffrey, Francis Pelletier, and Lee Morrill—died far from home (Lee's younger brother, Charles, working in Petoskey, also died). [456]

Phil Blankinship, as seen, lost a wife, daughter, daughter-in-law, and niece. Mr. and Mrs. Howard Reynolds both died, as did Mr. and Mrs. Edward Switzer. Brothers Charles and George Houghtelling died within days of each other. Moses and Lizzie Beaver, then working in Germfask, lost three children and a newborn grandson. The county was out $10,000 in costs. Mr. Campbell had to have his entire hotel "thoroughly disinfected, scrubbed and cleaned from cellar to garret" with all the bedding "put through a sterilizing process."[457]

It was a horrible time and a sobering rebuke to the spirit of progress.

Chapter Fifteen
The Times They Are A-Changing

"On every side today can be heard the hum of the binder, the whistle of the steam thresher, where only a few years ago could be heard the howl of the wolf. Today there are fine farm buildings, fine fields, churches and schools and some of the finest roads in the state. Sons of the pioneers of the county ride in automobiles where their parents were pleased to be able to ride behind a yoke of oxen."

— William S. Locke, Pioneer, in 1922

LUCE COUNTY WAS A BUSTLING, up-and-coming place in 1915, and one of the fastest-growing counties in Michigan. Newberry was the center, the county seat, with almost 2,200 people (nearly double what it had been ten years earlier) and hundreds more working out in the wood camps of the surrounding forests. It was a modern, forward-thinking community. Town residents now benefited from electricity, telephones, sewer, running water, graveled and graded streets, streetlights, dozens of stores, a weekly newspaper, barbershops, hotels and boarding houses, candy kitchens, and restaurants. Religion was met by Catholic, Presbyterian, Episcopalian, Methodist, and both Swedish and Finnish Lutheran churches.

Industry was booming. After several uncertain years, the furnace had recently been acquired by a new owner, who had promised improvements and prosperity. It was no longer the only major industrial concern, however. In 1914, the Horner Flooring Company opened an ultra-modern factory of steel and concrete that furnished work for one hundred men. It flourished. Within six years, it claimed to be the largest flooring factory in the country, producing one-fourth of all hardwood flooring in the United States.

The populace enjoyed moving picture palaces, baseball, football, basketball, community dances, temperance societies, study clubs, Shakespeare societies, "secret" societies, pool halls, and saloons. Ninety percent of children attended grade school. Nearly half of those were going on to high school. The village council had ordered old frontier-style wooden sidewalks replaced with cement walks in 1903. Cement sidewalks would not rot, nor break and trip up old ladies who would sue for damages, as had once been the case. Many businessmen were slowly replacing their old pine store buildings with new, solid brick ones.[458]

In 1915, a visiting Clyde Hecox described Newberry Avenue: "The main street, 100 feet in width, is being boulevarded with a grass plot down the center, clusters of arc lights beautify the streets, a Masonic temple is being erected, the premises, both business and residences, present a clean, neat appearance and the inhabitants are well dressed, cheerful and apparently contented." He continued, reminiscing, "It was in strange contrast to the village of 25 years ago, when the streets were ungraded, unpaved and most of them filled with stumps...."[459]

The wealthier merchants and professionals had all built themselves large houses, especially along Newberry Avenue. These modern homes featured intricate woodwork, hardwood floors, steam radiators, furnaces, hot and cold running water, indoor bathrooms, electric lights, verandas, and cold storage rooms. Dan McLeod installed a "plate heater" in his dining room to keep food warm. J. L. Richardson put a "billiard room and gymnasium for the children" on his third floor. His was the first brick home in town.[460]

Milton E. Beurmann, the land broker, built the largest house of all. In 1908, he spent over $10,000 constructing a three-story, fifteen-room behemoth plus a full basement, which besides all the modern conveniences (including a bathroom on each floor) boasted such amenities as a library, music room, sewing room, and eight bedrooms. Moreover, it was located on two acres of land designed by a "landscape artist." The newspaper called it the "most pretentious residence in Newberry," which it meant as a compliment.[*461]

The "city dads" who had founded Newberry as energetic young men now were settling into a well-to-do middle-age. They were optimistic by nature, believing in the progressive perfection of society. The future would always be bright. Newberry was a "wide-avenued, green-lawned, boulevarded-lamped town, so spick and span and polished that it reminds one of the freshly scrubbed boy ready for Sunday school," as the *Detroit Free Press* enthused. It was a "thoroughly modern, prosperous town."[462]

Surrounding Newberry like satellites were smaller communities like Dollarville and McMillan. Dollarville was still a company town with sawmills and factories and hundreds of workers in rented housing. McMillan and Lakefield Township were still farming centers, surrounded by nearly 200 small farms and 1,000 inhabitants. Laketon, just west of McMillan, had fifteen families at its peak, as well as a general store, post office, school, train stop, and gravel pit. It had begun life in 1894 as "Lakeside" or "Lakefield Siding," merely a cleared space by the tracks.[463]

To Newberry's south sat the "insane asylum," or "State Hospital," perched on the hill, almost a village of its own, with hundreds of residents, both patients and caretakers. They were at the forefront of modern, humane, compassionate care (such as it was). To the east was Hulbert, to the north Shelldrake, Emerson, Deer Park, and Grand Marais, to the west Seney and Germfask, and to the south Curtis, Helmer, Rapinville, Engadine, Naubinway, and Trout Lake.

Newberry was not the isolated wilderness it once was. Even the tiniest hamlet had its railroad and telegraph stations, like Sage Station with fifteen inhabitants, or Soo Junction with six households. One could jump on the line and reach Newberry, and journey to the wider world: Marquette, Detroit, New York, and parts beyond.[464]

The Bradley & Hurst lumbering firm installed the first telephone line in 1891, running from its camps at Deer Park to the depot at Newberry, used chiefly by them to order supplies. By 1895, this line also connected to the American House Hotel and State Hospital. By 1900, the Michigan Telephone Company completed a long-distance line reaching from St. Ignace to

---

*Thirty years later this mansion was destroyed by a fire—like seemingly everything else in town.

The Horner Flooring Company, circa 1929 (photo courtesy of the Luce County Historical Society).

Main Street, Looking North, Newberry, Michigan.

This postcard (postmarked 1912) shows a block of Newberry Avenue featuring Leighton's store (and a poster for the Bank Opera House, advertising "Remember Sweetheart")
(author's collection).

Marquette, and the Neil Drug Store bit the bullet and installed a "long-distance phone" of its own. Now, lumbermen and businessmen could speak directly to the far-flung corners of their empires.

A "local" or "hello" system was launched in 1903 with thirty-five phones installed all over town and an "exchange" run by a Mrs. Campbell. This early system was piecemeal and patchwork in nature. Lines were strung from whatever was handy, including rooftops and convenient trees. Folks often had to shout into the mouthpiece to be heard.[465]

For this crude service, they paid $2 per month for a business and $1.50 for a home (at that time $1 could get you a night at a hotel room). Still, six years later, the number of subscribers had tripled to ninety-seven. In 1908, the township farmers hopped on board. A cooperative called the Lakefield Telephone Company formed, running lines from Newberry to McMillan. By 1910, its telephone service had reached Germfask, and by 1912, Curtis. The rate in Lakefield, as of 1915, was $10 per year.[466]

It seems, though, that telephones also could be dangerous. In 1914, a number of town phones actually "burst into flames" during an accidental surge of electricity. The convenience, however, was worth it.[467]

The automobile (dubbed "buzz wagon" by local wags) was the next big innovation, but at the turn of the century, no one in Luce County had one. The train was the fastest and most direct way to travel. It only cost thirty-three cents to ride from Newberry to McMillan; however, you were dependent on the trains' schedules. Passenger trains stopped at least twice a day in Newberry, going east or west. To get to Marquette in 1900, for example, one had to board the westward-bound train at 11:05 a.m.[468]

Getting anywhere on your own time, under your own power, was much more difficult. There was a fairly well-established road between Newberry and Deer Park to the north, and Newberry and Naubinway to the south, but most other roads were dirt trails, and some barely that. The road between Curtis and Helmer was so bad that mail was sent via the lake instead. Alternately, travelers could go west from Helmer to Germfask, then south to an unmarked trail that led between the lakes and get to Curtis that way.[469]

The townships, when they could afford it, would remove the stumps and roots and put gravel down, which improved matters slightly. The next step was to grade the road, to give it a slope for better drainage. In the swampiest places, the road might be "corduroy." This work was slow and fragmentary. There was no organization in place, no systematic, efficient way to get from one place to another.

To get to Marquette by horse, wagon, or early automobile over these tiny trails was a difficult endeavor. According to the *Automobile Blue Book of 1921*, one would leave Newberry, travel southwest to Helmer, west to Germfask, north through Seney, and all the way to Grand Marais on the shore. Then you would continue on the Adams Trail, a rough sandy road full of pine stumps, along the shore to Munising (this took about four or five hours), drive southwest to Chatham, and then northwest to Marquette. In the end, it could be nearly a full day of travel.[470]

In 1925, after a new stretch of highway opened, the *Munising News* marveled that cars traveling on this lovely new gravel road (though "in spots, rather wavy") could reach speeds of thirty-three miles per hour! Moreover, one could now reach Newberry "with ease in less than 3 hours."

This postcard (dated 1912) shows the neighboring block. The school is at the far left and the Richardson House at the far right (author's collection).

This postcard shows (circa 1910) several of the fine homes built by Newberry's wealthiest citizens. The bank can be seen at the far right (author's collection).

Today, it takes about an hour to drive between Munising and Newberry, and the length of road that opened in 1925, called the "Seney Stretch," is almost universally loathed for being flat, straight, and deadly dull.[471]

Besides no roads, the countryside lacked gas stations and mechanics. A poor road for horse and wagon, with ruts, mudholes, and rough bumps, is even poorer for the delicate mechanics and higher speeds of the auto. Wintertime travel was further hampered by the blankets of snow that covered everything. Traditionally, in the winter, horse and buggies were switched for horse and sleighs. The townships that could afford to brought out their "snowrollers"—massive horse-drawn machines with giant metal or wood rollers that packed down snowfall into a harder, more solid surface for better sleighing.

Newberry's first automobile, as William Fretz reminisced decades later, is said to have belonged to Dr. H. B. Gregory, the local veterinarian.* He purchased a "red Orient" around 1907, which was "propelled by a single-cylinder, air cooled engine," with neither "headlights nor tail light" and crawled into town with a "weird 'put-put'" sound. It took an hour of cranking before it would start.

The inhabitants crowded around, as described by Fretz:

> John A. Shattuck protested that those darn contraptions were dangerous and should not be allowed to roam at large on the streets. That it would scare all the horses and cause the cows to give sour milk. It did all that and then some. The village fathers, in a spirit of levity, passed a special ordinance stipulating that the contraption should not be left standing without tying, specifying a speed not to exceed two miles an hour, imposing severe penalties should it elect to climb any telephone poles and warning the mothers to keep their children off the streets and out of the way of danger....

> There was one good feature about the Orient: it was easily shoved, and if it ran off the road, you could pick it up and place it on again. It burned more lubricating oil than gas, and its exhaust resembled that of a locomotive after the fireman had shoveled in a fresh supply of coal.[472]

Sour milk and scared horses aside, the automobile was here to stay. Many of the wealthier inhabitants followed in Doc Gregory's wake. James C. Foster, the merchant, bought a Buick in 1911 and later became a "local agent" from which others could place orders. Andrew Westin and Dr. Bohn both bought an electric R.C.H. in 1912. And John H. Hunter bought himself a Cadillac. By 1912, fourteen prominent citizens were proud car owners.[473]

Infrastructure crawled into place to service these expensive toys. James Foster purchased a "vulcanizing machine" in his hardware store for the repair of tires, and the Standard Oil set up a gasoline storage tank. Matthew Surrell began adding rentable automobiles to his livery business. Soon, the state began installing a "trunk line" highway all over to better and more directly connect its towns, villages, and farms. Gravel roads began, slowly but inexorably, to make way for "macadamized" roads. The snow roller would make way for the snow plow. The future was on its way. As the road system grew better and better, the rail system declined.[474]

---

* There is a passing mention of a "pneumatic tired run-about" in 1903 as belonging to Ed McDonald, but whether this is a bike, carriage, or some kind of early auto is unclear.

The Ford is lighter than any other car of its size and power. Yet stronger, studier, longer lasting. Vanadium steel, that's why. Vanadium is the hardest; strongest, toughest steel made. It is the only steel that is hard and tough at the same time. It is the highest priced steel that is used in automobile construction. Yet the Ford is very low in price. Its quality, terms, price and small cost of operation and upkeep, less than two cents a mile, have made it the nniversal necessity in town and country

Ford Coupelet $750; Sedan $975; Town Car $690; Touring Car $490; Runabout $440. All fully equipped, f. o. b. Detroit. For sale by

J. C. FOSTER, Agent
NEWBERRY, MICHIGAN

Brightens
One Up

There is something about Grape-Nuts food that brightens one up, infant or adult, both physically and mentally.

What is it?

Just its delightful flavor, and the nutriment of whole wheat and barley, including their wonderful body and nerve building mineral elements!

A crisp, ready-to-eat food, with a mild sweetness all its own; distinctive, delicious, satisfying—

Grape-Nuts
"There's a Reason"

Heavy and Light Draying on Short Notice

JAMES BARBER
Drayman

Local Standard Oil Co. Agent

Top: Newberry Avenue, 1922, showing many cars (photo courtesy of Dr. James Surrell).

Advertisement from *The Newberry News* of October 29, 1915.

Right: Advertisements from *The Newberry News* of October 5, 1916 and October 29, 1915.

Luce County's first car accident happened in October of 1912, when an unnamed, overly enthusiastic driver sped down a road in Lakefield, lost control, rolled down a ditch, and hit a stump. The second accident happened a week later when a little girl ran out in front of Duncan Campbell's car in Dollarville. The girl lost several teeth, but was otherwise unharmed. Another week later came the third accident, when Herman Myers was speeding along and hit a ditch, the car "turning turtle" and pinning him underneath. Perhaps the most...unusual...accident was in 1917, when Mrs. Peter Miller panicked when she thought her son was driving too fast and leapt from his car, knocking herself senseless.[475]

Electric light was another innovation that transformed life in Luce County. In the early 1880s, when the land was being settled, electric light was a brand-new technology, and it was one that was taken up by the big concerns: the factories, the furnace, and the larger sawmills. The entities built their own powerhouses and employed their own engineers. So did the State Hospital when it was built in 1894.

In Newberry, the furnace often produced more energy "on the Edison system" than it could use, and so offered for sale its surplus current. A few business places contracted to light their own buildings, including the Post Office, McLeod House, Newberry Hotel, Younglove's Jewelry store, and Board of Trade Saloon. Flickering oil lamps made way for bright, sparkling light.[476]

The furnace was an unreliable provider, however, because it was constantly going in and out of business, and in 1895, the Newberry Water & Light company was established, with investors such as Claude W. Case, the McMillan family, and two of John S. Newberry's grown children (Truman and John, Jr.). The new company immediately wired the village hall and also began installing streetlights—each one a "1200-candlepower arc light." The company also collected subscribers among the various businesses, many of which jumped eagerly at the chance. (There were a few holdouts, like Joseph Stafford, who preferred thirty-five acetylene gas lamps for his drug store).[477]

At first, electricity was only available during the evening hours, but in 1900, providers expanded to offer "all-night service." The demand for electricity only grew stronger as the years went on. By 1914, the Hotel Murphy was blazing away with an electric sign. Most well-to-do homes were now wired for light, as were most of the new buildings being built in town. Merchants advertised electric vacuum cleaners and electric Christmas lights. Residents pled for "twenty-four-hour electric light service," which was finally granted late in 1914.[478]

Not all of the original pioneers had stayed put to enjoy their bustling, modern, flourishing little city. Building up a new business, a new town, or a new county is exciting work. Once that had been accomplished, many of the more restless began looking for greener pastures, larger challenges, and bigger and better businesses. California called, as did the new lumber countries of the northwest. Many of the original pioneers moved on, leaving behind the town and country they had created from scratch to face the declining timber industry, declining railroad industry, and an uncertain future.

Robert Dollar was one of the first to go. He sold his little Michigan industries not five years after he had founded them, and moved out west to California, where he continued in the logging industry. Then he branched out into steamships. The Dollar Steamship Company became so successful that Robert Dollar was known as the "Grand Old Man of the Pacific." He never forgot the Upper Peninsula, though, and close to his death expressed a wish to return to his little Dollarville.[479]

Top: James C. Foster in his prosperous middle age (photo courtesy of Dr. James Surrell).

Center: William S. Locke, in later years (photo courtesy of Sterling McGinn).

Left: Advertisement from *The Newberry News* that appeared around the year 1918.

Right: Advertisements from *The Newberry News* of May 21, 1915, March 9, 1917 and May 9, 1913.

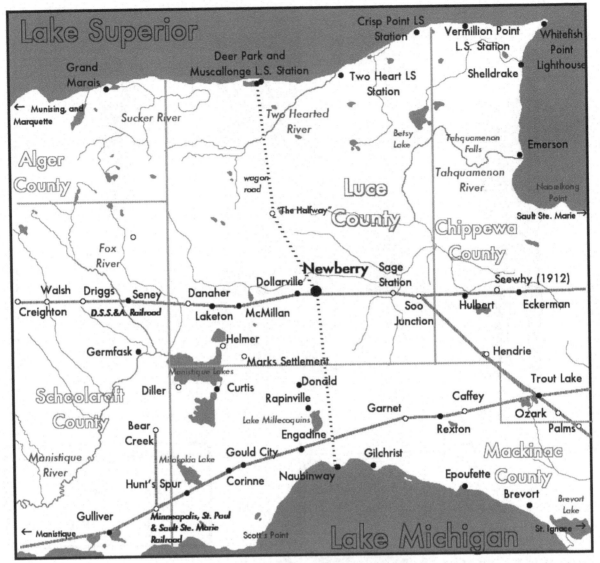

Luce County and Vicinity, circa 1920. Many of the "towns" shown here had their own schools, railroad stations, and post offices. Over the next century, many declined into little more than a few homes and a sign on the highway.

Above: Advertisement from *The Newberry News* of February 23, 1917.

The Willard Mark family, about 1907: Roy, Arthur, Margaret (Mrs. Arthur), Ruth, Willard, Daisy Bernice, Ferris, Dorothy, Lucinda, and Mina (Roat) Mark, holding Philip.

Another daughter, Ada, would be born a few years later. Willard and Mina had both moved to Luce County with their families in the early 1880s. Many members of the family would later move to Oregon (photo courtesy of Greg Marks).

Above: Advertisements from *The Newberry News* of October 29, 1915 and May 21, 1915.

The pull of sunny California, "the land of sunshine and flowers, oranges and gold dust," was strong. Many pioneer residents took the plunge. The Somervilles went to California, as did the Shattucks, Mr. and Mrs. Arthur A. Henderson, the Rosenthals, and the Fanjoys. Sanford N. Dutcher moved there permanently in 1905 after a political rival accused him of graft and his marriage fell apart.[480]

Robert Dollar's half-brother, William Dollar, left Newberry around the turn of the century, establishing himself in Kootenai County, Idaho, a booming region full of mining and timber interests. Many Newberry pioneers joined him there, settling in Couer d'Alene and nearby St. Maries, including the Brebners, McDurmons, Cases, Alexander Main family, Cyrs, Ambro and Evelyn Bettes, Frank and Ingeborg Erickson, and Miss Lodella Miller. So many immigrated to Kootenai County that in 1908, a full thirty-seven Newberry households subscribed to the *St. Marie's Gazette* (Charles Brebner's new newspaper), just to keep up with their old friends.[481]

The Pacific Northwest was another booming region, abounding in timber resources. Washington State claimed George Smathers and family. Hibbard Ingalls moved to Oregon, as did Webb Latham, Willard Mark, and his father-in-law, Frederick Roat.[482]

Minnesota attracted quite a few people, too, especially Duluth, and the state's northeast corner, which experienced a mining boom in the 1890s. Arthur Henderson (briefly), Doc Ingalls (briefly), Robert Langstaff, Robert F. Berdie, and others all moved there. The new town of Hibbing (established in 1893) attracted James Gandsey, and he was joined by fellow citizens James Vanmere, Robert S. Bradley (briefly), Ambro Bettes (briefly), Thomas Webster, and John Bergman. By 1910, Archie Kerr, Joseph Truman, Warren Smith, and James O. Myers had all moved to the nearby Virginia, Minnesota. They got out, as it were, while the getting was good, for the Luce County boom times were beginning to dry up.[483]

One by one, over the next century, the other cornerstones of the county's prosperity toppled.

The DM&M railroad lines still run, but they are not the life-giving byways they once were. Most of the narrow-gauge lines have been pulled up. Even their grades are grown over, although you can still tell where they used to be if you know what you're looking for.

The Vulcan Furnace Company, finally called the Newberry Lumber and Chemical Company, closed its doors for good in 1945. Nothing at all remains of the furnace. "Charcoal iron" (created with burning wood) proved to be less efficient than "coal iron" (created with burning coal).

The great forests are gone, replaced by a snarl of young, second-growth trees crisscrossed by a spiderweb of county roads. As early as 1901, the newspaper warned that "the timber in McMillan Township is being rapidly stripped from the land, and in a few years practically the last stick will be cut."[484] True pine logging could be replaced with hardwood logging, but now everyone actually understood that forests don't last forever. True enough, the hardwood forests were exhausted faster than anyone could have imagined. Although logging and lumber operations continue to this day, the scope is not what it was. By 1920, the great days were gone.

Over the first few decades of the twentieth century, most of the lumber boom towns began to fade, then totter. Grand Marais and Seney both declined from villages of several thousand people to tiny, struggling hamlets. By 1910, Grand Marais was down to four hundred people, and in 1911, the railroad tracks between Grand Marais and Seney were pulled out. By 1920,

Charles Surrell, 1912 (photo courtesy of Dr. James A. Surrell).

Bridge over Tahquiamenon River, Newberry, Mich.

This postcard (postmarked 1908) shows the new bridge over the misspelled "Tahquiamenon River." Someone (presumably the card's sender, "Ruby," writing to her friend Nell Ryan) has quietly corrected the spelling by crossing through the offending "i" (author's collection).

only 120 people remained. Seney dropped from a peak of three thousand people in the mid-1890s to "only thirty-five families" in 1899, "but a shadow of its former self." By 1920, its population stood at forty-four, and its hotels, saloons, drugstores, newspapers, and jewelry stores vanished.[485]

The smaller communities that had sprung up around the rivermouth sawmills, such as Shelldrake or Emerson, practically disappeared. Emerson, founded by lumber baron Alonzo Chesbrough, had at its peak 109 residents surrounding its sawmill. It lost its post office in 1914, while Alonzo's son Fremont B. Chesbrough went bankrupt in 1915.[486]

Shelldrake was once considered a "model" lumbering town, featuring hot running water, a school, and an icebox to store meat for the town. Its population once peaked at 350, but a ruinous fire and changing economies took their toll, there as elsewhere. Within the next twenty-five years, everything vanished. Post offices, schools, model homes: all faded away.

Little of either town remains.

Deer Park, with its electric-lit mill, two-room schoolhouse, telephones, railroad tracks, and regular stagecoaches, at one time had boasted a population of 300. Unfortunately, it was not able to survive the closing of its sawmill.[487]

Visiting in 1932, William G. Fretz sadly described what remained as follows:

> Where are the rows of houses, the mill and the docks that existed in this thriving little sawmill town some 40 years ago? It is 35 years since the last stick of timber was cut in the Deer Park mill, and today, not a vestige of the town remains.
>
> Here and there one may see the outlines of what was once a building, now overgrown with grass, and if one dug beneath the sod would probably discover rotting timbers. We searched for the site of the saw mill and could not find it. Along the beach a few piles which formed the dock are still standing like lonely sentinels, eroded and eaten away by the ever restless waves of Gitchie Gaume. A trace of the frameways, now rotted ruins, can be found overgrown with scrub, and nature is doing its best to hide the sawdust mountain. It takes a keen eye to distinguish it from the sand cliff, it is so overgrown with the scrub, and with here and there a tree at least a foot in diameter.[488]

By 1932 all that was left at Deer Park was the lifesaving station. Fretz took comfort in that, explaining that "the coast guard station stands today much as it did in those early years, gleaming white in the bright sunshine, everything spotlessly clean, and a well-kept lawn surrounding the premises."

The Horner Flooring mill, which could be considered the pinnacle of the lumber mill industry and had opened to such fanfare in 1914, moved off in the 1940s after a dispute with the village council.

While logging and the logging industry were on their slow decline, the residents were sure something else would come up. Newberry, still holding on with its government facilities and State Hospital, began to cast about for something to fill the void. Perhaps a hydroelectric plant could make use of the Tahquamenon River and run several new factories. Maybe the swamplands could be drained, which would naturally reveal fine, rich soil, and an agricultural bonanza would result.

J. C. Foster's "model farm" as it appeared in the pages of *Cloverland Magazine*.

They're Easy to Clean

Handsome
Washable
Sanitary

CONGOLEUM RUGS

For Every
Room in
Your Home

HERE are the rugs that have taken the "weep" out of "sweep"— The rugs that make cleaning-day a joy. But, this is only one advantage of Congoleum Rugs, a full line of which we are displaying this week. Come in and see them.

Our stock of the new Congoleum Art-Rugs will be a treat for your eyes. Such marvelous patterns in a low-priced rug have never before been possible. You will find here just what you want for every room in your home. Call around and solve your floor covering problems today

Chas. B. Beaulieu

Farm Machinery

It is up-hill-work trying to farm unless you are possessed of modern and up-to-date machinery with which to perform your work. Old methods of farming are being cast into the discard. The farm-

er of today, if he would succeed must employ modern methods. When you are in the market for farm machinery of any kind, remember we carry a full line and can sell you as cheaply as anyone. We also carry a full stock of repair parts.

J. C. FOSTER

Advertisements from *The Newberry News* of February 23, 1917 and May 9, 1913.

Everyone had long preached, from the lumber barons on down, that once the timber was gone, the "cut-over lands" could be transformed into a vast farming paradise. This was prophesied, this was predicted, this was counted on. Wild schemes were proposed over the years to drain the surrounding swamps and reclaim that land for the farmer. Inside these reclaimed swamplands, companies announced, would be many new towns (like the much-fanfared, never materialized 1911 town of New Seney). They further promised to entice "colonies" of desirable settlers, including Frankenmuth farmers, Minnesotans, Belgians, Italians, Poles, and Japanese. The grand drainage schemes never did accomplish much besides the digging of a few ditches. The new towns never appeared, and neither did the promised "colonies."[489]

This idealized vision of the U.P., this idea of an agrarian "Cloverland," never really staggered off the ground. There would always be some place cheaper, larger, or warmer in which to grow potatoes and raise sheep. Even the celery gardens—originators of the famed Newberry celery that was served in the best hotels in Chicago and New York—did not survive. The demand for Newberry's "golden" celery dropped, as a cheaper, less labor-intensive variety, the "green pascal," became more popular. And green pascal was more easily grown elsewhere. [490]

Limited farming remains. Satellite photos reveal large swatches of green fields in Lakefield Township, still clear, which correspond roughly to the farms of the original pioneers.

Finally, the State of Michigan, in its infinite wisdom, chose to shutter the State Hospital (called, at the last, the Newberry Regional Mental Health Center) just shy of its 100th birthday.

Many of the original buildings still stand, that quadrangle of brick buildings "in the Italianate style," which can be seen in aerial photos of the area. Because in 1996 the hospital was converted into a prison, access is limited.

Today, not much is left of those wild and woolly days, and more is lost every year.

Very few of the original wooden buildings still stand. A great chunk of the original pine downtown was destroyed in the 1920s by (you guessed it) a devastating fire. Other elderly buildings, damaged by decades of decline and neglect, fell into disrepair. One by one, they have been torn down. The brick buildings, built in a flush of prosperity, from the 1890s to the 1930s, have fared a little better. Many are still hanging on.

Yiddish, French, German, and Swedish are no longer spoken on the streets. Neither is Finnish, although saunas are still popular. The great Victorian mass of a courthouse, dignified and solid, was demolished in the 1970s, replaced by a modern, efficient, soulless municipal building. The neighboring Sheriff's House was saved by the heroic efforts of the Newberry Historical Society and is a museum today. The lumber camps, sawmills, docks, one-room schoolhouses, frontier hotels, saloons, and farms have all vanished, reabsorbed back into the land.

Advertisements from *The Newberry News* of
May 21, 1915 and June 23, 1905.

This postcard, dated 1926, shows a portion of Newberry Avenue, with several
factories in the background (author's collection).

An old railroad grade in 2015. The tracks here were laid about 1905 and probably removed in the 1920s (author's photo).

Postscript

W E'RE SUPPOSED TO LEARN FROM the mistakes of history. We look back and imagine the great forests, the marvelous trees, and shake our heads sadly. It took centuries for those forests to grow, and only forty years to destroy them forever. This is a terrible thing.

"Why didn't they realize?" we say. "Why didn't they *know*?"

Of course, it's easy to look back and judge. But our pioneers did not intend to be destroyers. They didn't see themselves that way. And it wasn't as though they hated nature.

Most people actually loved it—they really did. They loved the trees and the animals and the streams full of sturgeon. They loved camping, fishing, hunting, and the grandeur of nature.

They saw themselves as builders. They cut the trees so they might create. Out of the forests they built fortunes, families, and communities. It is sad, they said, but necessary. Anything else was just nostalgia or sentimentality, which had no place in a modern and efficient society. They were building the future.

They did not stop to think—they could not and would not stop to think—that maybe the future would wish it otherwise.

What's done is done and can't be undone. The lesson we can learn is to think twice before destroying resources, and think harder about managing and preserving them. This is a tricky balancing act, to be sure, but one that's worth doing.

However, in destroying one resource, the pioneers created another: history, their successes and failures, hopes and dreams, virtues and vices. History is also a resource. It's a precious resource, and finite. One that needs to remembered, preserved, and protected.

In our haste to create, it's very easy—too easy—to become destroyers as well. Let's not do that. Let's learn from the pioneers, learn from their mistakes, and learn from their triumphs.

So visit museums, preserve architecture, treasure antiques, tell family stories, write them down, and, above all, label your photographs.

Further Reading
and
Additional Resources

It's a little unnerving to stand in the local history section of the Peter White Public Library in Marquette and be confronted with row after row, and hundreds upon hundreds, of books about the Upper Peninsula and its inhabitants. Yoopers are, if nothing else, fascinated by themselves. Almost every facet of life in the UP, from its industries and immigrants, to its shipwrecks and recipes, has at least a couple of books behind it. It's simply not possible to read, evaluate, and appreciate each one. I have probably missed dozens and dozens of gems; however, here are a few tomes I have found useful as well as other resources.

For those in a traveling mood, I wholeheartedly recommend both the Luce County Historical Museum and Tahquamenon Logging Museum, both located in Newberry. They are most excellent resources. Also of interest would be Fayette State Park in Delta County, about ninety miles southwest of Newberry, on the shores of Lake Michigan. The park features a partially restored 1870s iron smelting town, which demonstrates exactly what was meant by a "neat, comfortable cottage."

The Place of the Pike by Charles E. Cleland (2001)

> A scholarly and readable book, this volume takes a look at the history of the Ojibwa tribes of the eastern UP, their culture and struggles, and in particular of the development of the Bay Mills Indian Community.

Tahquamenon Country: A Look at Its Past by Charles Sprague Taylor (1991)

> A local classic, this is a loving and affectionate look at some of the stories surrounding Tahquamenon country, its natives and lumberjacks.

Columbus Township History by Dutch Hanes and Delbert Musgrave (2000)

> This is an exhaustive volume chock-full of reminiscences, photographs, and news items from Columbus Township, Luce County, Michigan

Luce County: A History by Hilja Pekkarinen, Minnie Ida Matson, and Phyllis Brumm (1985)

> This is a rather rare volume created in celebration of Newberry's Centennial. It features photos, reminiscences, articles, and newspaper extracts. See also (if you can find them) its two-volume predecessor, *The History of Luce County: "Past Years"* by

Hilja Pekkarinen and Minnie Ida Mattson.

Upper Peninsula Hospital by William A. Decker (2012)

A coffee table book stuffed with information and photos detailing nearly 100 years of history of the Newberry State Hospital.

Vanishing Values: Louis W. Foster and 20th Century American Business by Robert Windeer (1994)

This is the biography of Louis Foster, a California businessmen who spent his childhood in Newberry. The first few chapters detail his family's experiences during the town's boom times.

The Duluth, South Shore & Atlantic Railway: A History of the Lake Superior District's Pioneer Iron Ore Hauler by John Gaertner (2009)

Just what it says, a history of the DSS&A, covering the initial railroad lines that were its predecessors (including the DM&M) until its merger with the Soo Line Railroad in the 1960s.

Incredible Seney by Lewis Reimann (1953)

Another classic of Michigan history, this slim volume relates many lively stories and legends from Seney's past, once a notorious lumbering "hell town" full of colorful characters and dramatic incidents.

Michigan Ghost Towns: Upper Peninsula, Volume III by Roy L. Dodge (1973)

This is an interesting and exhaustive cataloging of notes on many of the vanished towns of the Upper Peninsula, organized by county.

Remotely Yours by Jan McAdams Huttenstine (2010)

This book details the history of the nearby Whitefish Point area and its remote lumber camp communities, lighthouses, and isolated farms.

The Old Log School by the Lake and the Surrounding Area: A History of Portage Township, Mackinaw County, Michigan by E. W. Kiebler (1953)

and *The Lone Survivor, as related to the History of Germfask Township* by E. W. Kiebler (1956)

This pair of short and sweet booklets contains many interesting stories of the Manistique Lakes area pioneers during the early 1880s and beyond. They are available online at https://babel.hathitrust.org.

Curtis Remembered by the Curtis Centennial Committee (2007)

Issued to mark the centennial of the hamlet of Curtis, in nearby Portage Township. It features an eclectic collection of stories, memories, and photos.

The Blazed Trail by Stewart Edward White (1904)

This is work of fiction. It's old-fashioned in style and substance, and a bit odd besides, but it does paint a very thorough look at Michigan lumber camps. It also serves as an example of dual attitudes towards the forest that prevailed back then—both revering the woods and relishing their destruction.

Acknowledgments

Many, many, many, and much thanks goes to my encouraging editors, Dorothy Richards, Julia Diem, Nancy Diem (Mom!), and Tyler Tichelaar, as well as those whose praise and interest bucked me up when I was down, including James Diem (Dad!) and Chris Diem. Also, thanks Uncle Bill, for suggesting this project in the first place. I'm sorry there were no stories about wolves.

For photographs and illustrations, my heartfelt gratitude goes out to the following generous and enthusiastic people and organizations:

Sterling McGinn, Luce County Historical Society, the Tahquamenon Logging Museum, Dr. Jim Surrell, Robert and Cheryl Teed Bryers, Greg Marks, Roxanna Pentland Transit, Jeff Chown, Tom Whalen, Ned Barker, Avis Fretz, Larry Johnson, Patricia Proebstel, Joanne Jessee, Brandy Walsh, Billie Nicholson, and Kathy Fitzgerald. Your passion and dedication to the past is worth so much more than we all know.

For help with the editing and computer "clean-up" of the pictures, recognition must go to Jerry Stimac, Lauren Burton, Jeff Richards, and LarryAlexander who are so much more talented and patient than I am.

Finally, grateful thanks go out to all journalists, everywhere—preservers of tomorrow's history—and to the subscribers and advertisers who still support them.

Endnotes

DOCUMENTING THE MANY SOURCES USED for this book proved an exercise in frustration, bafflement, and ultimately exhaustion. I know that the style may not be exactly correct (apologies to my professors and teachers!), but hope there is enough detail to provide a useful provenance to those interested.

1   **Chapter One: How It All Began**

"Local," *Newberry News*, November 12, 1915.

(NOTE: Although she was listed in the paper as "Mrs. Ashbury," her actual name was Delphine Ashbaugh).

2   "Dollarville Doings," *Newberry News*, April 8, 1892.

3   "Will Celebrate 60th Anniversary," *Newberry News*, May 30, 1930.

4   Charles Sprague Taylor, *Tahquamenon Country: A Look at Its Past* (Ann Arbor, Michigan: Historical Society of Michigan, 1991), 48.

5   "Captain Dollar Sends Greetings," *Newberry News*, December 23, 1927.

6   R. C. Hulbert, "Hulbert Township Historical Sketch, 1936," retyped by Mary Frances Morden, Bayliss Public Library, Sault Ste. Marie, Michigan, http://www.uproc.lib.mi.us/bpl and http://www.baylisslib.org.

7   "Will Celebrate 60th Anniversary," *Newberry News*, May 30, 1930.

8   *History of the Upper Peninsula of Michigan* (Chicago: Western Historical Company, 1883), 547.

9   William S. Locke, "Pioneer Reminiscences," *Newberry News*, June 9, 1922;

"Will Celebrate 60th Anniversary," *Newberry News*, May 30, 1930.

10   42n12w, Survey Map, 1849, Guy H. Carleton, from the General Land Office Records, Bureau of Land Management, U.S. Department of the Interior, www.glorecords.blm.gov.

11   "Mrs. J.O. Myers," *Newberry News*, June 28, 1940;

"Lakefield," *Newberry Independent*, August 1, 1889;

"Many Pioneers Here Before Newberry A Town," *Newberry News*, Newberry's 100th Birthday Issue, September 1, 1982;

"Lakefield, the Banner Township," *Newberry News*, August 21, 1896

12   United States Census, 1880," database with images, *FamilySearch* (https://familysearch.org/ark:/61903/1:1:MWSR-MBH : 10 August 2016), Sanford Helmer, Newton, Mackinac, Michigan, United States; citing enumeration district ED 42, sheet 269A, NARA microfilm publication T9 (Washington, DC: National Archives and Records Administration, n.d.), roll 0592; FHL microfilm 1,254,592, page 5;

Ernest William Kiebler, *The Lone Survivor, as related to the History of Germfask Township*, (Lansing, Michigan, 1956), page 27 (digitized by the Hathi Trust (https://babel.hathitrust.org)

13   Locke, "Pioneer Reminiscences."

14   "Pioneer Resident Passes," *Newberry News*, January 17, 1930;

1849 Survey Map, William Ives from the General Land Office Records, Bureau of Land Management, U.S. Department of the Interior, www.glorecords.blm.gov.

15   "Moses Pentland (Obituary)," *Newberry News*, August 5, 1955;

Household of Thomas Pentland, "Canada Census, 1881," database, *FamilySearch* (https://familysearch.org/ark:/61903/1:1:MVNS-P8T : 18 November 2014), Thomas Pentland, Kinloss, Bruce South, Ontario, Canada; citing p. 60; Library and Archives Canada film number C-13274, Library and Archives Canada, Ottawa, Ontario; FHL microfilm 1,375,910.

(NOTE: Their name was almost always spelled as "Pentland." However, an early map of Luce County referred to "Pendleton Township." The family was also listed as "Pembleton" on the 1871 Canadian Census, and as "Pendleton" on the 1861 Canadian census.)

16   "Frederick Roat," *Newberry News*, June 8, 1928;

"Two Days of Pleasure," *Newberry News*, January 21, 1898.

17   "Some U.P. Triumphs," *Newberry News*, July 20, 1923.

18   "Newsites," *Newberry News*, June 24, 1886;

"Reminisces of an Old Pioneer," *Newberry News*, October 26, 1956;

Household of Theodore Calabaugh, "United States Census, 1880," database with images, *FamilySearch* (https://familysearch.org/ark:/61903/1:1:MW3D-LVV : 10 August 2016), Theodore Calabaugh, Greenwood, St Clair, Michigan, United States; citing enumeration district ED 377, sheet 228B, NARA microfilm publication T9 (Washington D.C.: National Archives and Records Administration, n.d.), roll 0604; FHL microfilm 1,254,604;

Kiebler, *The Lone Survivor*, page 47

19   "Lakefield," *Newberry Independent*, August 1, 1889.

20   Le Roy Barnett, "The Railroad," Dutch Hanes and Delbert Musgrave, ed. *Columbus Township History*, (Columbus Township, McMillan, Michigan, 2000), 10-11;

George Rintamaki, "Looking Back, Upper Peninsula Up for Grabs," *Newberry News*, February 25, 1987.

21   "Will Celebrate 60th Anniversary," *Newberry News*, May 30, 1930.

22   John Gaertner, *The Duluth, South Shore and Atlantic Railway: A History of the Lake Superior District's Pioneer Iron Ore Hauler*, (Bloomington & Indianapolis, Indiana University Press, 2009), page 45.

23   Gaertner, 15, 45-46, 15;

History of the Upper Peninsula of Michigan, 167-168.

24   "Capt. Dollar Sends Greetings," *Newberry News*, December 23, 1927;

"Old Pioneer Passes" (Obituary of Newby Allen) *Newberry News*, June 24, 1921;

Hanes and Musgrave, 14;

Gaertner, 47.

25   1854 Survey Map, G. H. Cannon from the General Land Office Records, Bureau of Land Management, U.S. Department of the Interior, www.glorecords.blm.gov;

"Ninety Years Young," *Newberry News*, April 14, 1950;

"Will Celebrate 60th Anniversary," *Newberry News*, May 30, 1930;

Walter Romig, *Michigan Place Names* (Detroit: Wayne State University Press, 1986), 392.

26   Rand McNally's 1881 Atlas, p. 648, accessed online from Michigan State University;

"A Look Back into History," *Newberry News*, May 30, 1963.

27   Plat of Town of Newberry, being part of Sections 26 and 26 of Town 46 North of Range 10 West, Owned and Divided by the Peninsular Land Company, limited, surveyed and drawn by Farrand, Henry, October 1883, accessed via http://www.dleg.state.mi.us/platmaps/sr_subs.asp;

"Postscript," *Newberry News*, January 25, 1890;

"Newberry, Its Past History and Rapid Growth; Its Bright Future Prospects and Natural Advantages," *Newberry Independent*, September 26, 1889.

28   Thomas A. Arbaugh, "John S. Newberry and James H. McMillan: Leaders of Industry and Commerce," *Tonnancour: Life in Grosse Pointe Along the Shores of Lake St. Clair, Volume 2 (1997)*, 79. *<www.gphistorical.org/pdf-files/tonnancour/jsn-jhm.pdf>*.

29   "Pioneer Woman Passes," (Obituary of Catherine Alice Miller), *Newberry News*, July 2, 1948.

30   "Land Department," *Newberry News*, July 8, 1886;

"A Glimpse of Early History," *Newberry News*, December 17, 1959

31   Newberry, Its Past History and Rapid Growth; Its Bright Future Prospects and Natural Advantages, *Newberry Independent*, September 26, 1889.

32   Gaertner, 60.

33   Arbaugh, 82.

34   "The New County," *Newberry News,* December 30, 1886;

J. P. Mills, "Friend Editor," *Newberry News*, December 30, 1886;

"Luce County," *Newberry News*, February 10, 1887;

"Luce County," *Newberry News*, February 24, 1887;

Rachel Sheer, "History of Newberry," *Newberry News*, May 28, 1920;

Romig, 7.

35   "Local," *Newberry News*, May 24, 1888.

36   "Newberry, Its Past History and Rapid Growth; Its Bright Future Prospects and Natural Advantages," *Newberry Independent*, September 26, 1889;

"Fifty Years Progress," *Newberry News*, August 28, 1936;

"New Village Dump," *Newberry News*, May 5, 1905;

"Newberry, including Dollarville," by the Sanborn Perris Map Co., limited, October 1893.

37   Taylor, 81-82;

Roy L. Dodge, *Michigan Ghost Towns, Upper Peninsula, Volume III* (Sterling Heights, Michigan: Glendon Publishing, 1981), 55.

38   "Here and There," *Newberry News*, November 22, 1888;

Newberry News, September 28, 1894.

39   Taylor, 74.

40   "Will Celebrate 60th Anniversary," *Newberry News*, May 30, 1930.

41   R. C. Hulbert "Hulbert Township Sketch."

42   "Lakefield," *Newberry Independent*, August 1, 1889;

"Reminisces of an Old Pioneer," *Newberry News*, October 26, 1956;

Romig, 194, 504.

43   "Local," *Newberry News*, July 7, 1887.

Chapter Two: Peopling the Place

44   Hanes and Musgrave, 7, 155;

"Local and County," *Newberry News*, January 10, 1896.

45   "Pioneer Citizen Passes," (Obituary of J. C. Holland), *Newberry News*, October 31, 1924; "Donald N. McLeod is Called," *Newberry News*, November 6, 1931;

Rintamaki, "Looking Back: A Look Back at Life in the Camps in the White Pine Days of Luce County," *Newberry News*, June 22, 1983.

46   Rintamaki, "Looking Back, A Look Back at Life in the Camps in the White Pine Days of Luce County," *Newberry News*, June 22, 1983.

47   Hanes and Musgrave, 356;

Frank P. Bohn, "This Was the Forest Primeval," *Michigan History Magazine* (Winter 1937);

Rintamaki, "Looking Back: Fred Sorenson Had Long Career as Camp Cook," *Newberry News*, October 26, 1983.

48   Rintamaki, "Looking Back, Logging Camps a Home Away from Home," *Newberry News*, March 16, 1983;

Hanes and Musgrave, 357.

49   "Local News," *Newberry News*, January 25, 1890.

50   "Woodville," *Newberry News*, December 21, 1889;

"The Wood Camp," *Newberry News*, May 29, 1891.

51   Rintamaki, "Looking Back: Romantic Aura Surrounds Fearless Breed of Log Drivers," *Newberry News*, August 29, 1984.

52   "Historic Woodsmen," *Newberry News*, March 26, 1915.

53   Frank P. Bohn, "This Was the Forest Primeval," *Michigan History Magazine* (Winter 1937);

Hanes and Musgrave, 354-355;

Columbus Township History by Dutch Hanes and Delbert Musgrave, 354-355;

"Passing of the Lumberjack," *Newberry News*, March 7, 1919.

54   Taylor, 56.

55   Ida R. Spring, "White Pine Portraits: Genial Dan McLeod," *Michigan History Magazine*, January-March 1946.

56   "In Full Swing," *Newberry News*, June 14, 1901.

57   Ida M. Spring, "White Pine Portraits: Genial Dan McLeod," *Michigan History Magazine*, January-March 1946;

"In Full Swing," *Newberry News*, June 14, 1901.

58   "Local News," *Newberry News*, May 15, 1891;

"Our Man About Town," *Newberry News*, July 27, 1889;

"Donald N. McLeod Is Called," *Newberry News*, November 6, 1931.

59   Ida M. Spring, "White Pine Portraits: Big Dave Ransom," *Michigan History Magazine*, September 1947;

Memorial Record of the Northern Peninsula of Michigan (Chicago: Lewis Publishing Company, 1894), 371-372.

60   Ida M. Spring, "White Pine Portraits: Norwegian John Ryland," *Michigan History Magazine*, September, 1948.

61   Ida M. Spring, "White Pine Portraits: Con Culhane," *Michigan History Magazine*, December 1947.

62   "Camps Breaking Up," *Newberry News*, March 20, 1903;

Rintamaki, "Looking Back: Spring River Drive Continued After Building of Railroads," *Newberry News*, July 30, 1986.

63   Rintamaki, "Looking Back," *Newberry News*, November 24, 1982.

64   "Historic Woodsmen," *Newberry News*, March 26, 1915;

"Camp Jumpers Jailed," *Newberry News*, July 1, 1910.

65   "Camp Jumpers Jailed," *Newberry News*, July 1,1910;

"Men Went to Work," *Newberry News*, July 8, 1910.

Chapter Four: Wild and Woolly Days

66   "The Last Pine is Being Cut," *Newberry News*, December 15, 1911;

"Historic Woodsmen," *Newberry News*, March 26, 1915;

"Forty Years of Progress," *Newberry News*, June 28, 1918.

67   "Local," *Newberry Independent*, May 8, 1890;

"Newberry, including Dollarville," by the Sanborn Perris Map Co., limited, October 1893.

68   Advertisement: Board of Trade Saloon, *Newberry Independent*, September 26, 1889;

"Local," *Newberry News*, April 25, 1890;

Advertisement: Board of Trade Saloon, *Newberry Independent*, May 29, 1890;

Advertisement: Beaulieu & Son, *Newberry News*, November 18, 1892;

"Local," *Newberry News*, May 5, 1893;

"Local," *Newberry News*, May 4, 1894;

Advertisement: Board of Trade Saloon, *Newberry News*, December 29, 1899.

69   "Advertisement: Oriental Saloon," *Newberry News*, July 4, 1890;

"Advertisement: Marquette City Saloon," *Newberry Independent*, October 11, 1890;

"Advertisement: Railroad Saloon" and "Advertisement: Palace Saloon," *Newberry News*, July 28, 1893;

"Here and There," *Newberry News*, March 30, 1889;

"Local," *Newberry Independent*, May 2, 1889;

"Advertisement: The Palace," *Newberry Independent*, July 3, 1890;

"Advertisement: Bank Sample Room," *Newberry News*, March 3, 1893;

"Advertisement: Blue Front Sample Room," *Newberry Enterprise*, February 8, 1894.

70   "In Trouble Again," *Newberry News*, February 24, 1899.

71   "A Retraction," *Newberry News*, April 7, 1899.

72   "Circuit Court," *Newberry News*, May 12, 1899.

73   "Fined Fifty Dollars," *Newberry News*, September 6, 1907.

74   "Local News," *Newberry News*, September 8, 1887;

"Advertisement: Hurrah for the Palace Saloon," *Newberry Independent*, September 26, 1889;

"Advertisement: Ed Ryan," *Newberry News*, July 4, 1890;

Advertisement: Blue Front Sample Room," *Newberry Enterprise*, February 8, 1894;

"Made Spurious Coin," *Newberry News*, March 10, 1905;

"Frank L. Harris," *Newberry Enterprise Special Edition*, October 1894;

"Local News," *Newberry News*, February 13, 1891.

75   "Should be Suppressed," *Newberry News*, December 14, 1900;

Newberry News, July 14, 1893;

Newberry Enterprise, March 22, 1894;

"Notes on Interview with News Editor," *Newberry News 100th Birthday Issue*, September 1, 1982.

76   Household of Jas. F. Wilkinson, "United States Census, 1870," database with images, *FamilySearch* (https://familysearch.org/ark:/61903/1:1:MHH1-XM5 : 17 October 2014), Clara Wilkinson in household of Jas F Wilkinson, Michigan, United States; citing p. 8, family 62, NARA microfilm publication M593 (Washington, DC: National Archives and Records Administration, n.d.); FHL microfilm 552,183;

Michigan Marriage Record, William S. Grismore to Clara Wilkinson, November 9, 1870, "Michigan Marriages, 1868-1925," database with images, *FamilySearch* (https://familysearch.org/ark:/61903/1:1:N3ZG-KHM : 4 December 2014), William S. Grismore and Clara Wilkinson, 09 Nov 1870; citing Attica, Lapeer, Michigan, v 2 p 181 rn591, Department of Vital Records, Lansing; FHL microfilm 2,342,451;

Michigan Marriage Record, Milan Canfield to Clarissa Wilkinson, October 5, 1873; "Michigan Marriages, 1868-1925," database with images, *FamilySearch* (https://familysearch.org/ark:/61903/1:1:N3DD-JBH : 4 December 2014), Milan Canfield and Clarissa Wilkinson, 05 Oct 1873; citing Elkland, Tuscola, Michigan, v 3 p 217 rn 147, Department of Vital Records, Lansing; FHL microfilm 2,342,457;

Michigan Marriage Record, Franklin Saulsbury to Clara Wilkinson Canfield, April 4, 1877, "Michigan Marriages, 1868-1925," database with images, *FamilySearch* (https://familysearch.org/ark:/61903/1:1:NQSX-9ZD : 4 December 2014), Franklin Saulsbury and Clara Wilkinson Cainfield, 04 Apr 1877; citing Imlay City, Lapeer, Michigan, v 2 p 219 rn 1744, Department of Vital Records, Lansing; FHL microfilm 2,342,461;

Household of Charles Harrington, "United States Census, 1880," database with images, *FamilySearch* (https://familysearch.org/ark:/61903/1:1:MW3X-WH5 : 10 August 2016), Charles Harrington, Evergreen, Sanilac, Michigan, United States; citing enumeration district ED 332, sheet 89C, NARA microfilm publication T9 (Washington, DC: National Archives and Records Administration, n.d.), roll 0605; FHL microfilm 1,254,605;

Michigan Marriage Record, William Rust to Clara Canfield Wilkinson, April 10, 1882, "Michigan Marriages, 1868-1925," database with images, *FamilySearch* (https://familysearch.org/ark:/61903/1:1:N3N4-9MN : 4 December 2014), William Rust and Clara Canfield Wilkinson, 10 Apr 1882; citing Gaylord, Otsego, Michigan, v 3 p 73 rn 6, Department of Vital Records, Lansing; FHL microfilm 2,342,471;

Household of Clara Strobridge, "United States Census, 1900," database with images, *FamilySearch* (https://familysearch.org/ark:/61903/1:1:M918-G1G : 20 January 2015), Clara Strobridge, Burt township, Alger, Michigan, United States; citing sheet 18A, family 311, NARA microfilm publication T623 (Washington, DC: National Archives and Records Administration, n.d.); FHL microfilm 1,240,698;

Michigan Death Certificate of Jason Canfield, June 26, 1876, "Michigan Deaths, 1867-1897," database with images, *FamilySearch* (https://familysearch.org/ark:/61903/1:1:N3NS-94Z : 12 December 2014), Jason Canfield, 26 Jun 1876; citing p 91 rn 1566, Cass City, Tuscola, Michigan, Department of Vital Records, Lansing; FHL microfilm 2,363,664

77   "Newsites," *Newberry News*, January 6, 1887;

"Our Man About Town," *Newberry News*, August 10, 1889;

"Newsites," *Newberry News*, November 11, 1886.

78   "Newsites," *Newberry News*, February 17, 1887;

"Local News," *Newberry News*, August 25, 1887;

Newberry News, September 1, 1887;

"Local," *Newberry News*, May 24, 1888.

79   "Our Man About Town," *Newberry News*, August 10, 1889.

80   *Newberry Independent*, August 8, 1889;

Michigan Marriage Record, Carrie [sic] Canfield to August Spooner, February 18, 1891, "Michigan Marriages, 1868-1925," database with images, *FamilySearch* (https://familysearch.org/ark:/61903/1:1:NQSR-36Z

: 4 December 2014), August Spooner and Carrie Cainfield, 18 Feb 1891; citing Cheboygan, Cheboygan, Michigan, v 1 p 357 rn 206, Department of Vital Records, Lansing; FHL microfilm 2,342,490;

Michigan Marriage Record, Joseph Lanway to Clara Wilkinson Canfield, July 21, 1894, "Michigan Marriages, 1868-1925," database with images, *FamilySearch* (https://familysearch.org/ark:/61903/1:1:NQSY-6YM : 4 December 2014), Joseph Lanway and Clara Wilkinson Canfield, 21 Jul 1894; citing South Arm, Charlevoix, Michigan, v 1 p 5 rn 329, Department of Vital Records, Lansing; FHL microfilm 2,342,498.

81   "A Happy Mother," *Newberry News*, April 20, 1900.

82   "Pinkey Arrested," *Newberry News*, September 6, 1901.

83   (NOTE: Pinky's ultimate fate is a frustrating mystery, as her many various legal names and aliases make her difficult to track. I have searched census records, death certificates, newspaper clippings, but can find no trace of her after 1901.)

"Stealing Camp Supplies," *Newberry News*, August 7, 1903;

"Bound Over to Trial," *Newberry News*, August 14, 1903;

"Collins Gets Two Years," *Newberry News*, October 23, 1903;

Michigan Death Certificate of Truman Strickland Strowbridge, November 5, 1936 <www.seekingmichigan.com>.

84   "Local," *Newberry News*, March 29, 1888.

85   "Malicious Depredation," *Newberry News*, December 23, 1910.

86   "Local," *Newberry News*, April 9, 1915.

87   "The Stone Pile Cure," *Newberry News*, September 15, 1905;

"Judge Harris Adopts New Plan to Get Rid of Tramp Nuisance," *Newberry News*, October 20, 1905;

"Prisoners to Work on Roads," *Newberry News*, April 21, 1916.

88   "The Last Pine Is Being Cut," *Newberry News*, December 15, 1911.

89   "A Small Riot," *Newberry News*, September 22, 1905.

90   "Dollarville Doings," *Newberry News*, August 15, 1890.

91   "Local," *Newberry News,* August 22, 1890.

92   "Knocked His Block Off," *Newberry News*, December 28, 1906.

93   *Newberry News*, June 16, 1887;

Newberry News, December 1, 1887;

Newberry News, January 5, 1894.

94   "Collecting a Debt," *Newberry News*, March 2, 1894;

"Threatens the Editor," *Newberry News*, May 20, 1892;

Frank H. Peters, "Letter to the Editor," *Newberry Enterprise*, March 8, 1894.

95   "Assault," *Newberry News*, September 28, 1894.

96   Robert Dollar, *Memoirs of Robert Dollar*, (San Francisco: W.S. Van Cott & Co, 1918), 26.

97   "Held for Trial," *Newberry News*, October 27, 1893.

98   "Marshal Crocker's Statement," *Newberry News*, September 1, 1887.

99   *Newberry News*, July 22, 1886; December 16, 1886; April 7, 1887; April 28, 1887; June 30, 1887; November 17, 1887.

100   "Escape of Prisoners," *Newberry News*, November 9, 1894.

101   *Newberry News*, May 10, 1888.

102   "Local," *Newberry Independent*, May 15, 1890;

"Local," *Newberry News*, April 25, 1890.

103   "Broke Jail," *Newberry News*, August 14, 1891.

104   "A Serious Charge," *Newberry Enterprise*, November 1, 1894;

"Escape of Prisoners," *Newberry News*, November 9, 1894;

"Is Pingree Crazy?" *Newberry News*, December 28, 1900;

"Did Good Work," *Newberry News*, May 24, 1895.

"Three More Pardons," *Detroit Free Press*, December 23, 1900, page 24.

105   Sterling McGinn, "Luce County's Original Courthouse," *Historical Society Notes*, Volume VII, Issue 1, Spring 2015.

106   "Took Leg Bail," *Newberry News*, September 27, 1901;

"Captured McLeod," *Newberry News*, March 28, 1902;

"Circuit Court," *Newberry News*, May 9, 1902.

107   "Took Leg Bail," *Newberry News*, December 19, 1902.

108   "Prisoner Escaped," *Newberry News,* June 27, 1913.

109   "Our Man About Town," *Newberry News*, May 18, 1889.

110   *Newberry News*, September 27, 1888; January 18, 1907;

"Candy Kitchen Burglarized," *Newberry News*, March 10, 1905;

"Got Twenty Days," *Newberry News*, November 4, 1904;

"Made Spurious Coin," *Newberry News*, March 10, 1905;

"Local," *Newberry News*, November 10, 1916.

(NOTE: Mary Tebo was employed by Oliver Labombard. She may have been committed to the State Hospital.)

111   "Youthful Wrongdoers," *Newberry News*, September 29, 1899;

"Local News," *Newberry News*, June 27, 1890.

112   "Thugs at Trout Lake," *Newberry News*, October 13, 1893; "Fleeced by Sharpers at Trout Lake," *Newberry News*, November 17, 1893; "Michigan Exhibits," *Detroit Free Press*, November 20, 1893, page 2.

113   "Local," *Newberry News*, August 26, 1898;

"Robbed," *Newberry News*, May 12, 1899.

114   "Thrashed the Toughs," *Newberry News*, July 7, 1899.

115   "Used a Shotgun," *Newberry News*, January 1, 1904.

116   "Finlander Runs Amuck," *Newberry News*, January 27, 1911;

(NOTE: His last name is also spelled in news reports as Payfanen and Pafanen.)

117   "Shooting Affray," *Newberry News*, June 7, 1912.

118   Rintamaki, "Looking Back: The Saga of Deadman's Farm," *Newberry News*, March 7, 1984, March 14, 1984, March 21, 1984, and March 28, 1984.

119   "A Trip on the Taquamenaw," *Newberry Enterprise*, June 21, 1894.

"Dead Man's Farm," *Newberry News*, November 3, 1905.

120   "Unsolved Mysteries of the North Woods," *Newberry News*, November 22, 1940.

121   "Oakley Rivers, "Mystery of the Tahquamenon," *Newberry News*, August 7, 1931.

122   "Man Killed," *Newberry News*, November 1, 1888;

"Murder at Wood Camps," *Newberry News*, March 23, 1906.

123   "Fatal Stabbing Affray," *Newberry News*, November 6, 1891;

"Local News," *Newberry News*, November 13, 1891.

124   "Local News," *Newberry News*, February 26, 1892.

125   "Fatal Stabbing Affray," *Newberry News*, December 28, 1894.

126   "Deliberate Murder," *Newberry News*, June 4, 1897;

"Circuit   Court,"   *Newberry   News*,   October   29,   1897;
    Michigan Death Certificate of Richard Palmer, April 22, 1922 <www.seekingmichigan.com>.

127   "Montgomery's History," *Newberry News*, August 9, 1907;

"Murdered," *Newberry News*, August 2, 1907;

Michigan Death Certificate of Frank Montgomery, July 27, 1907 <www.seekingmichigan.com>;

"Plead Guilty," *Newberry News*, October 18, 1907.

(NOTE: News articles say that Henry Colburn had a wife and child, but while he did have a wife, I could not find
    any evidence of a child. Good thing.)

128

Chapter Five: To Drink or Not to Drink

"Horrible Accident," *Newberry News*, October 21, 1886;

(NOTE: The news article mentioned that James "Clockesy" was from Point Edward, Ontario, and was traveling
    with his (unnamed) eighteen-year-old brother. The family actually appears to have been Cloghessy, an
    Irish-Canadian family, whose surname was variously spelled Clochecy, Clockesy, Cloghesy, Cloghessy,
    Clochnessy, Clohessy, Cloghessy, Cloghise, and Cloagrosy. However, as James Cloghessy *was* only eighteen
    years old in 1886, the article must have gotten the names mixed-up. The man whose ear was ripped off may
    be one of his older brothers, John, Thomas, or Patrick.).

129   *Newberry News*, February 23, 1889;

Newberry News, March 2, 1889.

130   "Met a Horrible Death," *Newberry News*, October 19, 1900;

"Killed by Train," *Newberry News*, August 3, 1906;

"Train Cuts Man to Pieces," *Newberry News*, October 6, 1911.

131   "Killed by Train," *Newberry News*, May 16, 1913;

"Train Strikes Indian," *Newberry News*, August 15, 1913;

"King Barleycorn Gets Another Victim," *Newberry News*, October 3, 1913; "Highway Robbery," *Newberry News*,
    March 30, 1917;

(NOTE: The George Asland killed in 1913 is not to be confused with George Arthur Asland who lived in Gould
    City at about the same time. They are two different men.)

132   "A Saloon Brawl," *Newberry News*, December 19, 1902;

"Given Knock Out Drops," *Newberry News*, March 3, 1905;

"Trouble at Trout Lake," *Newberry News*, May 18, 1900;

"Local and County News," *Newberry News*, December 29, 1893;

"Man Loses Proboscis in Drunken Brawl Sunday Afternoon," *Newberry News*, September 22, 1916.

133   "Another Victim," *Newberry News*, June 22, 1900.

134   "Run Down by Drunken Farmer," *Newberry News*, October 25, 1907.

135   "Here and There," *Newberry News*, February 2, 1889;

"Additional Local," *Newberry News*, September 27, 1907;

(NOTE: It is unclear who "Matt Hakala" is exactly, as there were several men with that name living in the area at the time, including one Matt Hakala who had two sons named Matt Victor and Matt Ivari.)

136   "Local," *Newberry News*, November 9, 1900;

"Death Claims His Own," *Newberry News*, December 14, 1900.

137   Michigan Death Certificate of Sanna Lizzie Anderson, December 26, 1910, <www.seekingmichigan.com>;

Household of David Riberg, "United States Census, 1900," database with images, *FamilySearch* (https://familysearch.org/ark:/61903/1:1:MS97-T4D : 20 January 2015), David Riberg, Newberry village, Luce, Michigan, United States; citing sheet 8B, family 150, NARA microfilm publication T623 (Washington, DC: National Archives and Records Administration, n.d.); FHL microfilm 1,240,726.

138   Michigan Marriage Record Sanna Lisa Riberg to John Jerrenpaa, February 1, 1890, "Michigan Marriages, 1868-1925," database with images, *FamilySearch* (https://familysearch.org/ark:/61903/1:1:NQW8-6R5 : 4 December 2014), John Jerrenpaa and Sanna Lisa Rieberg, 01 Feb 1890; citing Newberry, Luce, Michigan, v 3 p 118 rn 75, Department of Vital Records, Lansing; FHL microfilm 2,342,488;

Newberry News, February 6, 1890;

"A Determined Suicide," *Newberry News*, July 9, 1897;

Household of Victor Riberg, "United States Census, 1900," database with images, *FamilySearch* (https://familysearch.org/ark:/61903/1:1:MS9Q-TNZ : 20 January 2015), Victor Riberg, McMillan township (excl. Newberry village), Luce, Michigan, United States; citing sheet 9A, family 148, NARA microfilm publication T623 (Washington, DC: National Archives and Records Administration, n.d.); FHL microfilm 1,240,726;

Michigan Marriage Record Matt Anderson to Susan Mrs. Riberg Kokra, April 8, 1901. "Michigan Marriages, 1868-1925," database with images, *FamilySearch* (https://familysearch.org/ark:/61903/1:1:N38J-GSJ : 4 December 2014), Matt Anderson and Susan Mrs Riberg Kokra, 08 Apr 1901; citing Newberry, Luce, Michigan, v 3 p 124 rn 342, Department of Vital Records, Lansing; FHL microfilm 2,342,519;

Newberry News, April 12, 1901;

Household of Matt Anderson, "United States Census, 1910," database with images, *FamilySearch* (https://familysearch.org/ark:/61903/1:1:ML51-76X : 29 October 2015), Matt Anderson, McMillan, Luce, Michigan, United States; citing enumeration district (ED) ED 157, sheet 10A, NARA microfilm publication T624 (Washington, DC: National Archives and Records Administration, n.d.); FHL microfilm 1,374,671;

"Michigan Deaths and Burials, 1800-1995," database, *FamilySearch* (https://familysearch.org/ark:/61903/1:1:FHKD-J73 : 9 December 2014), Jacob Emili Koukkari, 01 Jun 1894; citing Newberry, Luce, Michigan, reference v 1 p 5; FHL microfilm 1,008,004;

Michigan Death Certificates for Mary Anderson (July 15, 1903), Matt Victor Anderson (September 17, 1903), Mamie Anderson (September 15, 1904), Toivo Anderson (September 25, 1910) <www.seekingmichigan.com>.

139   "Christmas Drunk," *Newberry News*, December 30, 1910;

"Plead Guilty," *Newberry News*, January 6, 1911;

Michigan Death Certificate, Matt Anderson, May 11, 1911 <www.seekingmichigan.com>;

"Died in Prison," *Newberry News*, May 19, 1911.

140   "Three are Burned," *Newberry News*, March 21, 1913.

141   "Local," *Newberry News*, September 30, 1898;

"Local," *Newberry News*, October 28, 1898.

142   Hanes and Musgrave, 153-154;

"Communicated," *Newberry News*, March 24, 1887.

143   "Will Locate Here," *Newberry News*, July 10, 1903;

"McMillan: Its Early History and New Found Prosperity," *Newberry News*, December 16, 1904.

144   Hanes and Musgrave, 60;

"New Livery Barn," *Newberry News*, February 10, 1905.

145   "Drug Store at McMillan," *Newberry News*, July 20, 1906;

"McMillan: Its Early History and New Found Prosperity," *Newberry News*, December 16, 1904.

146   Hanes and Musgrave, 7, 43, 64, 153-154;

"A Disagreement," *Newberry News*, October 19, 1906.

147   "Wholesale Arrests," *Newberry News*, July 20, 1906.

148   "The Fire Bugs," *Newberry News*, July 27, 1906;

"Circuit Court," *Newberry News*, May 11, 1906;

"Wholesale Arrests," *Newberry News*, July 20, 1906.

149   "The McMillan Fire Bug," *Newberry News*, June 8, 1906;

"Local," *Newberry News*, June 15, 1906.

150   "A Disagreement," *Newberry News*, October 19, 1906;

"The McMillan Firebug," *Newberry News*, June 8, 1906;

"Wholesale Arrests," *Newberry News*, July 20, 1906.

151   "Wholesale Arrests," *Newberry News*, July 20, 1906.

152   "Wholesale Arrests," *Newberry News*, July 20, 1906.

153   "The Fire Bugs," *Newberry News*, July 27, 1906.

154   "Held for Trial," *Newberry News*, August 3, 1906;

"Another McMillan Blaze," *Newberry News*, August 10, 1906.

155   "Circuit Court," *Newberry News*, October 12, 1906.

156   "A Disagreement," *Newberry News*, October 19, 1906;

"Circuit Court," *Newberry News*, October 12, 1906.

157   "Will be Tried at the Soo," *Newberry News*, October 26, 1906;

"The Mark Case," *Newberry News*, February 22, 1907;

"Not Guilty," *Newberry News*, March 1, 1907.

158   "Rutledge Confesses," *Newberry News*, March 15, 1907;

"Circuit Court," *Newberry News*, May 10, 1907.

159   "A Retraction," *Newberry News*, June 26, 1908;

"Circuit Court," *Newberry News*, October 16, 1908.

160   "Here and There," *Newberry News*, February 2, 1889;

"Here and There," *Newberry News*, March 9, 1889;

"Robbed Company Store," *Newberry News*, September 29, 1916;

"Local," *Newberry News*, May 2, 1930.

161   "In Contempt," *Newberry News*, November 23, 1906;

"Decision Confirmed," *Newberry News*, December 28, 1906;

"Circuit Court," *Newberry News*, January 25, 1907.

162   "Make McMillan Dry," *Newberry News*, April 23, 1915.

163   "Mark Is Acquitted," *Newberry News*, November 5, 1915;

"Dropped Dead," *Newberry News*, May 24, 1918.

164   "Prohibition was Defeated," *Newberry News*, April 8, 1910.

165   "Only Three Days to Live," *Newberry News*, April 26, 1918.

166   "Large Crowds See Rum Demise," *Newberry News*, May 3, 1918.

167   "Dray Load of Booze Seized," *Newberry News*, May 10, 1918.

Chapter Six: That Old Time Religion

168   "Council Proceedings," *Newberry News*, June 10, 1886.

169   "The Founders Don't Forget," *Newberry News*, June 28, 1918.

170   "Newberry Presbyterian Church," *Newberry Independent*, September 26, 1889;

"History of the Presbyterian Church," *The History of Luce County: Volume II Past Years*, ed. Hilja Pekkarinen and Minnie Ida Mattson (Newberry, Michigan: *Newberry News*, 1981), 757-759.

171   "The Founders Don't Forget," *Newberry News*, June 28, 1918;

"Doing Good Work," *Newberry News*, April 13, 1894.

172   "Thirty-Seventh Anniversary," *Newberry News*, October 14, 1927; "Methodist Church has Pioneer History in Village," *Newberry News*, September 25, 1958;

Methodist Episcopal," *Newberry Independent*, September 26, 1889;

Ronald A. Brunger, "Early History of the Methodist Episcopal Church," *The History of Luce County: Volume II Past Years*. ed. Hilja Pekkarinen and Minne Ida Mattson (Newberry, Michigan: *Newberry News*, 1981), 817;

(NOTE: The name of the first Methodist minister was spelled "Bigloe" in local news stories. However, other sources spell it Bigelow, and that is probably the correct one.)

173   "Local," *Newberry News*, March 6, 1914;

"The Newberry Presbyterian Church," *Newberry Independent*, April 5, 1894; "Doing Good Work," *Newberry News*, April 13, 1894.

174   "Fire Damages Parsonage," *Newberry News*, June 7, 1912;

"Pastor is Jailed," *Newberry News*, February 20, 1914.

175   "Trip to Europe Beneficial," *Newberry News*, August 23, 1912;

"Will Leave Newberry," *Newberry News*, August 30, 1912;

"Crank Burns Minister's Home," *Newberry News*, January 30, 1914.

176   "Crank Burns Minister's Home," *Newberry News*, January 30, 1914;

"May Never Face Trial," *Newberry News*, June 5, 1914.

177   "Out on Bail," *Newberry News*, February 27, 1914;

"May Never Face Trial," *Newberry News*, June 5, 1914;

"Rev. Joseph Cottam Found Not Guilty," *Newberry News*, October 23, 1914; "Clean Bill," *Detroit Free Press*, December 8, 1916, page 3.

178   "St. Gregory's Observes Centennial Year," *Newberry News*, January 8, 1986;

"Cornerstone Ceremonies," *Newberry News*, July 7, 1950;

"Newberry Catholic," *Newberry News*, September 1, 1887.

179   "Newsites," *Newberry News*, September 16, 1886;

"Cornerstone Ceremonies," *Newberry News*, July 7, 1950.

180   "The New Catholic Church Gone Up in Smoke," *Newberry News*, February 3, 1887;

"The Catholic Church Is to Be Rebuilt," *Newberry News*, February 10, 1887; "Newsites," *Newberry News*, February 17, 1887;

"The Catholic Church is to be Rebuilt," *Newberry News*, February 10, 1887; "Newberry Catholic," *Newberry News*, September 1, 1887.

181   "Local," *Newberry News*, October 21, 1898;

"Local," *Newberry News*, September 6, 1901;

"Father Manning's Birthday," *Newberry News*, May 19, 1893;

"Local," *Newberry News*, July 30, 1897;

"Our Man About Town," *Newberry News*, July 6, 1889;

"Heard on the Street," *Newberry News*, June 14, 1888;

"Death of Mrs. Manning," *Newberry News*, November 7, 1890;

"Death of Miss Manning," *Newberry News*, July 10, 1896;

"Death of Father Manning," *Newberry News*, October 30, 1908.

182   "Local News," *Newberry News*, October 6, 1887.

183   "Local and County News," *Newberry News*, May 5, 1893;

"Local," *Newberry News*, March 1, 1890;

"Local News," *Newberry News*, January 11, 1890;

"Finnish Church 75th Birthday," *Newberry News*, May 2, 1963.

184   *Newberry News*, May 27, 1892;

"Dedication Ceremony," *Newberry News*, August 19, 1898.

185   "Local and County News," *Newberry News*, July 1, 1892;

"Episcopal Church Dedicated," *Newberry News*, February 15, 1901.

186   Philip Abblebaum, "The Jews of Luce County, Michigan," *Michigan Jewish History*, Volume 21, Number 1, January1981, 3-9.

187   "Profile of Rosenthal," *Newberry News*, October 21, 1892;

"Local and County News," *Newberry News*, October 28, 1892;

"Local and County News," *Newberry News*, November 4, 1892.

188   Abblebaum, 3-9.

189   "Local News," *Newberry News*, December 15, 1887;

"Local," *Newberry News*, January 19, 1888;

"Local," *Newberry News*, April 11, 1890;

"Local and County News," *Newberry News*, June 24, 1892; "Misrepresented," *Newberry News*, May 11, 1894.

190   "Manistique Lake," *Newberry News*, July 8, 1886;

"Newsites," *Newberry News*, June 24, 1886;

"Correspondence," *Newberry News*, March 8, 1890;

"Rev. J.P. Mills and Wife," *Newberry Independent*, August 1, 1889.

191   "Communicated," *Newberry Independent*, July 24, 1890.

192   "Communicated," *Newberry Independent*, August 7, 1890.

193

Chapter Seven: School Bells

Household of Robert Bryers, "United States Census, 1880," database with images, *FamilySearch* (https://familysearch.org/ark:/61903/1:1:MWSR-MB9 : 10 August 2016), Robert Bryers, Newton, Mackinac, Michigan, United States; citing enumeration district ED 42, sheet 269A, NARA microfilm publication T9 (Washington, DC: National Archives and Records Administration, n.d.), roll 0592; FHL microfilm 1,254,592;

Rintamaki, "Looking Back," *Newberry News*, September 19, 1984;

Louise and Dan Gooseberry, "Working at the Charcoal Iron Company," *Luce County History: Centennial Edition*, ed. Hilja Pekkarinen, Minnie Ida Mattson, and Phyllis Brumm. (Chelsea, Michigan, Bookcrafters, 1985), 485.

194   "More Early School History," *Newberry News*, August 26, 1927;

Rintamaki, "Looking Back: McMillan Township Had Many Schools Before the First World War," *Newberry News*, September 12, 1984;

"School Report," *Newberry News*, June 24, 1886.

195   "Report of the Standing of Pupils in the Academic Room," *Newberry News*, July 14, 1887;

"Dollarville," *Newberry News*, December 8, 1887.

196   "Newsites," *Newberry News*, June 17, 1886;

"School Report," *Newberry News*, June 24, 1886;

"Newsites," *Newberry News*, September 9, 1886.

197   "Our Man About Town," *Newberry News*, August 17, 1889;

"Our Man About Town," *Newberry News*, October 5, 1889;

"Local and County News," *Newberry News*, June 24, 1892;

"Newberry Public Schools: Miss Estelle Jenney," *Newberry Enterprise Special Edition*, October 1894.

198   "Schools Opened," *Newberry News*, September 6, 1895;

"The School House," *Newberry News*, August 18, 1893;

"Annual Report," *Newberry News*, August 13, 1897;

"School House Improvements," *Newberry News*, August 20, 1897.

199   "Annual Report," *Newberry News*, August 13, 1897.

200   "Local and County News," *Newberry News*, March 10, 1893.

201   "Newberry Public Schools: Miss Clemie Somerville," *Newberry Enterprise Special Edition*, October 1894.

202   "Newberry School Report," *Newberry News*, December 8, 1893;

"School Notes," *Newberry News*, February 8, 1895;

"Newberry Public Schools," *Newberry News*, March 29, 1895.

203   "Annual Report of the Newberry Public Schools to the Board of Education," *Newberry News*, June 30, 1893;

"Newberry School Report," *Newberry News*, December 8, 1893;

"Newberry Public Schools," *Newberry News*, January 5, 1894.

204   "Newberry Public Schools," *Newberry News*, March 2, 1894;

"Newberry Public School Report," *Newberry News*, July 9, 1897;

"Newberry Public Schools, Intermediate Department," *Newberry News*, October 7, 1898.

205 "Newberry Public Schools," *Newberry News*, May 5, 1893;

"Local and County News," *Newberry News*, March 10, 1893;

"Annual Report," *Newberry News*, August 13, 1897;

"Newberry Public Schools: Miss Edith Bettes," *Newberry Enterprise Special Edition*, October 1894.

206 "Newberry Public Schools: Miss Sara A. Campbell," *Newberry Enterprise Special Edition*, October 1894;

"Local and County News," *Newberry News*, January 13, 1893;

"Newberry Public Schools," February 3, 1893;

"Local and County News," *Newberry News*, March 10, 1893.

207 "Newberry Public Schools: Miss Estelle Jenney," *Newberry Enterprise Special Edition*, October 1894;

"Annual Report," *Newberry News*, August 13, 1897.

208 School Notes," *Newberry News*, March 27, 1903;

Rintamaki, "Looking Back," *Newberry News*, July 5, 1984;

"Local," *Newberry News*, March 16, 1961;

"Joseph A. Pelletier" (obituary), *Newberry News*, March 8, 1946;

"Mrs. Emily Pelletier" (obituary), *Newberry News*, May 30, 1963;

"Household of Joseph Pelletier," "United States Census, 1940," database with images, *FamilySearch* (https://familysearch.org/ark:/61903/1:1:K4G4-JJW : accessed 19 August 2016), Joseph Pelletier, McMillan Township, Luce, Michigan, United States; citing enumeration district (ED) 48-4, sheet 61A, family 9, Sixteenth Census of the United States, 1940, NARA digital publication T627. Records of the Bureau of the Census, 1790–2007, RG 29. Washington, DC: National Archives and Records Administration, 2012, roll 1781.

"Household of Fred Beaudoin," "United States Census, 1900," database with images, *FamilySearch* (https://familysearch.org/ark:/61903/1:1:MS97-JKY : 20 January 2015), Fred Beaudoin, Newberry village, Luce, Michigan, United States; citing sheet 8A, family 144, NARA microfilm publication T623 (Washington, D.C.: National Archives and Records Administration, n.d.); FHL microfilm 1,240,726.

(NOTE: Joseph Pelletier, listed as "Afoe," was Fred's brother-in-law).

209 "Local and County News," *Newberry News*, August 25, 1893;

"Additional Local," *Newberry News*, August 30, 1907;

"Local," *Newberry News*, June 24, 1910;

"Cora M. Sherman," *Newberry News*, November 9, 1951.

210 "Newberry Public Schools: Prof. A. D. Chisholm," *Newberry Enterprise Special Edition*, October 1894;

"School Report," *Newberry News*, May 5, 1893;

"Roll of Honor," *Newberry News*, February 9, 1894;

"Newberry Public Schools," *Newberry News*, March 2, 1894;

"School Notes," *Newberry News*, February 8, 1895;

"School Notes," *Newberry News*, May 10 1895;

"Annual Report," *Newberry News*, August 13, 1897.

211 "School Notes," *Newberry News*, June 7, 1895;

"Household of Royal A. Jenney," "United States Census, 1900," database with images, *FamilySearch* (https://familysearch.org/ark:/61903/1:1:M9B5-Z9P : 20 January 2015), Royal A. Jenney, Ann Arbor city Ward 6, Washtenaw, Michigan, United States; citing sheet 12A, family 200, NARA microfilm publication T623 (Washington, DC: National Archives and Records Administration, n.d.); FHL microfilm 1,240,746;

Michigan Marriage Record Byron Fred Ott to Pearl Jenney, August 23, 1904, "Michigan Marriages, 1868-1925," database with images, *FamilySearch* (https://familysearch.org/ark:/61903/1:1:N3FG-Y54 : 4 December 2014), Byron Fred K. Ott and O. Pearl Jenney, 23 Aug 1904; citing Ann Arbor, Washtenaw, Michigan, vol 4 p 383 rn 1233, Department of Vital Records, Lansing; FHL microfilm 2,342,669;

Household of Byron Ott," "United States Census, 1910," database with images, *FamilySearch* (https://familysearch.org/ark:/61903/1:1:M5X4-J9X : 29 October 2015), Byron F Ott, Salt Lake City Ward 5, Salt Lake City, Utah, United States; citing enumeration district (ED) ED 142, sheet 1A, NARA microfilm publication T624 (Washington, D.C.: National Archives and Records Administration, n.d.); FHL microfilm 1,375,620;

"Local," *Newberry News*, August 20, 1897;

"Local," *Newberry News*, March 17, 1899;

"Popular Young Couple United in Marriage," *Newberry News*, October 13, 1905;

"Household of Hibbard J. Ingalls," "United States Census, 1910," database with images, *FamilySearch* (https://familysearch.org/ark:/61903/1:1:M2GJ-968 : 29 October 2015), Hibbard J. Ingalls, Coleraine, Itasca, Minnesota, United States; citing enumeration district (ED) ED 63, sheet 1A, NARA microfilm publication T624 (Washington, D.C.: National Archives and Records Administration, n.d.); FHL microfilm 1,374,720;

"Local," *Newberry News*, June 30, 1889; "Local," *Newberry News*, September 2, 1898;

"Household of Elmer McPhee," "United States Census, 1920," database with images, *FamilySearch* (https://familysearch.org/ark:/61903/1:1:MZQ6-G1K : 14 December 2015), Elmer R Mcphee, Marquette, Marquette County, Michigan, United States; citing sheet 3B, NARA microfilm publication T625 (Washington, DC: National Archives and Records Administration, n.d.); FHL microfilm 1,820,784

212   "Local," *Newberry News*, October 18, 1901;

"Local," *Newberry News*, July 3, 1903.

213   "School Bus in Operation," *Newberry News*, September 17, 1926; "Dollarville Public Schools," *Newberry News*, March 1, 1895.

214   "Rural Teachers Engaged," *Newberry News*, May 9, 1913;

"Local," *Newberry News*, August 1, 1902;

"Local," *Newberry News*, June 5, 1903.

215   "Local and County News," *Newberry News*, August 4, 1893;

"Local," *Newberry News*, May 10, 1912;

Hanes and Musgrave, 391-394.

216   "Newsites," *Newberry News*, June 24, 1886;

"Lakefield," *Newberry Independent*, August 1, 1889.

217   Angus D. Chisholm, "Our Schools," *Newberry News*, August 3, 1894; "Lakefield," *Newberry Independent*, August 1, 1889.

218   "Local," *Newberry News*, September 16, 1898;

"School Notes," *Newberry News*, November 15, 1901;

"School Notes," *Newberry News*, March 9, 1894.

219   "Roat School Report," *Newberry News*, June 8, 1906;

Rintamaki, "Looking Back: School No Longer Taught to the Tune of a Hickory Stick," *Newberry News*, September 5, 1984;

Household of John Fyvie, "United States Census, 1900," database with images, *FamilySearch* (https://familysearch.org/ark:/61903/1:1:MS9Q-PCZ : 20 January 2015), John Fyvir, Lakefield township, Luce, Michigan, United States; citing sheet 9B, family 68, NARA microfilm publication T623 (Washington, DC: National Archives and Records Administration, n.d.); FHL microfilm 1,240,726.

"Compulsory School Law," *Newberry* News, September 29, 1905.

220   E. W. Kiebler, *The Old Log School by the Lake*, (Newberry, Michigan: Luce County Historical Society, 1953), 30. <https://catalog.hathitrust.org/Record/003118922>.

221   Angus D. Chisholm, "Our Schools," *Newberry News*, August 3, 1894;

"Local," *Newberry News*, September 25, 1903.

222   "Teachers' Examinations," *Newberry News*, November 9, 1894.

223   "Teachers' Examinations," *Newberry News*, November 9, 1894.

224   "Saved by a Faithful Dog," *Newberry News*, September 2, 1898.

225   "School Notes," *Newberry News*, September 2, 1898.

226   "Schools Reopen," *Newberry News*, September 1, 1905;

"Local," *Newberry News*, August 12, 1898;

"A Model School," *Newberry News*, August 26, 1904;

"School Notes," *Newberry News*, November 25, 1904;

"New School Needed," *Newberry News*, December 20, 1901.

227   "School Notes," *Newberry News*, October 14, 1904;

"School Notes," *Newberry* News, October 9, 1903;

"School Notes," *Newberry News*, November 15, 1901.

228   "Standard Schools," *Newberry News*, February 11, 1916;

Hanes and Musgrave, 394. The requirements for a "Standard School" can be found in the *Seventy-Seventh Annual Report of the Superintendent of Public Instruction of the State of Michigan for the Year 1913-1914.*

229   "United States Census, 1900," database with images, *FamilySearch* (https://familysearch.org/ark:/61903/1:1:MS97-MPL : 20 January 2015) , Pentland township, Luce, Michigan, United States; citing sheet 1A, family 1, NARA microfilm publication T623 (Washington, DC: National Archives and Records Administration, n.d.); FHL microfilm 1,240,726. Sheet No. 1 (218A) to Sheet No 3 (220A);

"Lakefield," *Newberry Independent*, August 1, 1889;

"Two Days of Pleasure," *Newberry News*, January 21, 1898;

"Local," *Newberry News*, January 5, 1900.

230   See various monthly "School Notes," articles from the *Newberry News*, especially the years 1904-1905.

231   "Nearly Quarter Million Dollars," *Newberry News*, December 25, 1908.

232   "Schools Reopen," *Newberry News*, September 6, 1912;

"Schools Open August 30," *Newberry News*, August 27, 1915.

233   "Remain in School," *Newberry News*, June 20, 1913;

"Six and Six Plan," *Newberry News*, July 17, 1914.

234   "Six and Six Plan," *Newberry News*, July 17, 1914;

"Must Pay Tuition," *Newberry News*, August 29, 1913;

"To Pay School Fees," *Newberry News*, September 13, 1895;

Hanes and Musgrave, 185-177.

235   "Schools Open August 30," *Newberry News*, August 27, 1915.

236   "Dedication Services Tonight," *Newberry News*, June 10, 1927.

237   Hanes and Musgrave, 144;

"School Bus in Operation," *Newberry News*, September 17, 1926

"Local," *Newberry News*, January 16, 1920.

Chapter Eight: Taking Care of Business

238   Advertisement: Duluth, South Shore and Atlantic Railway Timetable, *Newberry News*, November 9, 1894;

Hanes and Musgrave, 20-21.

239   Rintamaki, "Looking Back: Slag Was Useful Product of Iron Making." *Newberry News*, May 30, 1984;

Rintamaki, "Looking Back: Old Iron Company Days Recalled by Louis Gooseberry," *Newberry News*, June 27, 1984;

Rintamaki, "Looking Back: Local 'Iron Men' Made Newberry Iron Industry Go," *Newberry News*, June 27, 1984;

"Newberry Furnace Co," *Newberry Independent*, September 26, 1889.

240   Rintamaki, "Looking Back: Louis Gooseberry Explains Iron Making Process at Newberry," *Newberry News*, May 16, 1984.

241   Rintamaki, "Looking Back: Louis Gooseberry Explains Iron Making Process at Newberry," *Newberry News*, May 16, 1984;

"Furnace Items," *Newberry News*, July 22, 1886;

"Here and There," *Newberry News*, March 9, 1889.

242   "No Noodles in Newberry," *Newberry News*, September 6, 1888;

Rintamaki, "Looking Back: Newberry Iron Company Had Many Names," *Newberry News*, May 23, 1984;

"Burrell Chemical Works," *Newberry Independent*, September 26, 1889.

243   "Change of Owners," *Newberry News*, May 26, 1893;

"Furnace Closed Down," *Newberry News*, May 25, 1894.

244   "Removing the Chemical Plant," *Newberry News*, October 8, 1897.

245   "Furnace will Surely Run!" *Newberry News*, February 2, 1900;

"Local," *Newberry News*, November 21, 1902.

246   "Buys Another Furnace," *Newberry News*, April 12, 1907;

"Joseph H. Berry Dead," *Newberry News*, May 24, 1907;

"Newberry Furnace Sold," *Newberry News*, May 6, 1903;

"Deal Not Complete," *Newberry News*, May 13, 1910;

"$20,000 Deal Closed," *Newberry News*, July 1, 1910.

247   "Furnace to Resume," *Newberry News*, August 21, 1914;

"Iron Furnace Changes Hands," *Newberry News*, July 9, 1915;

Rintamaki, "Looking Back: Newberry Furnace Had Many Names," *Newberry News*, May 23, 1984.

248   "Dollarville," *Newberry News*, July 21, 1887;

"Dollarville Happenings," *Newberry News*, May 31, 1888;

"The Dollarville Mill," *Newberry News*, November 8, 1895;

"The Dollarville Mill," *Newberry News*, July 29, 1886.

249   "Dollarville," *Newberry News*, July 21, 1887;

"Dollarville Happenings," *Newberry News*, May 31, 1888;

"The Dollarville Mill," *Newberry News*, November 8, 1895;

"The Dollarville Mill," *Newberry News*, July 29, 1886.

250   Hanes and Musgrave, 18-19.

251   "Newsites," *Newberry News*, June 10, 1886;

"Newberry Celery and Improvement Company," *Newberry News*, July 19, 1888;

"Newberry Celery Industry," *Newberry News*, May 25, 1894;

"First Newberry Celery Garden Started in 1886," *Newberry News*, July 4, 1930;

Eugene J. Sundstrom, "Newberry's Celery Gardens," *Luce County: A History: Centennial Issue* (Chelsea, Michigan: Bookcrafters, 1985), 501.

252   "The Palms Estate," *Newberry News*, July 30, 1897.

253   "Harry L. Harris Passes Away," *Newberry News*, January 29, 1943;

Rintamaki, "Looking Back: Deer Park Area Instrumental to Lumbering a Century Ago," *Newberry News*, February 1, 1984;

Rintamaki, "Looking Back: Ice Man Provided Important Service to Early Hospital," *Newberry News*, January 9, 1985.

254   "Newberry, including Dollarville," by the Sanborn Perris Map Co., limited, October 1893.

255   "A Business Change," *Newberry News*, August 23, 1912.

256   "M. R. Manhard," *Newberry Independent*, September 26, 1889;

"Profile of J. C. Foster," *Newberry News*, November 4, 1892;

"M. R. Manhard & Co." *Newberry Enterprise Special Edition*, October 1894;

"Two Newberry Firms Merge," *Newberry News*, April 7, 1950;

"Grand Opening New Hardware," *Newberry News*, May 16, 1963.

257   G. Rosenthal," *Newberry News*, July 1,1886; "Gustave Rosenthal" (Obituary), *Newberry News*, March 21, 1941;

Abblebaum, 3-9.

258   "Farewell Reception for Rosenthals," *Newberry News*, March 4, 1910.

259   "Business Sold," *Newberry News*, July 26, 1907;

"Farewell Reception for Rosenthal," *Newberry News*, March 4, 1910;

Abblebaum, 3-9.

260   "Local," *Newberry News*, April 11, 1890.

261   "Hotels," *Newberry News*, July 1, 1886;

"The Newberry Hotel," *Newberry News*, April 19, 1894;

"The Newberry Hotel," *Newberry Enterprise Special Edition*, October 1894.

262   "Newberry House Fire," *Newberry News*, February 14, 1896.

263   Advertisement: Clayton House," *Newberry News*, June 10, 1886;

"Newsites," *Newberry News*, June 17, 1886;

"Here and There," *Newberry News*, October 11, 1888;

"All Sorts," *Newberry Independent*, December 5, 1889;

"Local," *Newberry News*, May 27, 1892;

"The McLeod House," *Newberry Enterprise Special Edition*, October 1894;

"McLeod House Sold," *Newberry News*, July 10, 1896;

Memorial Record of the Northern Peninsula of Michigan, 608.

264 "Hotel Burns," *Newberry News*, February 13, 1914.

265 "P. S. Hamilton," *Newberry Independent*, September 26, 1889;

"Local," *Newberry Independent*, October 10, 1889;

"A Popular Hostelry," *Newberry Enterprise*, February 15, 1894;

"James A. Craig," *Newberry Enterprise Special Edition*, October 1894;

"Postscript," *Newberry News*, January 25, 1890;

Rachel Sheer, "History of Newberry," *Newberry News*, May 28, 1920;

"George Olson Compares Early Days," *Newberry News 100th Birthday Issue*, September 1, 1982;

"Local and County News," *Newberry News*, July 15, 1892.

266 "Local," *Newberry News*, August 1, 1919;

"George Olson Compares Early Days," *Newberry News 100th Birthday Issue*, September 1, 1982.

267 "Hotel Murphy," *Newberry Enterprise Special Edition*, October 1894; "Communicated," *Newberry News*, January 17, 1896;

"George Olson Compares Early Days," *Newberry News 100th Birthday Issue*, September 1, 1982;

"Local and County News," *Newberry News*, April 14, 1893.

268 "All Sorts," *Newberry Independent*, December 5, 1889;

"Here and There," *Newberry News*, October 18, 1888;

"Local and County News," *Newberry News*, August 12, 1892.

269 "Local," *Newberry News*, March 12, 1897;

"Hotel Changes Hands," *Newberry News*, April 26, 1907;

"Fire Frightens Hotel Guests," *Newberry News*, January 20, 1911;

"George Olson Compares Early Days," *Newberry News 100th Birthday Issue*, September 1, 1982.

270 Local and County News," *Newberry News*, July 22, 1892;

"Advertisement: Scandinavian House," *Newberry News*, November 4, 1892;

"Newberry, incl. Dollarville, Luce Co., Mich.," Sanborn Perris Map Co., Limited, Oct. 1893.

271 "A New Hotel," *Newberry News*, April 14, 1899;

"New Hotel Opened," *Newberry News*, July 7, 1899;

"Hotel Changes Hands," *Newberry News*, May 10, 1918;

"The Hotel Luce," *Newberry News*, September 27, 1918;

George Olson, "George Olson Compares Early Days," *Newberry News*, September 1, 1982.

272 "A New Hotel," *Newberry News*," December 8, 1911;

"Formal Opening," *Newberry News*, January 15, 1915;

"Falls Hotel Has 10th Birthday," *Newberry News*, February 29, 1952.

273

Chapter Nine: Newberry Nuthouse

"The Insane Asylum," *Newberry News*, July 14, 1893;

"Local and County News," *Newberry News*, July 28, 1893;

"Our Side of the Asylum Matter," *Newberry News*, November 10, 1893.

274 "Free Site for the Asylum" and "The Insane Asylum," *Newberry News*, August 4, 1893.

275 "Meeting of Asylum Committee," *Newberry News*, October 12, 1894.

276 "Local and County News," *Newberry News*, August 4, 1983;

"Local and County News," *Newberry News*, August 11, 1893.

277 "Reception to Mr. Case," *Newberry News*, November 10, 1893.

278 "Hurrah! Newberry Gets the Asylum!" *Newberry News*, November 3, 1893.

279 "Newberry Congratulated," *Newberry News*, November 10, 1893;

"Our Side of the Asylum Matter," *Newberry News*, November 10, 1893.

280 "The Upper Peninsula Asylum for the Insane," *Newberry Enterprise Special Edition*, October 1894.

281 "Hospital Arrivals," *Newberry News*, November 8, 1895;

"A Visit to the U.P. Hospital," *Newberry News*, February 14, 1896.

282 "A Visit to the U.P. Hospital," *Newberry News*, February 14, 1896.

283 A Visit to the U.P. Hospital," *Newberry News*, February 14, 1896.

284 "A Visit to the U.P. Hospital," *Newberry News*, February 14, 1896;

Michigan Death Certificate of Henry Van Dallen, May 20, 1920, <www.seekingmichigan.com>;

(NOTE: His name in the news story was spelled Van Allen, but his death certificate listed it as Van Dallen, which is probably the correct spelling.).

285 "Insanity Cases," *Newberry News*, July 14, 1911;

"Clinical Report," *Report of the Board of Trustees of the Newberry State Hospital for the Period Ending June 14, 1914*, (Lansing, Michigan: Wynkoop, Hallenbeck, Crawford Co., State Printers, 1915), page 28;

"Report of the Medical Superintendent," *Report of the Board of Trustees for the Newberry State Hospital for the Period Ending June 30, 1912*, (Lansing, Michigan: Wynkoop, Hallenbeck, Crawford Co., State Printers, 1913), page 22.

286 "Upper Peninsula Hospital for the Insane," *Newberry News*, December 16, 1910.

287 "Many Finns Go Crazy," *Newberry News*, January 4, 1907;

"Report of the Medical Superintendent," *Report of the Board of Trustees for the Newberry State for the Period Ending June 30, 1912*, (Lansing, Michigan: Wynkoop, Hallenbeck, Crawford Co., State Printers, 1913), page 22.

"Report of the Medical Superintendent," *Report of the Board of Trustees of the Upper Peninsula Hospital for the Insane, for the Period Ending June 30, 1910*, (Lansing, Michigan: Wynkoop, Hallenbeck, Crawford Co., State Printers, 1911), page 20.

288 "Insane Swede Deported," *Newberry News*, June 20, 1902;

"Murdered Mother and Sister," *Newberry News*, May 13, 1904.

289 "Will be Transferred to Flint," *Newberry News*, December 27, 1895.

290 "A Sad Case," *Newberry News*, October 21, 1904.

291 "Local," *Newberry News*, December 1, 1905.

292 "Monument Wrecker Capture," *Newberry News*, October 6, 1905.

293 "Local," *Newberry News*, December 11, 1903.

294 "Local," *Newberry News*, May 11, 1906.

295 "Perpetual Motion Victim," *Newberry News*, August 7, 1903.

296 "Very Sad Case," *Newberry News*, April 28, 1905;

(NOTE: Mrs. Eli King was the former Nellie Rapin. She married Eli King (also known as Eli LeBlanc) in 1897, and had several children. She, at least, recovered from her "insanity," and after her first husband died, married a second time to a Telesfore or Joseph Grenier. She died in 1918 of tuberculosis.)

297   "Joins Sister in Asylum," *Newberry News*, October 6, 1905.

298   "Insane Patients Suffer," *Newberry News*, January 8, 1898;

"Asylum Is Crowded," *Newberry News*, March 22, 1907.

299   "Hospital Is Crowded," *Newberry News*, August 18, 1911.

300   "Upper Peninsula Hospital for the Insane," *Newberry News*, December 16, 1910.

301   "Scandal at the U.P. Hospital," *Newberry News*, August 27, 1909;

"Upper Peninsula Hospital for the Insane," *Newberry News*, December 16, 1910;

Taylor, 5.

302   "Attacked by Patient," *Newberry News*, November 1, 1912.

303   "Scandal at the U.P. Hospital," *Newberry News*, August 27, 1909;

"Vote of Confidence," *Newberry News*, September 3, 1909.

304   "Report of the Medical Superintendent," *Report of the Board of Trustees of the Newberry State Hospital for the Period Ending June 14, 1914*, (Lansing, Michigan: Wynkoop, Hallenbeck, Crawford Co., State Printers, 1915), page 28.

305   "Local," *Newberry News*, February 26, 1904.

306   "Upper Peninsula Hospital for the Insane," *Newberry News*, December 16, 1910.

307   "Upper Peninsula Hospital for the Insane," *Newberry News*, December 16, 1910.

308   "Upper Peninsula Hospital for the Insane," *Newberry News*, December 16, 1910.

309   "A Gruesome Find," *Newberry News*, October 24, 1902.

310   "Insane Man's Long Walk," *Newberry News*, July 3, 1903;

Household of John Wojtehosi, "United States Census, 1900," database with images, *FamilySearch* (https://familysearch.org/ark:/61903/1:1:MS98-LJD : accessed 5 May 2017), John Wojtehosi, Menominee Ward 1, Menominee, Michigan, United States; citing enumeration district (ED) 137, sheet 15A, family 243, NARA microfilm publication T623 (Washington, DC: National Archives and Records Administration, 1972.); FHL microfilm 1,240,731.

Household of Victoria Vojcihoski, "United States Census, 1910," database with images, *FamilySearch* (https://familysearch.org/ark:/61903/1:1:MLR8-BJQ : accessed 5 May 2017), Victoria Vojcihoski, Menominee Ward 1, Menominee, Michigan, United States; citing enumeration district (ED) ED 213, sheet 6A, family 108, NARA microfilm publication T624 (Washington, DC: National Archives and Records Administration, 1982), roll 664; FHL microfilm 1,374,677.

311   "Local," *Newberry News*, January 19, 1906;

"Takes Long Hike," *Newberry News*, April 28, 1911.

312   Michigan Death Certificate, Nora Sweeney, June 5,1919; <www.seekingmichigan.com>;

"Body is Found," *Newberry News*, June 6, 1919.

313   "Report of the Medical Superintendent," *Report of the Board of Trustees of the Newberry State Hospital for the Period Ending June 14, 1914*, (Lansing, Michigan: Wynkoop, Hallenbeck, Crawford Co., State Printers, 1915), page 20.

314   "Clinical Report," *Report of the Board of Trustees of the Newberry State Hospital for the Period Ending June 14, 1914*, (Lansing, Michigan: Wynkoop, Hallenbeck, Crawford Co., State Printers, 1915), page 24.

Chapter Ten: A Tale of Two Newspapers

315 "Merle Fretz Recalls Early Days of News," *Centennial Edition Newberry News*, July 2, 1986;

"Clyde W. Hecox Dies (Obituary)," *Newberry News*, November 30, 1934; "Salutory," *Newberry News*, June 10, 1886.

316 "The Newberry News Printing and Book Publishing Co." *Newberry News*, December 8, 1888;

"Merle Fretz Recalls Early Days of News" and "Much Bickering Between News and Competition," *Newberry News Centennial Edition*, July 2, 1986.

317 "Salutory," *Newberry News*, December 15, 1888;

"Then and Now," *Newberry News*, April 13, 1889.

318 "Bob Wright Is Dead," *Newberry News*, July 26, 1940.

319 "Here and There," *Newberry News*, April 20, 1889; *Newberry News*, May 4, 1889;

"Local," *Newberry Independent*, May 23, 1889.

320 "Local," *Newberry Independent*, August 1, 1889;

"Local," *Newberry Independent*, August 8, 1889;

"Local," *Newberry Independent*, August 15, 1889;

"Boodlerism," *Newberry Independent*, October 17, 1889;

"Communication to the Independent," *Newberry Independent*, November 28, 1889;

"Local," *Newberry News*, April 11, 1890;

"Local," *Newberry News*, April 18, 1890;

"Local," *Newberry News*, March 29, 1890;

"Local News," *Newberry News*, October 3, 1890;

Newberry News, December 14, 1889.

321 "Communication," *Newberry Independent*, October 31, 1889;

"Our Man About Town," *Newberry News*, November 2, 1889.

322 "Communication," *Newberry Independent*, March 20, 1890;

"Local," *Newberry News*, March 29, 1890;

"In Reply to the News," *Newberry Independent*, April 3, 1890.

323 "Local," *Newberry News*, April 25, 1890.

324 "Local," *Newberry Independent,* December 26, 1889.

325 "Our Man About Town," *Newberry News*, August 10, 1889;

"Local," *Newberry Independent*, January 30, 1890.

326 "Our Man About Town," *Newberry News*, June 1, 1889;

"Our Man About Town," *Newberry News*, August 10, 1889.

327 "Local," *Newberry News,* May 16, 1890;

"Local," *Newberry Independent*, January 2, 1890;

"Our Esteemed Contemporary," *Newberry Independent*, April 24, 1890;

"Our Man About Town," *Newberry News*, August 17, 1889;

"Merle Fretz Recalls Early Days of News," *Newberry News Centennial Edition*, July 2, 1986;

"Charles Brebner Passes," *Newberry News*, December 29, 1933.

328 "Local News," *Newberry News*, January 30, 1891;

"To Our Readers," *Newberry Independent*, January 24, 1891;

Newberry News, February 5, 1892.

329   "Salutation," *Newberry Enterprise*, January 24, 1894;

"Local and County News," *Newberry News*, January 26, 1894;

"A True Exposition," *Newberry Enterprise*, July 12, 1894.

330   "Later Personal," *Newberry Enterprise*, August 30, 1894;

"No Half-Hearted Welcome Goes," *Newberry Enterprise*, March 1, 1894;

"Caught on the Fly," *Newberry Enterprise*, July 19, 1984;

"Notice to Subscribers," *Newberry Enterprise*, November 19, 1894;

"Local Lore," *Newberry Enterprise*, September 27, 1894.

331   "The News Has Flopped," *Newberry Enterprise*, July 19, 1894;

"A True Exposition," *Newberry Enterprise*, July 12, 1894.

332   Merle Fretz, "Ramblings," *The Newberry News*, June 26, 1969; *Newberry News*, September 28, 1894.

333   *Newberry Enterprise Special Edition*, October 1894

334   "City News," *Newberry Enterprise*, October 4, 1894.

"Democratic Convention," *Newberry News*, October 12, 1894;

"Personal and Local," *Newberry Enterprise*, November 15, 1894.

335   "Local and County News," *Newberry News*, November 9, 1894;

"In Luce County the Entire Republican County Ticket was Elected Last Tuesday," *Newberry Enterprise*, November 8, 1894.

336   "Local and County News," *Newberry News*, November 23, 1894;

"Notice to Subscribers," *Newberry Enterprise*, November 19, 1984.

337   "Local and County News," *Newberry News*, November 23, 1894.

338   "Clyde Hecox Dies," *Newberry News*, November 30, 1934.

339   "Local," *Newberry News*, December 3, 1897;

"Local," *Newberry News*, December 24, 1897.

340   "A Hot Time," *Newberry News*, April 8, 1898;

"Journal Editor Gone," *Newberry News*, June 24, 1898;

"Local," *Newberry News*, September 15, 1899;

"Local," *Newberry News*, September 22, 1899;

"Merle Fretz Recalls Early Days of News," *Centennial Edition Newberry News*, July 2, 1986.

341   "Merle Fretz Recalls Early Days of News," *Centennial Edition Newberry News*, July 2, 1986.

342

Chapter Eleven: Fun and Games

"Local and County News," *Newberry News*, March 31, 1893;

"Local and County," *Newberry News*, August 14, 1896;

"Local," *Newberry News*, March 11,1904;

"Local," *Newberry News*, June 5, 1903;

"Local and County News," *Newberry News*, July 28, 1893;

"Local and County News," *Newberry News*, April 21, 1893;

"Local," *Newberry News*, February 2, 1894.

343 "Local," *Newberry News*, March 10, 1893;

"Local and County News," *Newberry News*, June 30, 1893.

344 "Local and County," *Newberry News*, November 22, 1895;

"Cyr Brothers," *Newberry News*, April 14, 1893;

"Local," *Newberry News*, June 16, 1911;

345 "Local," *Newberry News*, December 2, 1898;

"Local," *Newberry News*, December 9, 1898.

346 "Local," *Newberry News*, January 12, 1900;

"Additional Local," *Newberry News*, September 13, 1907;

"Moving Picture Show," *Newberry News*, February 22, 1907.

347 "Moving Picture Theater," *Newberry News*, June 26 1908;

"Local," *Newberry News*, June 11, 1909;

"Local," *Newberry News*, April 21, 1911.

348 "Local," *Newberry News*, October 24, 1913;

"New Picture Theater," *Newberry News*, May 1, 1914;

"A Modern Playhouse," *Newberry News*, June 5, 1914;

"Local," *Newberry News*, July 3, 1914;

"The Grand," *Newberry News*, July 17, 1914;

"Local," *Newberry News*, January 15, 1915;

"Vaudette Theater Destroyed by Fire," *Newberry News*, January 28, 1916;

"Theatre Reopens," *Newberry News*, March 17, 1916.

349 "Local," *Newberry News*, December 25, 1914.

350 "A Gala Day," *Newberry News*, July 4, 1890.

351 "The Cycling Season," *Newberry News*, April 20, 1900;

"A Bicycle Path," *Newberry News*, April 28, 1899;

"Local," *Newberry News*, June 2, 1899.

352 "Foot Ball," *Newberry News*, October 10, 1902;

"Wanted for Fraud," *Newberry News*, October 28, 1904.

353 "Won Their First Game," *Newberry News*, November 18, 1904;

"Local," *Newberry News*, September 29, 1905.

354 "History of Women's Bowling in Newberry," *Newberry News*, June 15, 1967; "Bowling Averages," *Newberry News*, December 24, 1915; "Local," *Newberry News*, September 3, 1915; "Local," *Newberry News*, September 24, 1915; "Bowling League Organized," *Newberry News*, December 10, 1915.

355 "Local," *Newberry News*, November 14, 1902;

"The Peepers Trapped," *Newberry News*, February 2, 1908.

356 "Local News," *Newberry News*, November 13, 1891;

"Local and County News," *Newberry News*, July 28, 1893.

357 "The Tahquamenon Falls," *Newberry Enterprise*, September 13, 1894.

358 "Local," *Newberry News*, August 1, 1902;

Merle Fretz, "The Newberry News," *Luce County History: Centennial Issue*, ed. Hilja Pekkarinen, Minnie Ida

Mattson, and Phyllis Brumm (Chelsea, Michigan: Bookcrafters, 1985), 168.

359   "Local," *Newberry News*, April 16, 1915;

"Local," *Newberry News*, April 9, 1915;

"Boat Club Officers," *Newberry News*, April 23, 1915;

Merle Fretz, "The Newberry News," *Luce County History: Centennial Issue*, ed. Hilja Pekkarinen, Minnie Ida Mattson, and Phyllis Brumm (Chelsea, Michigan: Bookcrafters, 1985), 168.

360   "Whitefish Lake," *Newberry News*, September 11, 1914;

Windeler, 35.

361   "Newsites," *Newberry News*, July 8, 1886;

"Local," *Newberry News*, October 4, 1888;

"Local," *Newberry News*, July 19, 1888.

362   "Round the World," *Newberry News*, July 7, 1899;

"Fourth of July," *Newberry News*, June 30, 1899.

363   "The Fourth Was Appropriately Celebrated Here Yesterday," *Newberry News*, July 5, 1907.

364   "Hallowe'en Pranks," *Newberry News*, November 3, 1905;

"Our Man About Town," *Newberry News*, November 2, 1889.

365   "Local," *Newberry News*, November 7, 1902.

366   "Hallowe'en Party," *Newberry News*, November 6, 1903.

Chapter Twelve: Sportsmen and Nimrods

367   Manistique Lake Region Thirty Years Ago," *Newberry News*, January 15, 1926, reprinted from an 1898 *Forest and Stream.*

368   "Local News," *Newberry News*, June 26, 1891;

"Local," *Newberry News*, August 19, 1898;

(NOTE: Clarence Anderson was from Pittsburg, Pennsylvania.)

369   "A Deer Park Adventure," *Newberry News*, January 26, 1888.

370   "Manistique Lake Region, An Interesting Fishing 'Where to' Article by E. S. Whitaker, an Old Forest and Stream Expert, *Newberry News*, December 4, 1914.

371   "Whitefish Lake," *Newberry News*, September 11, 1914.

372   "Game and Fish Laws," *Newberry News*, June 14, 1901.

373   "Game and Fish Laws," *Newberry News*, June 14, 1901.

374   "Game and Fish Laws," *Newberry News*, June 14, 1901.

375   "Poor Hunting Weather," *Newberry News*, November 14, 1902.

376   "Those Detroit Hunters," *Newberry News*, November 29, 1895.

377   "Local," *Newberry News*, November 19, 1897;

"Local," *Newberry News*, November 26, 1897.

378   "Mary Ann Wrecked," *Newberry News*, November 3, 1916.

379   "Snowed In," *Newberry News*, November 20, 1914;

"Marooned Hunters Get Home," *Newberry News*, November 27, 1914;

"Local," *Newberry News*, December 11, 1914.

380   "Arm Shattered," *Newberry News*, August 1, 1913.

381   *Newberry News*, October 11, 1888;

(NOTE: *The Newberry News* believed that John Sanders was the nephew of Joseph Sander (calling him "the old gentleman"), while *The Mining Journal* reported that John and Joseph were cousins. John Sanders actually had both an Uncle Joseph Sanders and a cousin Joseph Sanders, but the uncle had died in 1885. Joseph Sanders the cousin was only fifty-five, but perhaps he looked much older than the forty-year-old John Sanders.)

382   "Hunter Still Missing," *Newberry News*, November 27, 1914;

"Body is Found," *Newberry News*, May 14, 1915.

383   "Hunter Lost," *Newberry News*, November 12, 1909.

384   "Unsolved Mysteries of the North Woods," *Newberry News*, November 22, 1940.

385   "Hunter Lost," *Newberry News*, November 12, 1909.

386   "Hope Abandoned," *Newberry News*, November 19, 1909.

387   "An Unsolved Mystery," *Newberry News*, November 26, 1909.

388   Household of Jay Doty, "United States Census, 1910," database with images, *FamilySearch* (https://familysearch.org/ark:/61903/1:1:MLRT-2XF : accessed 5 May 2017), Jay Doty, St. Charles, Saginaw, Michigan, United States; citing enumeration district (ED) ED 75, sheet 12A, family 229, NARA microfilm publication T624 (Washington, DC: National Archives and Records Administration, 1982), roll 671; FHL microfilm 1,374,684;

"May Solve Mystery," *Newberry News*, February 14, 1913.

389   "Mystery Solved," *Newberry News*, December 5, 1913.

Chapter Thirteen: Accidents, Fires, and Other Disasters

390   "A Horrible Death," *Newberry News*, April 12, 1888.

391   "Disastrous Explosion!" *Newberry News*, January 9, 1891;

"Local News," *Newberry News*, January 23, 1891.

392   "A Fatal Accident," *Newberry News*, February 24, 1899.

393   "A Druggist's Blunder," *Newberry News*, June 6, 1913;

"Physician Under Arrest," *Newberry News*, June 13, 1913;

"Committed Suicide," *Newberry News*, July 6, 1917.

394   "Met Horrible Death," *Newberry News*, October 4, 1912;

"Fatal Accident," *Newberry News*, March 3, 1896;

"Buried in Sand Slide," *Newberry News*, October 5, 1906.

395   "Local," *Newberry News*, June 23, 1916;

"Additional Local," *Newberry News*, August 30, 1907;

"A Sad Fatality," *Newberry News*, October 16, 1891;

"Newsites," *Newberry News*, January 6, 1887;

"Local and County News," *Newberry News*, August 5, 1892;

(NOTE: Just who is "Mrs. R. Bolton"? That is difficult to tell because there appears to be no gravestone and no official record of her death. My best guess is she was the wife of Richard Boulton, who lived in Newberry at the time. However, I have not been able find any proof of this.)

396   "Local," *Newberry News*, November 15, 1901;

"Local," *Newberry News,* June 30, 1911;

"Local," *Newberry News*, July 7, 1911.

397   "Our Man About Town," *Newberry News*, June 1, 1889;

"Our Man About Town," *Newberry News*, September 7, 1889;

"Newsites," *Newberry News*, July 29, 1886.

398   "Runaway Accident," *Newberry News*, December 31, 1909;

"First Hunting Accident," *Newberry News*, October 25, 1907;

"Local," *Newberry News*, October 23, 1914;

"Maimed for Life," *Newberry News,* October 20, 1905.

399   "Sad Accident," *Newberry News*, July 7, 1905;

"A Strange Accident," *Newberry News*, September 20, 1907.

400   "Little Child Killed," *Newberry News*, May 4, 1917;

"Deer Park Girl Killed," *Newberry News*, April 4, 1919.

401   "A Sad Accident," *Newberry News*, November 11, 1898.

402   "Newsites," *Newberry News*, June 17, 1886;

"Newsites," *Newberry News*, August 19, 1886.

403   "The American House," *Newberry News*, July 1, 1886;

"Local News," *Newberry News*, December 22, 1887;

"Court Proceedings," *Newberry News*, October 20, 1887.

404   "Local News," *Newberry News*, December 15, 1887.

405   "Local News," *Newberry News*, February 8, 1890.

406   "A Small Blaze," *Newberry News*, March 3, 1899.

407   "The Fire Fiend," *Newberry News*, October 11, 1901.

408   "Plunged Through the Flames," *Newberry News*, August 28, 1903.

409   "Gone Before," *Newberry News*, September 11, 1903;

"Local," *Newberry News*, September 18, 1903.

410   Michigan Death Certificate of Neola May Velma Cassiday, June 15, 1901 <www.seekingmichigan.com>;

"United States Census, 1910," database with images, *FamilySearch* (https://familysearch.org/ark:/61903/1:1:MLPW-
        YN6 : 29 October 2015), John Summerville, Munising, Alger, Michigan, United States; citing enumeration
        district (ED) ED 4, sheet 16B, NARA microfilm publication T624 (Washington, DC: National Archives and
        Records Administration, n.d.); FHL microfilm 1,374,647;

"California Death Index, 1940-1997," index, *FamilySearch* (https://familysearch.org/ark:/61903/1:1:VP65-T5Y :
        accessed 14 May 2015), Howard C. Cassady, 07 Oct 1971; Department of Public Health Services, Sacramento.

411   The man labeled "Sandy Terrance" on the picture I have identified as Alex Trerice, who was a known
        resident of Luce County at the time. His last name was often misspelled as Terrece, and Sandy was a common
        nickname for Alexander at the time.

412   "Used Gasoline to Kindle Fire," *Newberry News*, July 21, 1905; Michigan Death Certificate of Coral Anna
        Long, July 18, 1905 <www.seekingmichigan.com>;

Household of James McClure, "United States Census, 1910," database with images, *FamilySearch* (https://
        familysearch.org/ark:/61903/1:1:ML8Q-N8G : 29 October 2015), James Mc Clure, Damascus, Henry,

Ohio, United States; citing enumeration district (ED) ED 24, sheet 7B, NARA microfilm publication T624 (Washington, DC: National Archives and Records Administration, n.d.); FHL microfilm 1,375,211.

413 "Two Children Cremated," *Newberry News*, September 15, 1905;

"The Laketon Horror," *Newberry News*, September 22, 1905.

414 "Dollarville Burns," *Newberry News*, June 19, 1914;

"Saw Mill Closes," *Newberry News*, June 26, 1914.

415 Patricia Proebstel, letter to author, July 8, 2016.

416 "Hard Times," *Newberry Enterprise*, July 12, 1894;

"Local and County," *Newberry News*, October 12, 1894;

"The Care of the Poor," *Newberry News*, May 24, 1895;

"Annual Report of the Superintendents of the Poor," *Newberry News*, November 11, 1898.

417 "Local and County," *Newberry News*, November 8, 1895;

"The Care of the Poor," *Newberry News*, May 24, 1895.

418 "Local and County News," *Newberry News*, July 15, 1892;

"Local," *Newberry Independent*, September 20, 1890;

"Local," *Newberry News*, August 4, 1899;

"Local," *Newberry News*, April 8, 1892;

"School Notes," *Newberry News*, April 8, 1904;

"Local," *Newberry News*, February 17, 1911;

"Local," *Newberry News*, May 12, 1916.

419

Chapter Fourteen: In Sickness and Health

Newsites," *Newberry News*, July 29, 1886;

"The Cemetery Association," and "Local News," *Newberry News*, September 22, 1887;

"Our Village Cemetery," *Newberry News*, August 17, 1889;

"Local," *Newberry Independent*, October 31, 1889;

"Old Graves Found," *Newberry News*, September 14, 1934.

420 "Dollarville," *Newberry News*, June 15, 1894;

"Card of Thanks," *Newberry News*, November 3, 1898.

421 Michigan, Death Certificate of Emma Jacobson, January 17, 1906 <www.seekingmichigan.com>

Michigan Death Certificates of (unnamed) Boggs, April 10, 1919; Stillborn, February 8, 1918; Baby Boggs, July 29, 1922; Infant Boggs, May 8, 1932, all <www.seekingmichigan.com>;

"Michigan Deaths and Burials, 1800-1995," database, *FamilySearch* (https://familysearch.org/ark:/61903/1:1:FHK6-699 : 9 December 2014), Boggs, 03 Oct 1923; citing Pentland Twp., Luce, Michigan, reference v 1 p 128; FHL microfilm 1,008,004.

"Hamilton Funeral," *Newberry News*, May 25, 1928;

Household of David Davern, "United States Census, 1900," database with images, *FamilySearch* (https://familysearch.org/ark:/61903/1:1:MS97-44K : 20 January 2015), David Daveren, Newberry village, Luce, Michigan, United States; citing sheet 5B, family 96, NARA microfilm publication T623 (Washington, DC: National Archives and Records Administration, n.d.); FHL microfilm 1,240,726.

422 "Local," *Newberry News*, July 23, 1915.

423 "No Diphtheria in Five Years," *Newberry News*, October 3, 1930;

"Local News," *Newberry News*, April 8, 1892;

"Health Notice," *Newberry News*, March 15, 1895;

"Is Very Ill," *Newberry News*, July 12, 1907;

"Scarlet Fever," *Newberry News*, January 23, 1920.

424 "Whole Family Poisoned," *Newberry News*, March 3, 1905;

"Local and County," *Newberry News*, August 31, 1894;

"Local and County," *Newberry News*, September 28, 1894.

425 "Local," *Newberry News*, December 27, 1918.

426 "How to Prevent Tuberculosis," *Newberry News*, September 5, 1913.

427 "School Teachers and Tuberculosis," *Newberry News*, January 5, 1912;

"Throw Out Cups," *Newberry News*, April 18, 1913.

428 "Improvements," *Newberry News*, July 21, 1887;

"Sewage Plant Project OK'd," *Newberry News*, January 23, 1964.

429 "Local," *Newberry News*, December 26, 1902;

"School Closed," *Newberry News*, February 12, 1904.

430 "Dr. H. C. Farrand," and "Dr. S. John Fraser," *Newberry Independent*, September 26, 1889;

Newberry Independent, January 9, 1890;

"Our Man About Town," *Newberry News*, September 28, 1889.

431 "A Pioneer Passes," *Newberry News*, September 20, 1907;

"Dr. A. W. Nicholson," *Newberry Independent*, September 26, 1889;

"Local News," *Newberry News*, October 17, 1890.

432 "Local," *Newberry News*, October 16, 1891;

"Dr. Neal Retires," *Newberry News*, February 10, 1905;

"Death of F. W. Neal," *Newberry News*, June 3, 1910.

433 "Newsites," *Newberry News*, July 15, 1886;

"Returns After Many Years," *Newberry News*, August 17, 1917.

434 "A Man Worth While," *Newberry News*, July 16, 1926;

"A Pioneer Doctor," *Newberry News*, July 16, 1915;

"Celebrates Birthday," *Newberry News*, July 18, 1941.

435 "Local," *Newberry News*, September 23, 1898;

"Local," *Newberry News*, November 18, 1898;

"Death of Mrs. Bohn," *Newberry News*, June 2, 1899;

"Dr. F. P. Bohn Passes Away," *Newberry News*, June 2, 1944.

436 Frank P. Bohn, "This Was the Forest Primeval," *Michigan History Magazine* (Winter 1937);

"A Man Worthwhile," *Newberry News*, July 16, 1926;

"Bohn Came to Seney Forty Years Ago," *Newberry News*, September 27, 1929.

437 "Here and There," *Newberry News*, October 11, 1888.

438   "A Near Fatality," *Newberry News*, February 9, 1912.

439   *Memorial Record of the Northern Peninsula of Michigan* (Chicago: Lewis Publishing Company, 1894), 636.

440   "From McLeod's Camp," *Newberry News*, December 21, 1900.

441   "Should Be Suppressed," *Newberry News*, December 14, 1900;

"Notes on Interview with News Editor," *Newberry News*, Newberry's 100th Birthday Issue, September 1, 1982;

"Old Timers Return," *Newberry News*, July 25, 1930.

442   "Doctors Disagree," *Newberry News*, January 11, 1901;

"Notice by Health Officer," *Newberry News*, January 11, 1901;

"Lover and Smallpox Make Several Kinds of a Fool of a Man," *Newberry News*, January 11, 1901.

443   "Local," *Newberry News*, January 25, 1901;

"County Must Pay," *Newberry News*, May 24, 1901;

"The Smallpox Scare," *Newberry News*, November 18, 1910.

444   *Newberry News*, October 4, 1918.

445   "Died of Burns," *Newberry News*, June 28, 1918.

446   Deaths of the Week," *Newberry News*, October 11, 1918;

"Deaths of the Week," *Newberry News*, October 18, 1918;

"Death's Toll," *Newberry News*, October 25, 1918;

"Local," *Newberry News*, December 6, 1918.

447   "Flu Epidemic Still Raging," *Newberry News*, October 18, 1918.

448   "Flu Claims Many Victims," *Newberry News*, October 25, 1918.

449   "Death's Toll," *Newberry News*, October 25, 1918;

"Death's Toll," *Newberry News*, November 1, 1918.

450   "Local," *Newberry News*, October 18, 1918;

"Local," *Newberry News*, October 25, 1918;

"Local," *Newberry News*, November 1, 1918;

"Flu Epidemic Is on Decline," *Newberry News*, November 8, 1918;

"Death's Toll," *Newberry News*, November 1, 1918;

"Death's Toll," *Newberry News*, October 25, 1918.

451   "Flu Epidemic Still Raging," *Newberry News*, October 18, 1918;

"Flu Claims Many Victims," *Newberry News*, October 25, 1918.

452   Email communication with Kathy Fitzpatrick, March 12, 2016.

453   "Flu Epidemic Still Raging," *Newberry News*, October 18, 1918;

"Twenty Deaths This Week," *Newberry News*, November 1, 1918;

"Spanish Flu Closes School," *Newberry News*, October 11, 1918.

454   "Twenty Deaths This Week," *Newberry News*, November 1, 1918.

455   "Newberry Is Free of Flu," *Newberry News*, November 22, 1918;

"Influenza Ban Is on Again," *Newberry News*, December 13, 1918;

"Nine Flu Cases," *Newberry News*, December 27, 1918;

"Influenza Deaths," *Newberry News*, January 3, 1919.

456   "Flu Epidemic on Decline," *Newberry News*, November 8, 1918;

"Death's Toll," *Newberry News*, November 1, 1918;

"Death's Toll," *Newberry News*, October 25, 1918.

457   "Emergency Hospital Closed," *Newberry News*, November 29, 1918.

Chapter Fifteen: The Times, They Are A-Changing

458   "Cement Walks," *Newberry News*, August 14, 1903.

459   "Recalls Old Memories," *Newberry News*, June 25, 1915.

460   "The McLeod House: History on the Move," *Newberry News*, October 11, 1989;

"Nearly Quarter Million Dollars," *Newberry News*, December 25, 1908.

461   "Nearly Quarter Million Dollars," *Newberry News*, December 25, 1908.

462   "Forty Years of Progress," *Newberry News*, June 28, 1918.

463   Hanes and Musgrave, 7, 43, 144.

464   Household of Milton Stewart, et al.," United States Census, 1920," database with images, *FamilySearch* (https://familysearch.org/ark:/61903/1:1:MZQ4-GQB : 7 December 2015), McMillan, Luce, Michigan, United States; citing sheet 8A, NARA microfilm publication T625 (Washington, DC.: National Archives and Records Administration, n.d.); FHL microfilm 1,820,782.

465   "Forty Years of Progress," *Newberry News*, October 11, 1940.

(NOTE: This article refers to Newberry's first telephone operator as "Mrs. Sam Campbell," but the 1910 census lists a "Mrs. Sarah Campbell" as a telephone operator (along with her daughter, Agnes). Sarah was the widow of Dougald Campbell and I suspect the "Mrs. Sam" is a typo.)

466   "A Hello System," *Newberry News*, December 5, 1902;

"Forty Years of Progress," *Newberry News*, June 28, 1918;

"Local," *Newberry News*, May 15, 1908;

"Lakefield Items," *Newberry News*, March 4, 1910;

"Lakefield Items," *Newberry News*, May 24, 1912;

"Local," *Newberry News*, February 5, 1915.

467   Hanes and Musgrave, 163.

468   Advertisement: Duluth South Shore & Atlantic Railway, The Marquette Route, *The Newberry News*, January 19, 1900.

469   Hanes and Musgrave, 139.

470   *The Automobile Blue Book, Volume 10* (New York and Chicago: the Automobile Blue Book Publishing Co., 1921), 244-246;

Hanes and Musgrave, 169.

471   "Road Opens to Seney," *Newberry News*, September 11, 1925.

472   "Ghosts of a Bygone Age," *Newberry News*, January 29, 1932.

473   "Local," *Newberry News*, April 7, 1911;

"Local," *Newberry News*, August 2, 1912;

"Local," *Newberry News*, May 10, 1912.

474   Local," *Newberry News*, March 29, 1912;

"Burned to a Crisp," *Newberry News*, October 27, 1916;

"Good Roads," *Newberry News*, July 5, 1907;

"Give the Kids a Show," *Newberry News*, June 17, 1910;

"Trunk Line Highway," *Newberry News*, December 18, 1914;

"Build New Roads," *Newberry News*, April 14, 1916;

"Forty Years of Progress," *Newberry News*, June 28, 1918.

475 "Local," *Newberry News*, October 11, 1912;

"First Auto Accident," *Newberry News*, October 18, 1912;

"Auto Turns Turtle," *Newberry News*, October 25, 1912;

"Local," *Newberry News*, September 7, 1917.

476 "Electric Lights," *Newberry Enterprise Special Edition*, October 1894;

"Our Man About Town," *Newberry News*, November 30, 1889;

"Local," *Newberry Independent*, August 1, 1889;

"The Newberry Hotel," *Newberry Enterprise*, April 19, 1894;

"Local," *Newberry Independent*, October 31, 1889;

"Our Man About Town," *Newberry News*, December 21, 1889.

477 "Electric Light Company," *Newberry News*, January 18, 1895;

Stafford "Local," *Newberry News*, July 29, 1898.

478 "All Night Service," *Newberry News*, December 28, 1900;

"Local," *Newberry News*, March 6, 1914;

"Local," *Newberry News*, May 8, 1914;

"Danger of Fire at Christmas," *Newberry News*, December 1, 1911;

"A Day Service," *Newberry News*, May 15, 1914.

479 "Old Timers Return," *Newberry News*, July 25, 1930;

"Capt. Dollar Dead," *Newberry News*, May 20, 1932;

"Capt. Dollar Sends Greetings," *Newberry News*, December 23, 1927.

480 "Local," *Newberry News*, March 28, 1902;

Will Leave Newberry," *Newberry News*, September 29, 1916;

"Former Resident Passes," *Newberry News*, January 8, 1932;

"Farewell Reception for Rosenthal," *Newberry News*, March 4, 1910;

"Cowardly Attack," *Newberry News*, October 4, 1907;

"To the Golden State," *Newberry News*, May 5, 1905.

481 Pioneering in His New Home," *Newberry News*, July 10, 1903;

"Likes the West," *Newberry News*, April 14, 1905;

"Another Business Change," *Newberry News*, Aug 23 1907;

"Local," *Newberry News*, October 2, 1903;

"Makers Wager Good," *Newberry News*, December 8, 1911;

"Pioneer Woman Passes" (Obituary of Catherine Alice Miller), *Newberry News*, July 2, 1948;

Household of Edward LaVeine (including Ambro Bettes), "United States Census, 1910," database with images, *FamilySearch* (https://familysearch.org/ark:/61903/1:1:MLHL-V8S : 29 October 2015), Ambro Bettes in household of Edward N La Veine, Sherman, Kootenai, Idaho, United States; citing enumeration district (ED) ED 173, sheet 17A, NARA microfilm publication T624 (Washington, DC: National Archives and Records Administration, n.d.); FHL microfilm 1,374,238.

"Brebner Grows Reminiscent," *Newberry News*, February 7, 1908;

"Joseph Wilson Trueman (obituary)," *Newberry News*, April 15, 1910.

482   Household of George Smathers, "United States Census, 1910," database with images, *FamilySearch* (https://familysearch.org/ark:/61903/1:1:MGJG-XMK : 29 October 2015), Geo F. Smathers, Union, Snohomish, Washington, United States; citing enumeration district (ED) ED 305, sheet 2A, NARA microfilm publication T624 (Washington, DC: National Archives and Records Administration, n.d.); FHL microfilm 1,375,682;

"Local," *Newberry News*, November 5, 1909;

"Local," *Newberry News*, May 2, 1890;

"Local News," *Newberry News*, July 11, 1890;

"Frederick Roat," *Newberry News*, June 8, 1928;

Tombstone of Willard Mark, 1858-1929, Grants Pass Masonic Pioneer Cemetery, Grants Pass, Josephine County, Oregon <http://www.findagrave.com >;

Household of Fredrick Roat, "United States Census, 1920," database with images, *FamilySearch* (https://familysearch.org/ark:/61903/1:1:M489-P37 : 14 December 2015), Mina C. Mark in household of Fredrick Roat, Fruitdale, Josephine, Oregon, United States; citing sheet 2A, NARA microfilm publication T625 (Washington, DC: National Archives and Records Administration, n.d.); FHL microfilm 1,821,495.

483   Local and County News," *Newberry News*, August 4, 1893;

"Local," *Newberry News*, April 19, 1907;

"Former Resident Passes (Obituary of Arthur Henderson)," *Newberry News*, January 8, 1932;

"Local and County News," *Newberry News*, December 9, 1892;

"Local and County News," *Newberry News*, April 21, 1893;

"Local," *Newberry News*, May 2, 1890;

"Local," *Newberry News*, June 22, 1934;

Household of Hibbard J. Ingalls, "United States Census, 1910," database with images, *FamilySearch* (https://familysearch.org/ark:/61903/1:1:M2GJ-968 : 29 October 2015), Hibbard J. Ingalls, Coleraine, Itasca, Minnesota, United States; citing enumeration district (ED) ED 63, sheet 1A, NARA microfilm publication T624 (Washington, DC: National Archives and Records Administration, n.d.); FHL microfilm 1,374,720;

"Local," *Newberry News*, July 8, 1910;

"Local," *Newberry News*, September 15, 1905;

"Joseph Wilson Trueman (obituary)," *Newberry News*, April 15, 1910.

484   "New School Needed," *Newberry News*, December 20, 1901.

485   "Local—Seney is but a shadow of its former self..." *Newberry News*, January 20, 1899;

Department of the Interior Census Office, *Census Bulletin, Eleventh Census of the United States: 1890, Population of Michigan by Minor Civil Divisions* (Washington, DC: United States Census Printing Office, 1891) 3, 16;

Department of Commerce and Labor, *Thirteenth Census of the United States Taken in the Year 1910, Statistics for Michigan*, (Washington, DC: Government Printing Office, 1919), 574, 587;

Department of Commerce, Bureau of the Census, *Fourteenth Census of the United States, State Compendium Michigan* (Washington, DC: Government Printing Office, 1924), 12, 21;

"Would Save Town," *Newberry News*, January 20, 1911.

486   Dodge, 55;

"Lumberman Fails," *Newberry News*, April 2, 1915.

487   Dodge, 183-184.

488   "Memories of Early Lumbering Days at Deer Park," *Newberry News*, June 3, 1932.

489   New Seney "Form New County," *Newberry News*, December 1, 1911;

"Frankenmuth Colony," *Newberry News*, July 4, 1913;

"New Settlers Coming," *Newberry News*, January 28, 1916;

"Local," *Newberry News*, May 19, 1911;

"Italian Colony," *Newberry News*, November 19, 1915;

"Colonize Poles Near Trout Lake," *Newberry News*, March 20, 1914;

"Japanese Coming Here," *Newberry News*, June 19, 1914;

"Reported Settlement of Japanese Colony in Alger County Creates Furor Throughout State," *Newberry News*, July 10, 1914.

490   Eugene J. Sundstrom, "Newberry's Celery Gardens," *Luce County: A History: Centennial Issue* (Chelsea, Michigan: Bookcrafters, 1985), 501-503.

Index

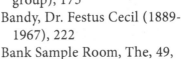

ONE OF THE COTTAGES.

❋ SPECTACLES ❋

Last Night

Was

Chilly !

X

Y

Z

Made in USA - Kendallville, IN
33464_9780578973654
06.28.2022 1023